Continuous Business
Improvement

SERIES EDITOR
BARRIE DALE
UMIST

Continuous Business Improvement

Linking the Key Improvement Processes for Your
Critical Long-term Success

Barry Povey

The McGraw-Hill Companies

London · New York · St Louis · San Francisco · Auckland
Bogotá · Caracas · Lisbon · Madrid · Mexico · Milan
Montreal · New Delhi · Panama · Paris · San Juan
São Paulo · Singapore · Sydney · Tokyo · Toronto

Published by
McGraw-Hill Publishing Company
Shoppenhangers Road, Maidenhead, Berkshire SL6 2QL, England
Telephone: 01628 23432   Fax: 01628 770224

British Library Cataloguing in Publication Data
Povey, Barry
Continuous business improvement: linking the key
improvement processes for your critical long-term success.
– (Quality in action)
1. Total quality management 2. Re-engineering (Management)
3. Strategic planning
I. Title
658.4'01

ISBN 0-07-709124-8

Library of Congress Cataloging-in-Publication Data
Povey, Barry
Continuous business improvement: linking the key improvement
processes for your critical long-term success / Barry Povey.
        p.   cm. – (Quality in action)
Includes bibliographical references and index.
ISBN 0-07-709124-8 (pbk. : alk. paper)
1. Total quality management. 2. Benchmarking (Management)
3. Re-engineering (Management) 4. Consumer satisfaction. I. Title.
II. Series. III. Series: Quality in action (London, England)
HD62.15.P68   1996
658.5'62–dc20   96-11406
                                                                    CIP

McGraw-Hill
A Division of The McGraw·Hill Companies   ı | ıo | 9⁸

12345 BL 99876

Typeset by BookEns Ltd, Royston, Herts.
Printed and bound in Great Britain by Biddles Ltd, Guildford, Surrey

Printed on permanent paper in compliance wth ISO Standard 9706

To Mary, Daniel and Gregory

Contents

Series Preface

Quality is regarded by most producers, customers and consumers as more important than ever before in their manufacturing, service and purchasing strategies. If you doubt this, just think of the unsatisfactory examples of quality you have personally experienced, the bad feelings it gave, the resulting actions taken and the people you told about the experience and outcomes. The concept of total quality management (TQM) is increasingly being adopted by organizations as the means of satisfying the needs and expectations of their customers.

Total quality management has been practised by the major Japanese manufacturing companies for the last 30 or so years. Their commitment to continuous and company-wide quality improvement has provided them with the foundation by which they have been able to capture markets the world over. In response to this competitive pressure Western manufacturing companies, first in America and then Europe, started to embrace the TQM ethic, followed later by commercial and service type organizations. The superior performing Western organizations have now 15 years or so operating experience of TQM. They have developed a series of plans for the improvement of their business, and over this time-scale have put the plans into place in a systematic, consistent and reliable fashion. These organizations in their development and deployment of such plans take into account the common themes arising from new initiatives such as business process re-engineering, total productive maintenance and self-assessment and integrate the principles and practices into overall long-term objectives for improvement of the business.

Superior performing organizations know that TQM is crucial to achieving significant and lasting improvement to the business. This is one indicator of its effectiveness. Senior management are judged on results and if TQM does not improve business performance, they would simply rechannel the resources in other directions.

Total quality management is a subject and management philosophy in which there appears to be an unquenchable thirst for knowledge, despite the considerable volume of published material. In recent times the interest in TQM has been fuelled by the Malcolm Baldrige National Quality Award and the European Quality Award. These awards, based on a model of TQM or business excellence, are being increasingly used by organizations as part of their business improvement process. This interest in the subject has continued in spite of some surveys and reports indicating that TQM is not working. There is also evidence that the concept is being regurgitated under a number of other guises. The objective of the 'Quality in Action' Series is to help satisfy this need and fill what we believe are gaps in the existing range of current books. It is also obvious from the arguments advanced from some quarters that there is still a lack of understanding of TQM and what it is about. Hopefully the books in the series will help to improve the level of understanding.

McGraw-Hill has already published books by three of the best known and internationally respected quality management experts – Crosby, Feigenbaum and Juran. The 'Quality in Action' Series will build upon the work of these three men; this in itself will be a challenge.

I was honoured when asked by McGraw-Hill to be the 'Quality in Action' Book Series Editor. I have personally been involved in industrially-based TQM research for the last 15 or so years and from this experience believe I am well placed to identify the aspects of TQM that need to be addressed by new books on the subject.

The prime focus of the series is management and the texts have been prepared from this standpoint. However, undergraduate and postgraduate students will also find the books of considerable benefit in understanding the concept, principles, elements and practices of TQM, the associated quality management systems, tools and techniques, the means of introducing, developing and sustaining TQM and the associated difficulties, and how to integrate TQM into the business practices of an organization.

One objective of the series is to provide some general TQM reading as guidance for management in introducing, developing and sustaining a process of continuous and company-wide quality improvement. It will focus on manufacturing, commercial and service situations. We are looking for recognized writers (academics, consultants and practitioners) who will be able to address the subject from a European perspective. The books appearing on this theme will not duplicate already published material, rather they will build upon, enhance and develop the TQM wisdom and address the subject from a new perspective. A second objective is to provide texts on aspects of TQM not adequately covered by current books. For example, TQM and human resources, sustaining TQM, TQM: corporate culture and organizational change, supply chain management and TQM and business strategy. It is likely that the authors of these books will be from disciplines (e.g. accounting, economics, psychology, human resources) not traditionally associated with quality management. A third objective is to provide texts that deal with quality management systems, tools and techniques in a practical 'how-to' manner.

The first six books in the series, dealing with understanding Japanese-led companies to make them your customers, making quality of service really work, achieving business success through reward and recognition, communicating change, leadership for quality, and self-assessment for business excellence, have been well received by the business community and are helping to address these objectives.

My commitment to this series is that I am prepared to allocate time from my considerable research, teaching and advisory activities in order to ensure that it meets and hopefully exceeds the needs and expectations of our readers.

B.G. Dale, Series Editor

About the Series Editor

Barrie Dale is Professor of Quality Management at the Manchester School of Management, UMIST and Director of the UMIST Quality Management Centre. The Centre is involved in three major activities: research into Total Quality Management, the Centre houses the Ford Motor Company Northern Regional Centre for training suppliers in Statistical Process Control, and the operation of a Total Quality Management Multi-Company Teaching Programme involving collaborators from a variety of industrial and business environments. The Centre has an extremely strong research base, and since 1981 its members have undertaken a wide range of research across a breadth of topics. The work has received funding to the order of £800 000 in addition to £1.84 million of funding for the TQM Teaching Programme. Professor Dale is also a Non-Executive Director of Manchester Circuits Ltd, a company specializing in the manufacture of high technology and complex printed circuit boards.

He is co-editor of the *International Journal of Quality and Reliability Management,* now in its thirteenth volume. Professor Dale is co-author of *Managing Quality, Quality Costing, Quality Improvement Through Standards, Total Quality and Human Resources: An Executive Guide* and *The Road to Quality,* and has published more than 260 papers on the subject of quality management. Professor Dale has also led four missions to Japan of European executives to study the application of TQM in major Japanese manufacturing organizations. He is the international quality management adviser to the South African Quality Institute. Professor Dale has also been closely associated with the Hong Kong Government Industry Department in preparing a series of booklets on quality management for their 'Make it Better in Hong Kong' campaign.

Preface

I was originally asked to write a specialist book on 'benchmarking' while I was on secondment from IBM as the first General Manager of The Benchmarking Centre in the UK. However, I did not feel that there was a need for another specialist book on that subject, which is already well served by many excellent books. I also felt that there is a very real danger that books that treat benchmarking as a separate subject in isolation, reinforce the impression that benchmarking is something that should have a separate existence rather than be treated as another, but very powerful, tool for business improvement. I therefore decided to write a book that addresses the total subject of business improvement, putting benchmarking and the other tools in the correct overall context in which they should be used.

This book is aimed at all managers and professionals who have a responsibility for establishing corporate strategies and implementing improvement plans. Many organizations start their goal setting and strategic planning by reviewing what they achieved in the previous year. They then aim to continuously improve their business performance and set future goals to achieve some level of improvement on what they have already achieved; either as an arbitrary improvement percentage over previous years, or (hopefully) based on competitive comparisons and best-practice benchmarks. Goal setting and strategic planning should be aimed at providing the answer to three questions:
• Where are we?

- Where do we want to get to?
- How do we get there?

This book reviews various approaches that can help provide the answers, and puts them into an overall business context. It provides real practical guidance that will help managers and professionals in their search for the answers. In order to help busy people who may not have the time or inclination to read business books from cover to cover, this book has been written in three parts: Part 1 gives a clear understanding of the principles of continuous business improvement. Part 2 gives a thorough understanding of the various approaches to continuous business improvement, while Part 3 gives detailed 'how to do it' case studies drawn from industry.

An appropriate title for this book could be 'Don't mention the "Q" word'. In many companies, quality programmes have been implemented in a fairly haphazard manner (often as a series of flavours of the month). The result has been that anything associated with the title 'quality' in those companies gets tainted. Quality initiatives are greeted by a compliant workforce on the basis that they only need to make a couple of token gestures before the management focus shifts on to something else, leaving them to carry on just as they did before. Worse still, management can treat the whole thing as the responsibility of the quality manager and nothing to do with them; while the marketing, sales and administrative functions think that the approaches are interesting, but that they only apply to manufacturing!

Improvement programmes have to be consistently applied over a period of years. Improvement comes from the long-term application of sound approaches, not from a series of quick fixes. Commitment and dedication from the workforce comes from it believing in a consistent message delivered by its leaders. The reason why these programmes should start with the construction of vision and mission statements is to allow business leaders to do exactly that – communicate a consistent message to the employees about what their organization is trying to achieve now, and where it wants to get to in the future.

All the tools and techniques involved in business improvement are easy to learn and use. What makes them effective is using them correctly and appropriately, which is dependent on the leaders in the organization, its culture and its employees. Leadership and the excellence of the management team are the key; all of these tools provide information to management, but it is management that have to interpret the information and take action. *None of these tools can replace good management.*

The purpose of this book is to address the key approaches to business improvement and to show how they can be integrated into a comprehensive framework for improvement. In-depth books exist on each of the individual elements and, where the reader might be interested in specific reading on a particular topic, texts worth further study are recommended. The purpose of this book is not to present a single approach and then to recommend it above all others, nor is it to provide another 'cook-book' approach to business improvement. Cook-books rarely work; what does work is to have a management team with a very clear understanding of what it needs to achieve and a good grasp of the various improvement methodologies that can be employed. Successful companies use this knowledge to develop their own customized approaches to business improvement. They do not slavishly follow the 'n' step approach of any particular guru but evolve their own approach, which has been refined by pilot tests and proven to be effective within their own company culture.

The purpose of this book is to introduce the key ingredients and to explain how they link together, so that the reader can then use them in the way that best suits their business and its environment. The book finishes by giving some guidance to the reader on the way forward.

RECOMMENDED READING

Balm, G. (1992). *Benchmarking: A Practitioner's Guide for Becoming and Staying Best of the Best.* QPMA Press, Schaumburg.

Bendell, T., Boulter, L., and Kelly, J. *Benchmarking for Competitive Advantage.* Pitman Publishing, London.

Camp, R. (1989). *Benchmarking: The Search for Industry Best Practices That Lead to Superior Performance*. ASQC Quality Press, Milwaukee, Wisconsin.

Codling, S. (1992). 'Best practice benchmarking'. *Industrial Newsletters*. Industrial Newsletters Ltd, Toddington, Dunstable.

Zairi, M. and Leonard, P. (1994). *Practical Benchmarking: The Complete Guide*. Chapman & Hall, London.

Acknowledgements

First, I cannot pretend by any stretch of the imagination that every word and idea in this book are originally mine. Wherever possible I have acknowledged sources and listed them at the end of each chapter. However it is inevitable after a long career in industry that my knowledge has been acquired from a large number of sources: a lot of first-hand experience, talking to others in the field, company education programmes, conferences, formal education, and wide-ranging reading on the subject. In these circumstances it is impossible to identify the original source of every idea or approach, and if I have inadvertently omitted to give credit to someone for their original work, then I humbly apologize.

Second, I would like to acknowledge the specific advice and support given to me by Professor John Bessant from the University of Brighton. Professor Bessant led the research team (of which I was proud to be one of the industrial partners) that generated much of the material used in the chapters on continuous improvement. John has been my mentor now for several years.

Introduction to Continuous Business Improvement

What is continuous business improvement?

There is no more delicate matter to take in hand, nor more dangerous to conduct, nor more doubtful in its success, than to set up as a leader in the introduction of changes. For he who innovates will have as his enemies all those who are well off under the existing order, and only lukewarm supporters in those who might be better off under the new.
(Niccolo Machiavelli)

Continuous business improvement requires all the people in the organization to accept and welcome change. This, in turn, requires the establishment of a new culture in which change and improvement are constantly occurring. The new culture cannot be established without addressing the issue raised by Machiavelli when he says that the introduction of change creates many enemies and gains few friends. Many will be hoping that the introduction of change fails, firstly because they are more comfortable with the familiar situation, secondly because it was that familiarity with the existing system that allowed them to achieve their present position and the introduction of change means that they will have

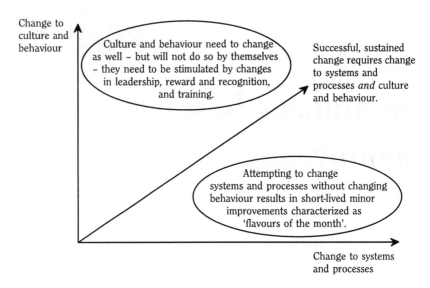

FIGURE 1.1   Successful change programmes involve both culture and system

to prove themselves all over again, and finally because change or improvement are too often used as a euphemism for job cutting.

In order to be successful in the introduction of change the hearts and minds of all the people involved need to be won (those affected either directly or indirectly), as well as getting the mechanics of the change right (the new methods, processes, working approaches, education, etc.). Successful change programmes need to proceed on two axes – culture and system.

This can clearly be seen in Fig. 1.1, which demonstrates in particular, that attempting to make changes to systems and processes without making parallel changes to the behaviour of employees and the culture of the organization results in short-lived 'flavours of the month'. This theme of behaviour and culture as an equal requirement with systems and processes is one that recurs throughout this book, because it really is fundamental to achieving sustained change – a purely mechanistic approach to systems, processes, and their improvement is doomed to failure.

BACKGROUND TO CONTINUOUS BUSINESS IMPROVEMENT

Improvement initiatives should be focused on one objective: improving the overall performance of the business. This is accomplished by improving the performance of the individual activities that comprise the business. Improvement initiatives should be structured strategically by the senior executives in order to avoid duplication and contradictory objectives, and to send the clear message to all employees that improvement is vital. They must draw on the ideas and participation from staff and middle management, so that the improvement direction is set from the top down, while the improvement ideas are generated from the bottom up.

Without careful and active management, improvement programmes can assume lives and purposes of their own, served by their own group of specialists. The tools and techniques of continuous business improvement are straightforward and do not require an army of specialists; in fact specialists, unless used as 'centres of competence', become a hindrance or worse, because they reinforce the mechanistic approach to change, concentrating on the tools and techniques rather than the people. The people using the tools and techniques should be those involved in the work activities, the processes and procedures, on a day-to-day basis. They are the ones who know how things work, what the real problems are, and they are in the best position to implement changes, which can be done by them with a feeling of ownership instead of as an imposition by outsiders.

Continuous business improvement is really concerned with harnessing the creative ability of the entire workforce to identify and solve the problems that impact their ability to perform their job. This may not seem too novel, but Western industry has matured with the principle of management control and worker conformity. In the days before the industrial revolution the craftsman was responsible for the whole job (what we would now call the seamless process!), from taking the customer order and understanding the requirements, making the product, through to delivering it to the customer and confirming that the finished product met all requirements. The industrial revolution changed two things; it took large numbers of unskilled and uneducated agricultural labourers into the new factories; then, in order to be able to use these people productively, it introduced the division of labour. Rather than each worker doing the whole job as had been the case with skilled craftsmen, it was broken down into small steps which enabled the unskilled and uneducated to be taught each small step quickly, and therefore to become productive quickly. These unskilled factory hands needed a layer of supervisors and engineers to control the total job, design the work flows, control quality and take the decisions. This created a legacy that survived long after the problem of uneducated farm labourers had gone – the belief that it was not the responsibility of the process operators to look for better ways of working (and to make changes to their work processes whenever they thought that would make an improvement). Their job was to do what they were told. Their thinking was done for them by the managers, professionals, and engineers that designed the work patterns. If changes or improvements were required, it was those specialists who decided what would be done, with the worker merely implementing their decisions. This approach to work reached its zenith with Ford's mass production factories in the early part of this century.

This situation is now changing. One reason for this is the final arrival of the technological revolution. Activities that required armies of workers a few years ago can now be performed by far fewer people, production line automation has removed much of the routine and put it in the hands of machines. The same has happened in the office; photocopiers, fax machines, computers, networks, e-mail, expert systems, etc. have all combined to remove much of the routine and increase efficiency significantly. New technologies continually emerge that enable new solutions to work problems that could not be considered before. It is this availability of technology that has highlighted the need for much of the improvement activity, and the need to take a business process rather than a functional view of the way work is performed. The introduction of CIM (computer-integrated manufacturing) technologies in the 1980s brought home the simple fact that you have to analyse, simplify and improve the process

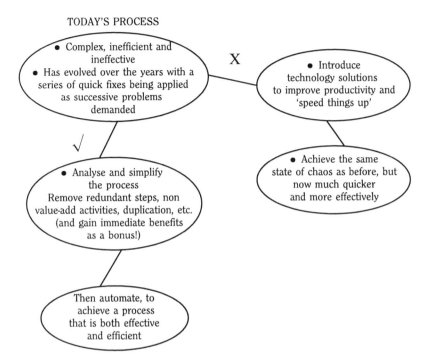

TODAY'S PROCESS

- Complex, inefficient and ineffective
- Has evolved over the years with a series of quick fixes being applied as successive problems demanded

X

- Introduce technology solutions to improve productivity and 'speed things up'

✓

- Analyse and simplify the process
Remove redundant steps, non value-add activities, duplication, etc. (and gain immediate benefits as a bonus!)

- Achieve the same state of chaos as before, but now much quicker and more effectively

Then automate, to achieve a process that is both effective and efficient

FIGURE 1.2   Simplification before automation

before you automate it. Failure to do so does not prevent automation speeding up the work, it just results in the achievement of a state of chaos quicker that under the old manual system. It also means that once inefficient, ineffective work practices have been enshrined in the computer system they are much more difficult, if not impossible, to clean up. This was true for CIM in the past, and it is true for business and support processes now. The route to efficient and effective processes is shown in Fig. 1.2 – first simplify, *then* automate!

Another reason for the changing situation is that the workforce is much better educated than it was a generation or two ago; production lines and offices are no longer staffed by throngs of men and women who left school at the age of 13 or 14, barely literate. Workers now can question, analyse and make sensible decisions on their own (with the right company culture providing support via involvement programmes and education and training).

Many of the preceding points were covered by Juran who, with Deming, has dominated the total quality field for a good part of the 20th century (they started their work on quality in the US prior to the Second World War, then took their approaches to Japan after the war and were credited with much of Japan's subsequent success; finally they were instrumental in reintroducing total quality in the US after Japanese competition rekindled interest) in his final appearance at the ASQC's (American Society for Quality Control) annual quality congress:[1]

- High product quality has always been achievable by Western manufacturers, but it was achieved at great expense by removing manufacturing defects by inspection and rework. This strategy was effective as long as everybody followed it, but its inherent weakness was exposed by the arrival of the Japanese quality revolution.

- The requirement for large numbers of quality inspectors led to the establishment of dedicated quality departments. Upper managers soon delegated responsibility for 'quality' to this department and subsequently became completely divorced from quality, focusing their attention on productivity instead.

- On the premise that workers and supervisors lacked the education to perform any planning, Taylor [see below] gave that function to the managers and engineers, and effectively created a division between those who planned (managers and engineers) and those who executed (workers and supervisors). Taylorism is still with us at the end of the 20th century, and as a result companies are still failing to utilize their greatest asset, the experience and creativity of the workforce.

Frederick Taylor was the pioneer of the mass production methods introduced into the US automobile manufacturers in the early part of the 20th century. The fundamental change he introduced was the division of labour between management and workers; he is considered to be the father of 'scientific management'. Continuous business improvement, encompassing all the tools and techniques of quality management, continuous improvement, and business process management, is in many ways trying to undo the damage inflicted on Western industry by almost a century of Taylorism.

BENEFITS OF CONTINUOUS BUSINESS IMPROVEMENT

The benefits can be measured in two ways. One is the tangible effect that continuous business improvement can have on the bottom line, the other is the intangible effect due to the improved morale and commitment of the workforce that is achieved in a continuous business improvement environment.

In order to be sure that the business is benefiting from continuous business improvement, it is necessary to measure performance accurately. First, know the baseline (current performance), then measure the effect of the improvements that are implemented. Measuring the things that are critical to the success of the organization and then using the measurement system to manage them actively is a major factor in ensuring that the expected improvements are actually obtained – that there is real improvement rather than just change.

There is always debate about what to measure. Should the company implement a full-scale 'cost of quality' measurement system? Should it have clearly defined quality goals? What measurements should there be? One organization, very successfully coming out of the doldrums under a new management team, had a set of goals that, at first glance, did not include any internal quality goals at all – they were nearly all financial. However, when considering what would be a good top-level indicator of quality improvement, one that would confirm that quality improvement really was hitting the bottom line, then the use of Return on Assets (ROA) as an indicator can be very effective.

An apparently pure financial measurement, but one that captures the benefits that continuous business improvement should be expected to provide, ROA is a simple calculation:

$$\frac{R - C}{V}$$

where R is revenue, C is cost and V is the asset value.

Continuous business improvement activity should reduce cost by improving process yields, reducing waste and process cycle-times, reducing the headcount required to operate the process, and improving product quality. Asset value should be reduced by continuous business improvement because it will reduce inventories – high value inventories tied up as incoming parts in warehouses, work-in-process (WIP) buffer stocks being held in the process, and finished product inventories being held by sales pending a customer order.

A variation of this has been described in the *Harvard Business Review* by Hayes and Clark.[2] Their research showed that most managers are subjected to a 'blizzard' of monthly reports that ultimately tell them little (sometimes described as being data rich and information poor!). They devised a measure of efficiency that they have called Total Factor Productivity (TFP) – the ratio of total output to total input. An advantage of their approach is that it integrates the contribution of all factors of productivity into a single measure. Their research showed that because their measure TFP (like ROA) put management focus on WIP and waste, it is a good indicator of overall performance improvement.

PRINCIPLES OF CONTINUOUS BUSINESS IMPROVEMENT

Continuous business improvement requires a never-ending cycle (see Fig. 1.3) of obtaining feedback from the organization's stakeholders, customers, employees, and from internal assessments; using that information as inputs for planning and goal setting; establishing the critical success factors needed to deliver the goals; developing and improving the processes that deliver the CSFs (critical success factors); then repeating the cycle by obtaining feedback from customers again.

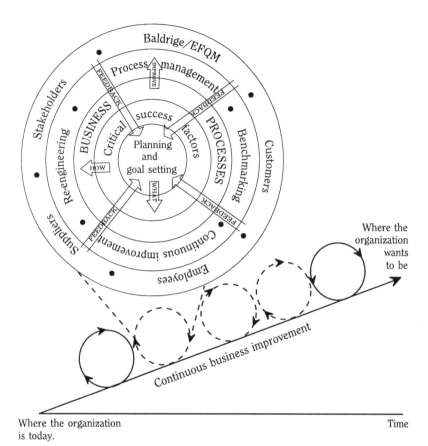

FIGURE 1.3   Total improvement model – the improvement wheel

This 'wheel of improvement' requires certain fundamentals to be in place if it is to take the organization up the slope to where it wants to be. These fundamentals are:

- using the customer perspective to drive improvement
- involving the entire workforce in improvement
- having effective measurement systems in place
- creating the right environment for innovation

- understanding the tools and techniques of improvement and knowing when and how to use them.

PROCESS OF CONTINUOUS BUSINESS IMPROVEMENT

The sequence of the activities contained within the improvement wheel is shown in Fig. 1.4, which is a flow chart of the process of continuous business improvement. They key points are:

1 The starting point is an analysis of 'where we want to get to' (vision, mission and goals) and 'where are we now' (the results of self-assessment and customer and employee feedback).
2 This analysis will identify many problems, which must be prioritized and sorted into three major groups for action:
   - Organizational problems that must be solved by management.
   - Process problems that can be addressed by process improvement teams.
   - Operational problems that can be addressed by problem-solving teams.

Processes and systems

Prior to the industrial revolution, and indeed in the small one or two person companies of today, there was no need to explain the concept of business processes – the business had only one or two people involved from start to finish; the start being the discussion with the customer about their wants and needs, the finish being the delivery of a product or service that satisfied those wants and needs. In between the start and finish was some form of design and production process, usually performed by the same person who was involved at the start and finish.

The problem comes with growth. There comes a time when the business is too big for one or two people, and they have to take on additional staff. These are inevitably specialists. Specialist salesmen, specialist purchasers, specialist production workers, specialist packers and shippers, specialist accountants, administrators and engineers. Specialists

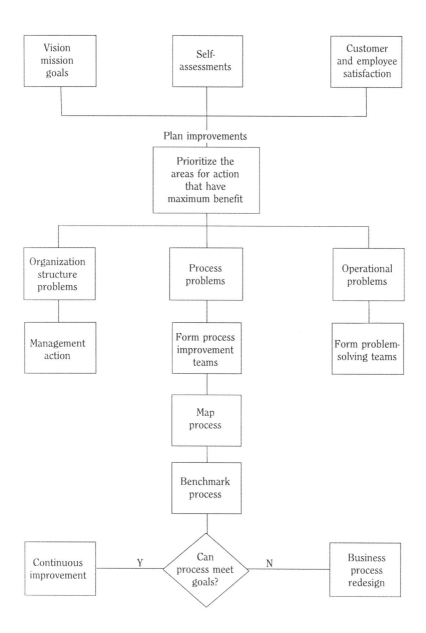

FIGURE 1.4   The process of continuous business improvement

build compartments to protect themselves. Continued growth builds hierarchies within each specialist function. Soon the concept of satisfying the customer is forgotten and each individual function concentrates on optimizing its own performance and fighting their internal battles with the other functions within the expanding organization. This may be tolerated while the organization and its market are growing, but inevitably at some point the growth stops. To get the organization back on track requires a 'back to basics' policy, starting with the introduction (really reintroduction) of the concept of a business process that starts and ends with the customer. This is shown in Fig. 1.5 which shows the three principal trajectories that the business life cycle can take. The three trajectories are:

1 The business grows initially but quickly stabilizes (or is limited) at a volume of work that can be contained by the original team. The business continues to be moderately successful until the market environment changes, when it declines quickly.

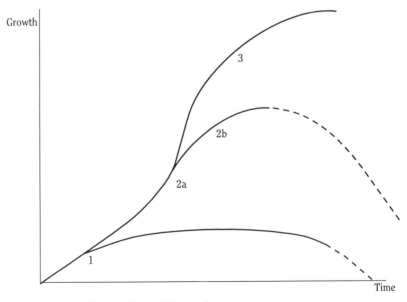

FIGURE 1.5   The business life cycle

14

2 (a) The business grows strongly; additional staff are recruited and formed into specialist functions; career paths are introduced; and (b) the business growth slows or stops. Continued functional conflicts and lack of focus send it into decline.

3 The decline can be halted and growth restimulated by abandoning the old functional structures and replacing them with a process structure focused on delivering delighted customers.

The first two trajectories always end with the business failing. Continued success can only be achieved by adopting option 3.

What is a process?

A definition of a process is:

> A definable, repeatable, predictable and measurable set of work activities consisting of people, equipment, procedures, and materials organised to produce a specific result. Any job can be analysed as a process, and most processes cross organisational boundaries.[3]

A process is simply a structured sequence of activities designed to take a set of inputs and use them to produce a specific output for a particular customer or market. All organizations have more than one process, which can be shown as a model that includes the processes directly involved in the production and delivery of its product or service, and those processes that provide support.

- Direct processes can be; design, production, delivery, after-sales, selling, purchasing, order entry, etc.
- Support processes can be; information management, recruitment, education and training, finance, etc.

The processes interrelate in a complex manner and collectively form a system. To be able to understand processes properly in order to manage and improve them, it is first necessary to understand them in the context of the total system. This will be examined in more detail in the following chapters.

Vertical organization and horizontal processes

Few organizations have made significant progress towards a process-based structure, although some companies have imposed process management as an additional responsibility, assigning process ownership to managers who also have functional responsibilities.

The reasons are, according to Davenport:[4]

- The high degree of change from functional to process-based organization might be too much to be able to manage.
- Fear that functional skills will be lost if functions are no longer the basis for organization.
- A belief that process is an unstable basis for organization because processes change more rapidly than functions.

Figure 1.6 shows a typical vertical functional organization, and illustrates why the process view is important. Functions are organized by specialization, which was and still is, necessary when the degree of education, training and experience required to do each job is high. However, modern technology is removing these as reasons for a functional, specialist organization. Any specialist spends significant amounts of time on routine work, and a surprisingly small amount on work that really demands the full extent of their specialist knowledge. Modern information technology applications can remove the routine from the specialist and put it into the hands of the generalist. This allows the organization the freedom to organize effectively on process lines, only involving the specialist in the small percentage of occasions when their knowledge is really required. Thus an organization can move from the vertical, functional model shown in Fig. 1.6 (where even the simple organization shown requires eight separate departments to process a customer order), to one in which there is a seamless process operating, one whose start and finish points are both with the organization's customer.

The idea of the 'seamless' process is an important one. The organization as shown in the diagram has nine 'handover' points, where responsibility and action are handed from one part of the organization to another. Each of these 'handover' points (the unmanaged 'white spaces') is

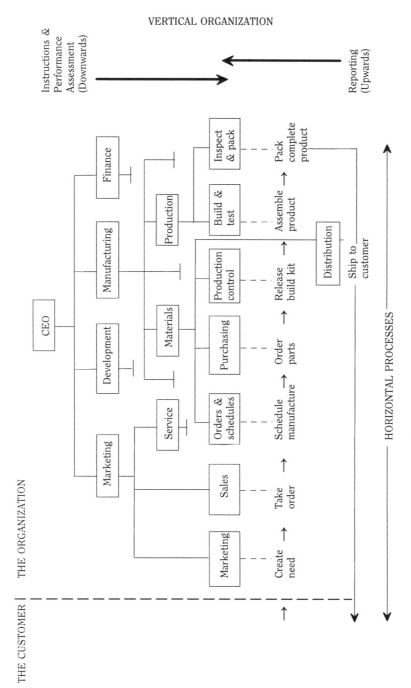

FIGURE 1.6 Vertical functions, horizontal process

a friction point, an opportunity for failure where mistakes are made, communication fails and delays occur. A seamless process does not suffer from these, therefore it is less costly, more efficient, produces a better quality product or service, and ultimately results in a delighted customer.

At one end of the organizational spectrum there is the purely functional organization which will clearly be rich in problems due to the reasons given above. At the other end of the spectrum is the purely process-oriented organization. As Davenport says, these do not really exist yet, although there is a steady movement in that direction. A typical, forward-thinking organization of today would probably have a hybrid organization. It would still need to have a vertical, functional organization because the specialization upon which functional structures are built still exist. But onto that functional structure they have grafted a process model. The business has been analysed in terms of the processes involved in delivering its goals, and each process has been given an owner; a senior executive with end-to-end responsibility for the process, its inputs and outputs, its performance, making improvements to it, and solving problems within it.

Issues involved with continuous business improvement

The issues fall into three basic categories: people, technology and methods.

People

The entire workforce of production workers, office staff, engineering, marketing and the entire management team, must become involved in the improvement activity. This requires motivation – a risk-free environment, appropriate rewards and recognition, empowerment. It requires education and coaching in the new techniques. It requires management to change from controlling and directing to coaching, mentoring, and leading. Creating the right cultural environment for change is probably the most important aspect of continuous business improvement. It is relatively straightforward to design an elegant business process on paper, but nothing can be achieved unless the new process can be successfully implemented – and this requires the wholehearted support of all the people affected by it.

Technology

Information technology (IT) is the great enabler of the age. It allows new functions to be performed or existing ones to be combined into new ways of working that could not be contemplated until now. Effective use of the new technologies requires two things:

1 Knowledgeable, creative gatekeepers who can understand the capabilities of the new technologies and see novel applications for them that yield quantum leaps in performance improvement. Normal user/ customer research is ineffective when faced by new technologies and new capabilities. When users or customers are asked what improvements they want, the majority will ask for the same again, but a little smaller, a little faster, a little cheaper ... only the few will have the vision to see that work processes can be radically changed or even eliminated. (For example, in the 1940s the projected total worldwide market for computers was around 40 units – because the research only looked at the few applications in existence at that time required high computing power. In the 1950s the photocopier was only expected to replace the need for carbon copies in the office.)

2 The removal of fear. Even in leading edge companies there are large numbers of staff who do not understand IT, are frightened of it, and only use it at the most basic level. The full benefits of the introduction of new technologies cannot be realized if the users struggle with it. They need thorough tra ning, help desk and coaching support, and the IT professionals need to deliver high quality, user friendly solutions.

Methods

There are many methods associated with continuous business improvement, and this book will examine the most important ones. As with technology, a company needs to have a 'methods' gatekeeper – a person who keeps up to speed with the new approaches that are emerging from the universities and business schools, and that are being developed and used successfully in other organizations. Once again, these people need to be knowledgeable and creative, so that they can understand the capabilities of the new approaches and see how they can be incorporated into their own organizations.

REFERENCES

1   Juran, J.M. (1994). 'The upcoming century of quality'. *Quality Progress*, August, pp. 29–37.

2   Hayes, R. and Clark, K. (1986). 'Why some factories are more productive than others'. *Harvard Business Review*, September/ October.

3   IBM (1992). *The Transformation of IBM: A Market-Driven Quality Reference Guide.* IBM internal document G325-0670-00.

4   Davenport, T.H. (1993). *Process Innovation: Reengineering Work through Information Technology.* Harvard Business School Press, Boston.

CHAPTER 2

How to succeed

We trained hard – but it seemed that every time we were beginning to form up into teams, we would be reorganized. I was to learn later in life that we tend to meet any new situation by reorganizing, and a wonderful method it can be for creating the illusion of progress while producing confusion, inefficiency and demoralization.

(Gaius Petronius)

We often view the past as a golden age of stability when little changed from one century to the next. However, it would appear that the challenge of change faced by today's managers is little different from that faced by their predecessors. Being able to cope with change is important to every organization; all the current management techniques such as restructuring, re-engineering, benchmarking and continuous improvement are really techniques for introducing changes of varying degree from the incremental to the radical. When failure occurs, it is seldom because the required changes were not correctly identified but because the organization was not able to manage the introduction of the changes. If an organization is not able to change, it ultimately stagnates and is overtaken by the competition. Unfortunately, Petronius's words are as true today as they were 1900 years ago; we often just create the illusion of progress or improvement, while in reality continuing exactly as we were before. The philosopher's stone that organizations search for is the magic substance that turns change into genuine improvement.

The following chapters provide some help to managers in their search for ways to implement genuine improvement.

All organizations exist to serve their stakeholders: their shareholders, employees, government and customers. Success is dependent on many factors including:

- the marketplace (market growth and degree of competition)
- the product range (competitive superiority, dictating the market)
- the management system (the collective effectiveness and efficiency of the processes used to run the business).

The relative importance of each of these factors varies over the product life cycle, as it goes through periods of:

- *Growth* (a period of rapid growth for the business, when its products actually create and define the market).
- *Maturity* (market growth slows as it begins to reach saturation. Clear product domination by the major market players has been lost and the product itself becomes a commodity. Competition is fierce and differentiation is on cost, cycle time, responsiveness and quality).
- *Decline* (as profits erode as the result of fierce price competition, players start to withdraw from the market and look for other products and opportunities that will put them back on the growth part of the S curve).

A company's culture, organization and system need to be aligned to the market in which it operates. The culture, organization and systems that are appropriate in a young, growing industry will still not be appropriate when it reaches maturity.

In an effort to maintain profit margins during the transition from growth to maturity, the focus moves from the product to the underlying processes such as production, support and management. Improving these processes (and thus reducing cost and cycle time, and improving quality) has the same effect on the bottom line as increasing revenue. This shift of focus is even more pronounced in times of economic recession. A 1992 survey[1] showed that priorities shift in a recession towards cutting costs, improving competitiveness, and improving response time. This business process focus, which allows cost, cycle time and quality to be continuously improved, is essential to the health of an organization. However, long-term prosperity requires revenue growth as well as cost reduction; if the focus remains only on cost reduction over an extended period of time, there is one inevitable conclusion – a well-managed decline.

Process improvement in the manufacturing production environment is now well established, having been introduced in the 1980s in parallel with Just-In-Time (JIT) manufacturing and computer-integrated manufacturing (CIM). These same approaches are now being migrated to the support and business processes to drive improvement; improvement which may be either incremental (as the result of continuous improvement programmes), or radical (as the result of process re-engineering and benchmarking).

There is a tendency inherent in many of the techniques of continuous improvement for the improvement focus to be purely internal. They are based on the premise that the processes and their outputs are necessary, and work to identify ways by which they can be improved. However, in order for these activities to make a real contribution to improving business performance, they also need some external focus which techniques such as benchmarking can help provide. Benchmarking, comparing oneself to what best practice is achieving externally, highlights the point at which the current process can no longer be enhanced to deliver what is required of it and indicates that fundamental reappraisal via business process re-engineering is required. It is vital that improvement is driven from the customer perspective, by knowing what their needs are and by knowing how well those needs are being satisfied by the organization.

ORGANIZING FOR CONTINUOUS BUSINESS IMPROVEMENT

A manager wants to know what to do first: is there a preferred sequence, or road map, that guarantees the successful implementation of continuous business improvement? Is there an organizational environment in which continuous business improvement will be more likely to succeed?

The manager's problem is that there is a wide variety of tools and techniques available and it is difficult to understand them all, so their temptation is to pick one or two and use them in all circumstances. This puts the manager into the situation described by Mark Twain; if the only tool you have is a hammer, then all your problems look like nails. The key to effective and sustained improvement is that all of these tools and techniques have a part to play. The manager and professional need to understand them all, so that they can select and use the most appropriate ones for their particular circumstances.

It is easy for the manager to fall into the trap of sub-optimizing at the individual department level – care must be taken to ensure that all the improvement activities actually do make a contribution to improving the overall performance of the organization. The fundamental causes of sub-optimization are the functional organization and not driving improvement strategically from the top down. Improvement in these circumstances can be characterized by:

- The department manager will pick things to improve that are important to him, not necessarily to the whole organization.
- The department manager's authority to implement changes is limited to the department which he manages.
- The functional reporting line's view is considered, not that of the customer.
- The effects on other departments upstream and downstream in the process flow are not considered (one person's improvement is another person's new problem!).

This is illustrated in Fig. 2.1, which shows sub-optimization at work. In Fig. 2.1a each individual department is working at improving itself, but few are actually contributing to the organization's strategic direction, indeed some are actually doing just the opposite. In Fig. 2.1b department improvement has been aligned to the functional direction, but still the focus on the overall goals of the organization is missing. In Fig. 2.1c sub-optimization has been eliminated completely by aligning the departments and the functions to delivering what the customer wants and therefore focusing all improvement on the customer.

(a) *Sub-optimization at the department level*

(b) *Sub-optimization at the functional level*

(Departments improve their own individual internal performance, but are focusing on what is important to them, not to their function)

(a)

(Departments are now aligned with each other and with their functions, but the functions still are not aligned)

(b)

(c) *Full optimization with strategic alignment based on the customer*

(Departments and functions are now all aligned and improvement is focused on the customer, ensuring strategic benefit to the organization)

(c)

FIGURE 2.1   Avoiding sub-optimization: (a) at the department level; (b) at the functional level; (c) full optimization with strategic alignment based on the customer

In order to achieve this alignment, there needs to be an effective framework for using the tools of continuous business improvement. Figure 2.2 shows a basic framework with a top-down approach from goals and critical success factors down to problem-solving teams, which can also be fed from the bottom up, from the employees themselves. (Having an effective bottom-up approach is essential to harnessing the creative problem-solving potential of employees. They will not remain motivated if they are not empowered to make some changes on their own, while also participating in the top-down improvement programmes.) This whole process is assessed on a periodical basis to measure progress and identify additional areas for improvement.

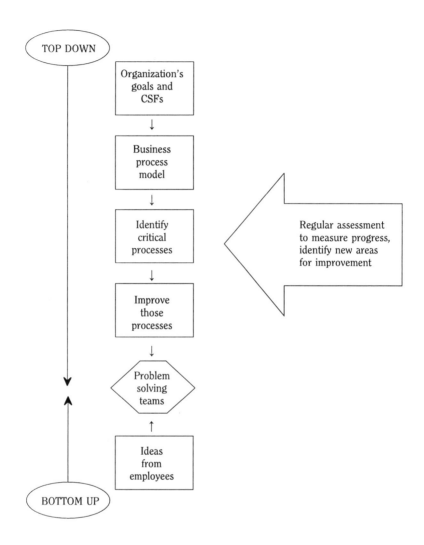

FIGURE 2.2 A basic framework for using the business improvement tools

In answer to the question asked earlier, 'is there a preferred sequence or road map that will guarantee the successful implementation of continuous business improvement?', the answer is *no*, no single method will guarantee success. The approach shown in Fig. 2.2 is a good starting point, which will be built on throughout the following chapters, and we will return to this question in the concluding section of the book. The basic approach shown in Fig. 2.2 is:

1 Start with developing goals and critical success factors.
2 Define the processes that deliver them.
3 Identify the processes that are critical (an assessment of their importance and their performance).
4 Improve those processes.
5 Pass the improvement items to process improvement teams for implementation.
6 Measure improvement by self-assessments.

SUCCESS FACTORS

A survey of 100 UK companies by A.T. Kearney[2] identified three key differences between organizations that are achieving improvement and those that are not. They split their survey respondents into two groups: the 20 per cent who reported significant performance improvement over the previous 12 months and the other 80 per cent who did not. They then compared the two groups.

Performance measurement

The 'improvers' were twice as likely to measure on-time delivery, product per cent defective, lead times, and to benchmark the competition.

The saying is, 'what gets measured, gets managed'. There are several reasons why this is true:

1 The act of defining a measurement for a particular performance parameter sends a signal to the organization that top management consider it to be important. Staff within the organization will respond by paying more attention to that point, and because of this performance improvement may start even before any other 'improvement' actions are taken.

2 Establishing a rational system of measurements for a process or system requires that there is a clear understanding of the factors that are critical to its success; such as meeting the customer's requirements, achieving cost, time and quality requirements, and understanding performance in comparison to direct competitors and to 'best practice'. The measures identified by A.T. Kearney are good generic measures that capture the performance of most of these parameters.

3 Establishing a system of measurements with a baseline of current performance allows the effect of changes to be measured. Do changes actually yield the anticipated improvements? Can cause and effect relationships be identified? Can improvements in results actually be related to changes in process caused by management action, or are apparent improvements really the effect of random fluctuations?

These findings (in particular the first point) echo the experience in the US with the Baldrige award. In a report[3] to Congress in April 1991 on the Malcolm Baldrige National Quality Award, it was stated that:

> the deficiencies noted in the lower scoring applicants include a lack of understanding of competitive comparisons, lack of process measurements, and a weakness in creating a prevention basis for quality.

Focus on customer programmes

The 'improvers' were five times more likely to include their customers in joint project teams.

In the years immediately following the Second World War, the concepts of 'customer' and 'customer satisfaction' were alien to manufacturers and retailers. Demand for goods and services far outstripped industry's ability to provide – anything that they could make could be sold. (For example, I bought my first new car in 1972. I was severely restricted in my choice of colour, trim and features; I had to join a six-month waiting list; I had to accept two price rises while I waited; I had to tolerate further delivery delays caused by strikes. When the car was finally delivered I had to record the long list of faults that became apparent in the first few weeks of use, so that they could be corrected during the first service. I didn't think there was anything to complain about over my shoddy treatment or the poor quality of the car, because that was my level of expectation; all other manufacturers were just as bad, if not worse!)

The revolution led by the Japanese manufacturers has made all this a thing of the past. Naïve consumers no longer exist in commercially viable quantities. In order to succeed, companies now have to put their customers first – it is no wonder that everybody's vision statements now talk of 'delighting the customer'! But saying it and doing it are two different things. How do you delight the customer? How do you know that your product or service is exactly right? The answer is to involve the customer at every point in the design; focus groups to gather requirements, review of prototypes, involvement in functional and usability testing, etc. This takes the original concept of concurrent engineering to the ultimate. Concurrent engineering was originally a strategy to stop the 'over the wall' attitude of development towards manufacturing; changing the game from a relay race, where the new product was handed sequentially from one group to another, to a rugby game, a team game with all the players from manufacturing and development involved from the beginning. The game now needs to be even bigger, to involve everybody: the customer, designer, manufacturer, suppliers, marketing, sales and service, all working as one coherent team.

Behaviour/culture
The 'improvers' were more likely to adopt cross-functional approaches and to support employee empowerment. It was much more likely that a director (rather than the quality manager) would be responsible for the TQM programme.

Cross-functional approaches are essential. As described in the introduction, functional organizations are vertical whereas the business process is horizontal; the work product is handed from one functional group to another as it progresses through the process. In the traditional functional organization, no one manages the 'white space' between departments, because no one has any responsibility outside of their own department. It is in these 'white spaces' that many of the problems occur. The only way to find an owner for the 'white space' is to keep escalating problems up the chain of command until the two departments with the 'white space' in between meet at a common reporting point. (Apart from the obvious time wasting and continued friction between departments, this also ensures that senior managers are continually dragged into resolving basic operational problems.) Experience now shows that the most effective way of addressing this problem is to have process owners for all business processes, responsible for the process achieving its performance targets, making performance improvements, and resolving problems as they arise.

Improvement programmes require employees to act in new ways, to look outside the narrow confines of their immediate job and take the responsibility to resolve problems and to implement improvements. This requires them to feel confident that firstly they will not be punished if they fail and secondly that their new behaviour patterns meet with the approval of their managers. The management team therefore have to demonstrate that improvement is important to them. This importance cannot be demonstrated if senior executives delegate responsibility for improvement to a specialist staff group, but it is demonstrated when senior executives show by their own behaviour that improvement activity is important to them (to use the fashionable clichés, 'to walk the talk' and 'to be role models'). This view of the role that top management have to play is further reinforced by recent research conducted by Hodgetts[4]. His research among Baldrige winners in the US identified eight lessons that need to be learned by organizations hoping to get ahead of the pack and achieve world-class status:

1 Formulate a vision of quality.
2 Having top management involved from the start.
3 Focus on customer needs.
4 Develop the planning and implementation processes.
5 Train employees to use statistical process control (SPC) tools.
6 Empower employees.
7 Recognize and reward employees.

8 Make continuous improvement an ongoing challenge.

Continuous business improvement is fundamentally about behaviour, not tools. A characteristic of programmes that have failed is that they have concentrated on the tools, whereas those that have succeeded have concentrated on the behavioural aspects. If the culture of the organization, and the behaviour of the individuals within it, are attuned for continuous business improvement, then the maximum benefit will be derived from the use of the tools, and new tools can be introduced easily whenever they are appropriate.

The answer to the original question 'Is there an organizational environment in which continuous business improvement will be more likely to succeed?', is a clear 'Yes', as has been demonstrated in the preceding discussion, and which can be summarized by reviewing the conditions for successful innovation identified by Professor Rothwell,[5] who has been studying innovation since the early 1970s (Table 2.1).

TABLE 2.1   Organizational rules for success

1 Top management commitment and visible support for the innovation.
2 A long-term corporate strategy in which the innovation plays a key role. Innovation must have direction and purpose.
3 Long-term commitment, not based on short-term returns on investment considerations.
4 Corporate flexibility and responsiveness to change.
5 Top management acceptance of risk. Innovation is a high-risk business in which failures will occur. Management must accept this and not use one failure as an excuse for withdrawing from the innovation.
6 An environment in which innovation can flourish: freedom from rigid rules, participative and informal, face-to-face communication, interdisciplinary teams, emphasis on creative interaction, willing to take on external ideas, risk accepting, flexible in the face of changing needs, non-hierarchical, two-way communication flows.

ENABLERS AND INHIBITORS

A recent survey conducted by the author has identified the enablers and inhibitors to the successful implementation of continuous business improvement in UK industry (Table 2.2).

TABLE 2.2 Enablers and Inhibitors

ENABLERS	INHIBITORS
Common to all respondents	*Common to all respondents*
– Top-level commitment	– Lack of commitment by some managers
– Customer focus	– Organizational 'empires'
– Management style	– Lack of knowledge
– Related to business plan	– Cross-company processes but functional organization
Unique to an individual respondent	– Lack of resource
– Some areas of the company are already process aligned	– Resistance to change
– Partnership with other companies	
– Small site for implementation	
– Dedicated teams	
– A will to improve	

The common enablers and inhibitors identified in this small sample of UK companies can be related to the findings of more extensive industrial surveys and academic research.[6] Surveys in the UK and US show that a high proportion of companies that embark on TQM programmes do not realize the benefits that they expected (an Arthur D. Little[7] survey of 500 US companies showed that only a third of them felt that total quality management (TQM) was having a significant impact on competitiveness, and the A.T. Kearney survey showed that 80 per cent of quality programmes fail to produce any tangible benefit). A study of more than 2800 civilian and Department of Defense establishments in the United States, commissioned by the General Accounting Office[8] showed that:

1 Embedding TQM into the culture takes time – it takes five years to move

from the phase of deciding to implement TQM to having it fully institutionalized.

2 There are several barriers to initiating TQM. They are, in descending order of importance, leadership, strategic planning, training, employee involvement, measurement, customer focus.

3 Most establishments pursuing TQM programmes report a positive impact on performance (defined as a composite of productivity, quality, timeliness, cost reduction, overall customer service, and customer satisfaction). They also report a positive impact on internal operating conditions (attention to customer requirements, group process and problem solving, management by fact).

4 They identified various barriers that impede TQM progress. In descending order of importance these are:
- employees don't believe they are empowered
- funding constraints
- employees lack information on TQM tools
- resistance to participatory management
- lack of information on TQM concepts
- employee resistance to changing roles
- personnel regulations
- senior management not spending time
- lack of long-term planning.

KEY PEOPLE FOR CONTINUOUS BUSINESS IMPROVEMENT

The research by A.T. Kearney highlights some of the differences between success and failure. The implementation of improvement programmes is fundamentally a question of introducing innovation, which itself is a subject that has been extensively researched over the past 20 years. Most of the studies have concentrated on successful product and process innovation in the design and manufacturing environments but their conclusions can, in the main, be applied to any organization because continuous business improvement requires the same environment as any other form of innovation in order for it to be successful.

Rothwell[5] makes the following observation about management:

> Success is people centred. Formal management techniques can enhance the performance of competent managers, but they are no substitute for management of high quality and ability, that it, innovation is essentially a people process and simply attempting to substitute formal management techniques for management talent and entrepreneurial flair is not a viable option.

Although no precise prescription or recipe for success exists, the research does identify some of the characteristics of successful innovation. These are summarized in Tables 2.3 and 2.4.

It can be seen from the above that the research into innovation generally supports the conclusions of the more focused surveys into TQM and the evidence provided by the Baldrige experience. Improvement programmes are not delivering what senior executives want, and one reason for this is that the programmes lack focus. Quality is not something to seek for its own sake. The reason for improving quality is because it helps to achieve the ultimate goal – to improve profit. An effective improvement programme must be able to show the link between:

Improving quality → Improving customer satisfaction → Improving market share → Improving profit.

This linkage is emphasized in the Baldrige (MBNQA) framework, where one of the questions is: 'How does the company relate overall improvements in product/service quality and operational performance to changes in overall financial performance?'

In order for improvement programmes to be successful, they need to be treated like any other product or process innovation. The preconditions for success need to be established before the programme is started. Rather than randomly trying improvement tools and techniques, they need to be

TABLE 2.3   Innovation success factors

1 The establishment of good internal and external communication. Effective linkages with external sources of knowledge, and a willingness to take on external ideas.
2 Treating innovation as a corporate-wide task. Effective functional integration involving all departments in the project from its earliest stages.
3 Implementing careful planning and project control procedures. Regular appraisal of projects.
4 Efficiency in development work and high quality production. Implementing effective quality control procedures.
5 Strong market orientation. Emphasis on satisfying user needs, efficient customer linkages, involving potential users in the development process.
6 Providing a good support service to customers, including training where appropriate.
7 The presence of certain key individuals. (See below)
8 High quality of management. Dynamic and open-minded managers able to attract and retain talented managers and researchers. A commitment to the development of human capital.

TABLE 2.4   Key individuals

PRODUCT CHAMPION	TECHNOLOGICAL GATEKEEPER
• Enthusiastically supports the innovation, especially during critical phases and is personally committed to it. • Particularly effective at maintaining impetus and support when difficulties are encountered. • Has sufficient power and authority to influence the course of events and to break down internal barriers to change.	• Attends conferences and seminars, has a comprehensive network of external contacts and is an avid reader of the primary literature. Thus brings a considerable volume of technical information into the firm. • Also an effective internal communicator who disseminates the information via a gatekeeper network.

appropriate and focused on the goals of the organization and the critical success factors required to achieve those goals; in particular they must focus on the customer.

In summary, the reason why we need continuous business improvement is that any enterprise, however successful, will be overtaken by its competitors as soon as it thinks that it is in the lead and starts to relax and get complacent. The answer is to keep watching the others; if you are in the lead, look over your shoulder to make sure that no one is catching you; if you are behind, keep measuring the gap between yourself and the leaders, and keep taking action to close it. Running a successful business is as much a race as any Olympic event.

The improvement activities within a company are not undertaken in the pursuit of some mystical holy grail of perfect quality, but because they will ultimately affect the bottom line. All improvement activities need to be aligned to what is strategically important to the organization's continued success.

KEY PLAYERS

The most important players in the pursuit of improvement are the process owner and the gatekeepers.

Process owners

Process owners have a difficult job. Invariably they are senior managers who also have a functional responsibility. They are given a process owner job to perform in addition to their normal role, which often means that process ownership becomes the subordinate role with insufficient attention paid to it. This results in the wrong signal being given to the staff; they then see process improvement as less important than their normal department job and therefore place as little emphasis on it as possible. If business improvement is important to the organization it must, like justice, be seen to be done; the responsibilities of process ownership must be given equal weight to the manager's functional responsibility. The responsibilities of a process owner are:

- Drive cross-functional alignment so that all process workers are focused on satisfying the needs of the process customer, and not just those of their functional management.
- Ensure that there is a simple system of measurements in place which will measure the parameters that the customer and stakeholders have decided are important. (It should not be a system that only measures what is easy to measure, or what 'we have always measured'.)
- Ensure that the total process is actively managed and is being subjected to a rigorous improvement methodology, which the process owner leads with a cross-functional process improvement team.
- Ensure that all problems are promptly resolved and root causes eliminated.
- Ensure that process workers obtain feedback from the process customers that confirms that they are meeting all requirements and have totally satisfied their customers.
- Compare their process performance and approaches to those of the 'best practice' that they can find.

Gatekeepers

There are two gatekeeper roles: one for new technologies, the for new methodologies. Both would be expected to provide a 'centre of competence' service to the rest of the organization, providing education and training, help and guidance, and ensuring, with the process owners and process improvement teams, that the new approaches to process management and improvement are used to their full effect, and that emerging technologies are evaluated for their potential to provide novel solutions to what are often old problems. As the name 'gatekeeper' implies, they provide the link between the outside world and the internal workings of the organization. They do this by attending conferences and seminars, having a comprehensive network of external contacts and reading primary literature, thus bringing a considerable volume of technical information into the firm. They must also be effective communicators who disseminate the information via an internal network.

REFERENCES

1 Ingersoll Engineers Ltd. (1992). *Commitment: implementing the vision. A survey of the management of change in manufacturing businesses.* Ingersoll Engineers Survey.

2 Cottrell, J. (1992). 'Favourite recipe'. *TQM Magazine*, February.

3 Interim Report to the President and to the Congress on the MBNQA, US Department of Commerce, April 1991.

4 Hodgetts, R.M. (1994). 'Quality lessons from America's Baldrige winners'. *Business Horizons*, July/August.

5 Rothwell, R. (1992). 'Successful industrial innovation: critical factors for the 1990s'. *R&D Management*, 22 March.

6 Povey, B. (1993). 'Continuing improvements'. *TQM Magazine*, December.

7 Tetzely, R. (1992). *Fortune Magazine*, 18 May.

8 *Quality Management: Survey of Federal Organisations.* United States General Accounting Office, Washington, DC. October, 1992.

RECOMMENDED READING

Goldratt, E.M. and Cox, J. (1989). *The Goal.* Gower Publishing Company Limited, Aldershot.

Denning, W.E. (1990). *Out of the Crisis.* Cambridge University Press, Cambridge.

Tools and Techniques

CHAPTER

3

Systems and processes

Study the past if you would divine the future.
(Confucius)

Sustained, continuous business improvement comes from a focus on the system and processes through which the business is executed. It is therefore necessary to start with an understanding of 'systems' and 'processes' in the context of a business organization, which can be taken to mean any organization, whether profit-making or not.

A simple definition of a system is:

A set of processes that interrelate in a complex manner and collectively form a system.

However, this simple definition needs to be expanded in order to gain a full understanding of 'systems' and 'processes'. The concepts and ideas of systems have been developed by Beer[1] and Checkland,[2] and interpreted by Waring[3] and Flood,[4] among others. A fuller definition of a system, based on their work, is:

A set of interactive components that transform inputs and have outputs, distinguished from its external environment by a boundary. The system should be described as a structured set of verbs – actions which the people employed in the system could directly carry out.

The following is a brief introduction to systems theory, drawing on the original work of Checkland and Beer, but concentrating on the points that are particularly relevant to continuous business improvement.

CHARACTERISTICS OF A SYSTEM

Certain characteristics common to all types of system are:
- a system has inputs
- a system does something (there are outputs)
- addition or removal of a component changes the system
- inclusion of a component affects the component
- a system has emergent properties (the whole is greater than the sum of the parts)
- a system has a boundary
- a system has an environment (outside the boundary) that affects it
- someone owns the system.

These characteristics can be more easily understood by considering the familiar example of a restaurant (which will be used throughout this chapter).

1 *A system has inputs.* The restaurant system has inputs such as raw ingredients and hungry customers.

2 *A system does something (there are outputs).* The restaurant system transforms the inputs into the principal output of a satisfied, replete customer. (The customer is the principal output – there are secondary outputs as well.)

3 *Addition or removal of a component changes the system.* The restaurant system is made up of many components such as the staff and fixtures and fittings. Removing any one of these affects the system; for example, removing the tables from the system changes it from a 'sit-down restaurant' system to a 'take-away food' supply system.

4 *Inclusion of a component affects the component.* We are all affected by the systems in which we work. In the case of the restaurant system, the waiter is a component of the system that takes and delivers food orders while contributing to the ambience of the restaurant. The waiter is

affected by being a component of the system because while he is within the system he is treated only as a part of that system – a mechanism that performs a function.

5 *A system has emergent properties (the whole is greater than the sum of the parts)*. For example, an aeroplane is a system that has the ability to fly through the air, although any of its individual components cannot fly by themselves, they can only fly as a part of the system. The emergent property of this system is flight. In the case of the restaurant, the emergent property is the ability to feed and satisfy the customer wants; the individual components cannot do this by themselves.

6 *A system has a boundary*. In the restaurant case the boundary is obvious – it has physical boundaries of walls, roof and floor.

7 *A system has an environment (outside the boundary) that affects it.* The restaurant system operates in the environment of the society in which it is placed; this environment provides it with its customers, supplies it with ingredients, specifies the regulations under which it operates, collects taxes from it, collects its waste, etc.

8 *Someone owns the system*. Clearly, the system owner in this case is the restaurant owner, who could be an individual, a bank or a group.

Types of System

Four major types of system have been identified. Being able to recognize the various types of system is a significant contribution to understanding the basic problem that afflicts business improvement in all organizations. The tools and techniques of process analysis were developed in the world of abstract and engineered systems, but they are now being applied in the world of human activity systems – and experience of working in human activity systems shows time and time again that it is one thing to design an elegant solution on paper, but a totally different thing to get it effectively implemented in the office! The four types of system are:

- *Natural systems*
  (for example, biological systems)

- *Abstract systems*
  (for example, computer programs)
- *Engineered systems*
  (for example, machines)
- *Human activity systems*
  (for example, a restaurant).

The various elements of the system communicate with each other and with their environment to provide information with which to control their activities. As the amount of information increases, the amount of variety that the management system must deal with also increases. There comes a point when management by exception occurs because management functions can no longer deal with the amount of variety of information.

There is a hierarchy of systems; each system is a sub-system (micro system) of a larger system, and is also a macro system itself, containing smaller sub-systems of its own. The system is defined by drawing boundaries around it and identifying the inputs and outputs that cross the boundary. This can be done in two ways; either by relying exclusively on the inputs and outputs, in which case the system is treated as a 'black box', or by describing the activities that take place within the system that produce the transformation of inputs into outputs. For example, a shareholder could view a company as a black box system which takes certain inputs and converts them into dividends, whereas the chief executive would view the company as a set of activities (business processes) that transform certain inputs into outputs, one of which is a shareholder dividend.

No single view of a system can fully describe it. It needs to be viewed from a variety of perspectives through the use of a series of metaphors, each of which will illuminate the system differently and which will collectively add to the understanding of the total system. The more useful metaphors are: *machine, organic, brain, culture,* and *political*.[5]

This can best be illustrated by returning to the example of the restaurant. It has boundaries, inputs and outputs, and performs a transformation. It is part of a larger system, yet contains sub-systems of its own. It is a part of the system which is the local community and possibly part of a system of other restaurants owned by a chain. It contains sub-systems such as the storage, preparation and delivery of food and refreshments. It has a boundary – the brick walls which contain it; it has inputs – customers, and supplies of drinks and raw ingredients. Finally it has a set of outputs – satisfied customers, rewarded staff, enriched owner. Its system has performed many transformations: hungry customers into replete ones, raw ingredients into culinary masterpieces, etc. It can also be viewed through a series of metaphors, as follows.

Machine

In what way is a restaurant like a machine? Some of its operations can be seen clearly through the machine metaphor. For example, the actions of the waiter can be viewed as purely mechanical – take the order, bring food, take money, put money in till, give change. It is possible to imagine a robot performing those tasks. Seeing these activities as mechanistic allows the analysis, simplification and improvement of them. But only viewing the restaurant and its components as a machine will not provide a complete picture – quite clearly the waiter is a person, not a robot! The operation of the restaurant needs to be viewed through other metaphors as well, in order to gain a complete picture.

Organic

In what way is the restaurant like an organism, an organized body with connected interdependent parts sharing a common life? Many parts share a common life within the boundary of the restaurant – each customer, the staff, the owner. Each have individual wants and needs from the system, and different roles to play within it. Relationships between the various members are constantly forming and reforming.

Brain

In what ways is a restaurant like a brain? There is a nervous system based on the owner or manager as the central control point taking input from a range of receptors and responding to these stimuli (from the external environment, the customers, and the staff) and issuing commands to limbs and muscles – in this case, the staff.

Culture

What is the culture of the restaurant? It may have its own rituals, theme, and certainly an ambience that make the customer want to return. Then again, its internal culture may be dictated by a rigid set of franchise rules, or it may have a relaxed, homely culture centred around an owner manager.

Political

What is the political structure of the restaurant? Are there leaders, followers, rebels, and malcontents? How do they relate to each other? Are there conflicting aims and aspirations evident among the constituent parts of the system?

Having used a series of metaphors to examine the restaurant, a much clearer understanding of it as a complete system is gained. There is an instinct to view organizations and activities in a purely mechanistic way, as a series of programmed activities that can be documented, mapped, analysed and improved. The need to look at the organization in other ways as well is often overlooked, with the all too frequent result that the simplistic mechanistic approach fails!

HARD AND SOFT SYSTEMS

Systems can be classified as either hard or soft. Hard systems tend to be the engineered and abstract systems such as machines or computer applications. Soft systems tend to be the natural and human activity systems (such as the organizations in which people work). The differentiation between hard and soft systems is the degree of predictability and repeatability. A hard system is both predictable and repeatable unless a catastrophic breakdown occurs. Soft systems are predictable and repeatable to a far smaller degree than hard systems.

Hard systems

As described by Waring,[1] these have readily quantifiable and measurable attributes and have fewer unpredictable properties than soft systems. They are characterized by well-defined structures and processes and readily quantifiable features, all of which aid prediction and control. World views (described later in this chapter) need to be taken into account but are not a dominant feature of hard systems analysis.

Hard systems approach

The hard systems approach to problem solving assumes that:
- Problems can be identified, described and solved.
- There is an optimal solution which is superior to others.
- Measures of performance are quantifiable.
- Systems models depend largely on mathematical relationships.
- There is a large level of agreement among the client set on the nature of the problem.
- The client set largely agrees about the overall goal.

Hard systems analysis evolved from the defence industry in the US, and grew to maturity within the information technology (IT) departments of organizations around the world. Years of experience in the computer systems environment have demonstrated that this approach is very effective – in environments where there is little or no human activity, where it is a genuinely machine-like environment. This success with systems engineering led to many attempts to use the same approach with problems in social (human activity) systems, with disappointing results. It was this failure of hard systems analysis in the human activity situation that stimulated Checkland[2] to develop his soft systems ideas.

Soft systems

Soft systems have a much higher degree of unpredictability because they involve people's attitudes and behaviour. They typically have properties that are difficult to quantify or measure. Soft systems are the human activity systems. Unlike hard systems analysis it is usually not possible to describe accurately a problem to be solved, because all the people involved in the system are to some degree a part of the problem.

Typical responses to attempts to make improvement in the soft systems environment are statements such as: 'We have always done it this way', and 'I don't know why I have to do this operation, it's what I was told to do when I joined this group'. What were initially effective business processes have degenerated over time to the status of rituals; things are always done like this, we no longer know why, but we shall continue doing things this way because it often produces the right result.

Soft systems approach

At the centre of soft systems analysis is the need to move from the real world to the idealized world of what might be. The objective is to build a hypothetical model of the system that performs all the functions necessary to produce the transformation of inputs into outputs required of the system. To understand properly what the desired transformation is, a root definition of the ideal world system needs to be constructed. Checkland has developed a method of developing root definitions using the mnemonic CATWOE:

- **C**ustomers of the system
- **A**ctors who carry out the activities
- **T**ransformation process
- **W**eltanschauung (the world view of the system)
- **O**wnership of the system
- **E**nvironmental constraints on the system

Each of these points needs to be addressed in order to construct a comprehensive root definition of the system – a complete definition of the human activity system. Before using this mnemonic to develop an example root definition of a restaurant system, the concept of *Weltanschauung* needs to be understood (taking a world view, looking at the system from the perspectives of all the people affected by it). Systems in the business world are usually systems of human activity. Human activity systems (any organization that employs people) can be described in different ways by each individual affected by it. There will never be one single complete view of a human activity system; as each of the individuals affected by the system will have a different perception of it. In the restaurant example, it is viewed differently by each of the individuals affected by it; the owner may view it as a system for transforming raw ingredients into profits; the staff view it as a system for transforming work into pay; the government views it as a system for transforming a basic human need into tax revenue; and finally, the customers view it as a system for transforming hunger into satisfaction.

A root definition of the restaurant system can be developed using the above mnemonic:

- **C**ustomers of the system: the primary customers are the clients who go to the restaurant in order to eat.
- **A**ctors who carry out the activities: these are the staff – the waiters, chefs, cleaners, dishwashers, etc.
- **T**ransformation process: hungry customers are transformed into replete ones, raw ingredients are transformed into meals.
- **W**eltanschauung (the perceptions of the individuals affected by the system):
  - *social customer*: a system for transforming hunger to satisfaction
  - *business customer*: a system for conducting business in an informal atmosphere
  - *chef*: a system for creatively producing gourmet meals
  - *waiter*: a system for earning money in exchange for work
  - *owner*: a profit-generating system
  - *dustman*: a system for producing waste material.
- **O**wnership of the system: the owner of the restaurant owns the system.
- **E**nvironmental constraints on the system: environmental health regulations, local government by-laws, car parking regulations.

Having used the mnemonic to examine the system from a variety of perspectives, it is then possible to construct a root definition that encompasses the salient points. The root definition can be considered to be the purpose or objective of the system. Our restaurant system is:

A system for providing excellent food for customers in a relaxed, informal atmosphere, while providing a reasonable financial return for its owner and staff and obeying all regulatory constraints.

Once the root definition has been developed, it is possible to think about how a system in the ideal world could perform the required transformation, and then to compare it to the system that actually exists in the real world and draw conclusions about the differences. This soft systems methodology developed by Checkland (see Fig. 3.1) has seven steps, moving from the real world into the ideal world of systems thinking, and then back again into the real world.

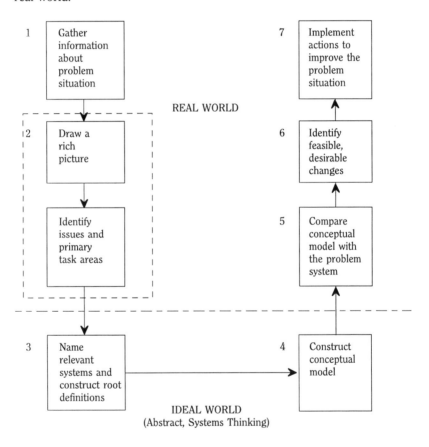

FIGURE 3.1   Soft systems methodology

Source: Checkland, P. (1981) *Systems Thinking, Systems Practice*. John Wiley & Sons. Reproduced by permission of John Wiley & Sons Ltd.

Real world
1 The problem – unstructured.
2 The problem situation – defined (the function of stages 1 and 2 is to describe the situation in the real world so that a range of possible and relevant alternatives can later be identified).

Systems thinking
3 Construct root definitions of the relevant systems.
4 Construct conceptual models – make a model of the activity system needed to achieve the transformation described in the definition. The definition is a description of what the system *is*; the conceptual model is an account of the activities the system must *do* in order to be the system named in the definition. There is a tendency for conceptual model definitions to slip into becoming a description of the actual problem system from the real world. This confusion of the 'as-is' and 'to-be' systems prevents the subsequent comparison of the two from yielding any new solutions or approaches. The activities contained within the conceptual model must be individually necessary to affect the system transformation, and collectively sufficient to do so.

Back in the real world
5 Compare stage 4 with stage 2 – the comparison of the conceptual model to the real world is not aimed at telling people what ought to be done, but to suggest possible changes for consideration.
6 Identify feasible, desirable changes.
7 Develop actio s to improve the problem situation.
The changes identified as a result of comparing the real and ideal worlds must meet two criteria; they must be systematically *desirable* and they must be culturally *feasible*.

BUSINESS PROCESSES AND PROCESS MODELS
Having started by examining and understanding the complete system, it is now possible to view business processes in their proper context – that

processes are collectively the means by which a system transforms its inputs into outputs. Once the system has been described by its root definition, a model can be constructed of the business processes required to perform the transformations contained within the root definition. Each process that is part of the system also has inputs, and performs a transformation on them to provide a set of outputs.

Processes, because they are contained within systems, share many system characteristics. One of these is that they are recursive – that is, there are successive decompositions from the top level right down to the work instruction level. The top level would share the same definition as its owning system. Other shared characteristics are that processes should also be described with a verb/noun combination, thus ensuring that the focus is on the activity performed within the process, and that processes have inputs on which work is performed to transform them into outputs. Figure 3.2 illustrates these points using the restaurant example.

A common point of confusion within organizations is that they believe that they have their processes well defined, when what they actually have is a set of working procedures. The difference between a process and a work procedure (which documents what happens at the bottom of the hierarchy) is:

- a process describes *what* is done
- a working procedure describes *how* it is done.

PROCESS ANALYSIS AND MAPPING

The reason for mapping a process is to provide a visual representation of it on paper that can be used to aid communication (particularly cross-functional) and thus enabling it to be easily understood in its totality, with the relationships between individual steps understood, and inconsistencies, bottlenecks, duplications and the unmanaged 'white spaces' identified. Mapping has two essential parts:

1 *The process flow diagram*

A visual representation of the process that shows the sequence in which

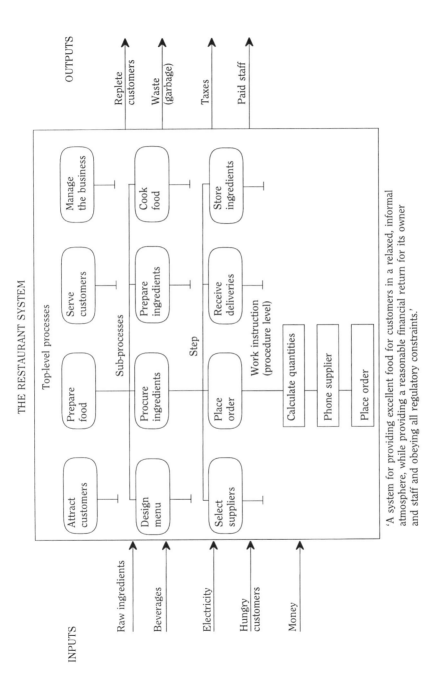

THE RESTAURANT SYSTEM

INPUTS

Raw ingredients

Beverages

Electricity

Hungry customers

Money

Top-level processes

Attract customers

Design menu

Prepare food

Serve customers

Manage the business

Sub-processes

Procure ingredients

Prepare ingredients

Cook food

Select suppliers

Place order

Receive deliveries

Store ingredients

Step

Work instruction (procedure level)

Calculate quantities

Phone supplier

Place order

OUTPUTS

Replete customers

Waste (garbage)

Taxes

Paid staff

'A system for providing excellent food for customers in a relaxed, informal atmosphere, while providing a reasonable financial return for its owner and staff and obeying all regulatory constraints.'

FIGURE 3.2 The hierarchy of processes within a system

53

activities are performed, and who performs them. Analysis of the flow diagram can reveal whereabouts in the process delays, breakdown and errors are most likely to occur.

2 *A process overview*

More information about the process, in text form, that defines the scope of the process, its customer and suppliers, its owner, its inputs and outputs, what process measurements exist, what activity it starts with and ends with, what activities it includes and, just as importantly, what activities it excludes.

Cost, cycle time, and defect data are required in order to complete the understanding of the process and its problems. These data can be recorded either on the process flow or in the accompanying overview.

Mapping methods

The purpose of the process map or model is to help answer questions about the system being modelled, and there are several modelling methods that can be employed. Three of the most useful ones are flowcharts, process activity charts and IDEF0.

Flowcharts

This is the simplest way to create a visual representation of a process and is quite suitable in the case that all that is needed is to be able to show the sequence in which activities occur. However, flowcharts have a limitation when there are many people or functions involved in the process. For this reason, flowcharts are most often used to represent the activities at the lowest level of process – the work instruction or procedure level, where a sequence of activities is carried out by the same person or group of people. An example of the simple flowchart is given in Fig. 3.3, using the restaurant process as an example. As can be seen, just by using a rectangle for activities, diamonds for decisions, and lines to join them, a very effective representation of the process is produced.

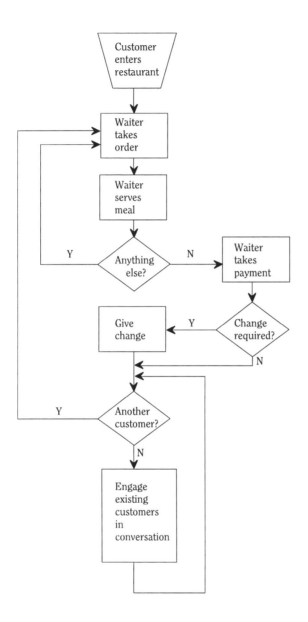

FIGURE 3.3   Basic flowchart of 'Serve Customer' process

Process activity charts

These are an enhancement to the basic flowchart. They still show clearly the sequence of activities, but now also show each individual or group performing the task, which is a real advantage when many people are involved in the process. They also have the major advantages of:

- Showing clearly where activity transfers from one person or function to another. This is a very important point, as it is at these transfer points that the majority of process breakdowns, such as delays or mistakes, occur.
- Including the customer of the process. It is amazing how often standard process flowcharts completely ignore any interaction with the customer, and therefore fail to highlight the fact that each of these interactions is a moment of truth[3] at which the customer forms his opinion of the organization. Omitting the customer from the process chart also contributes to subsequent improvement activity being internally focused.

Figure 3.4 shows an example of a process activity chart, once again from a restaurant.

IDEF0

This activity modelling system seems to divide people quickly into two opposing camps; there are those that love it, and those that shy away from it because they feel that it is too complicated. IDEF (Integrated Definition method) was defined by the US Air Force as part of its integrated computer-aided manufacturing programme. IDEF0 was developed as the standard for modelling function (activity), and IDEF1 for modelling the information structure (IS). IDEF was developed with the needs of the manufacturing systems developer in mind (which may account for the two opposing camps; those who love it tend to be concerned with the IS function). At its heart it is a straightforward approach that visually captures the key information required to allow a process to be understood. One of its strengths is that it allows easy decomposition from a top-level process down through successive levels of sub-process. IDEF0 analysis shows:

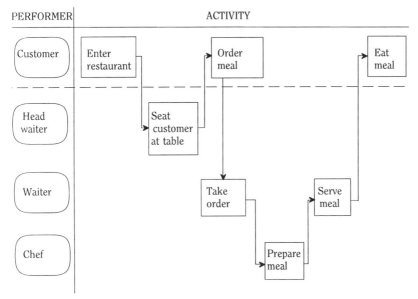

FIGURE 3.4   Process analysis chart – restaurant 'Serve Customer' process

- the activity
- what resources it uses (people and equipment)
- what controls it
- the process inputs (that are transformed into outputs by the activity)
- the process outputs
- the relationship of this process to others in the hierarchy.

The basic representation is shown in Fig. 3.5. In this context, *inputs* are data, information, or material used by the process step or activity to produce the outputs; *controls* are items that regulate the activity; *outputs* are the result of the activity; and *mechanisms* are the people, machines or resources that the activity uses.

A set of activities that collectively make up a sub-process can be shown in one IDEF0 chart, allowing the relationships between the steps to be easily seen. As a rule of thumb, four or five activities are enough for one chart. If more detail is required, then further decompositions of the process

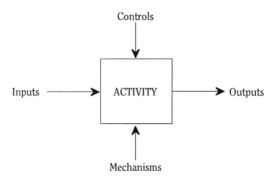

FIGURE 3.5 Basic IDEF0 diagram

should be used. Figure 3.6 is an IDEF0 chart representing the restaurant process. The problem for IDEF0 beginners can now be seen: the number of connecting lines on the chart can appear confusing at first glance, which leads to the common conclusion that these charts are over complicated. This has led to the development of an improved version of IDEF0, called Quality Management Activity (Q-MAP).[4] This shares many common features with IDEF0, but Q-MAPs are generally much easier to use and understand.

The choice of process modelling technique is really a 'horses for courses' one. If multiple decompositions are not required, or if the people involved in the process analysis work are not familiar with IDEF0, then the process activity chart technique should be used; it is certainly more intuitive and allows the capture of the main items required. Experience has shown that people are comfortable using the process activity chart format within a few minutes of being introduced to it. Until recently there was not one single methodology that was entirely appropriate for use at all levels – the top-level processes, the sub-processes, and the individual job level. To overcome this, I personally have found IDEF0 to be a good tool to use at the top, strategic level when I needed to understand the major activities that occurred within an organization and how they interrelated with each other. I then switch to using process activity charts to map the individual business processes, as these are ideal aids for the identification of unnecessary

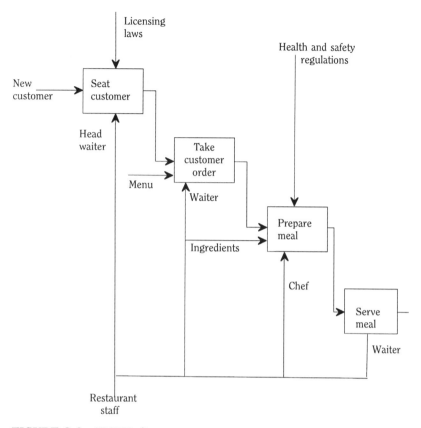

**FIGURE 3.6   IDEF0 diagram – restaurant 'Serve Customer'
process**

activities and excessive 'handovers'. I then switch again to using standard
flowcharting in order to represent the activities that occur at the individual
job level. Fortunately, good methodologies, supported by PC applications,
that cover each of these uses of process maps, are now becoming available.

PRIORITIZING PROCESSES FOR IMPROVEMENT

Before business processes can be improved or re-engineered, it is necessary
to understand what processes are actually required to deliver the

organization's mission, and in what order of priority they should be addressed. Trying to improve all of an organization's processes simultaneously is generally a recipe for failure. An effective method for identifying an organization's business processes, and then prioritizing them for improvement, is Process Quality Management (PQM).[6] This is basically a straightforward procedure, most effective when carried out by the senior executive team guided by an independent facilitator. (One of the reasons why this approach is so effective is because senior management are involved from the outset, which gains their 'buy-in' to the whole exercise.) The essence of PQM is shown in Table 3.1.

TABLE 3.1   Process quality management

STEP	ACTIVITY	COMMENTS
1	Develop mission statement	• The mission is what the executive team are collectively paid for • The mission statement should not be longer than 3 or 4 sentences • The mission statement should be worded so that you can tell when it has been achieved
2	Develop goals (critical success factors)	• Critical success factors (CSFs) are the things that the team must accomplish in order to achieve its mission • They should each start with 'We need ...', or 'We must ...' • The test for CSFs is that each should be *necessary* to achieve the mission, and that collectively, they are *sufficient* to achieve it
3	Identify the processes that accomplish the CSFs	• Each process must be named as verb/noun • Each process must have an owner within the executive team • The list of processes must be necessary and sufficient to accomplish the CSFs

STEP	ACTIVITY	COMMENTS
4	Rank processes to identify the most important to the mission	<ul><li>Construct a matrix of processes and CSFs</li><li>Ask for each CSF in turn, 'which processes must be performed particularly well in order for this CSF to be achieved?'</li><li>Indicate in the matrix those processes that are essential to each CSF</li><li>The processes that are essential to the most CSFs are then clearly the most important to achieving the mission</li></ul>
5	Rate process performance	<ul><li>Assess each process subjectively as: A = Excellent performance B = Good performance C = Fair performance D = Bad performance E = Embryonic performance</li></ul>
6	Compare process importance and performance	Plot process performance against importance. The top priority for attention comprises those processes that are most important to the mission but which are performing badly

The subjective rating of processes from A to E in Table 3.1 can be supplemented by more rigorous approaches such as process maturity assessment, if that is considered necessary.

Process maturity assessment

The approach to process maturity assessment was developed for use in the software development field,[7] and it has its roots in the Quality Management Maturity Grid first developed by Crosby[8] who identified five stages (uncertainty, awakening, enlightenment, wisdom, certainty) with which to evaluate certain categories of quality management.

There is nothing intrinsically unique about software development processes that prevents the process maturity assessment technique from

being used for any other business process. It allows each process to be
categorized into one of five levels, from initial to optimized. For software
development processes a detailed questionnaire has been developed that
allows the process to be accurately categorized. However, the definition of
each category has sufficient detail to allow a business process to be
categorized fairly accurately without resorting to over-detailed questionnaires. The categories and definitions are shown in Table 3.2.

The final step of PQM is to compare the process performance to the
importance of the process (established in the preceding step of the PQM
technique) as shown in Fig. 3.7. Those processes that fall into the quadrant
of poor performance/high importance are the ones that need to be
addressed as the priority. However, there is a flaw in this approach – the

TABLE 3.2 Process maturity assessment

MATURITY LEVEL	DEFINITION	CHARACTERISTICS
1 Initial	Ad hoc, chaotic	● Ill-defined procedures and controls ● May have serious cost/schedule problems
2 Repeatable	Dependent on individuals, intuitive	● Costs and schedules managed ● Standard methods and procedures used
3 Defined	Defined process	● Process well characterized and understood ● Improvements are being made ● Systematic process controls are in place
4 Managed	Measured process	● Process is well understood, quantified, measured, and controlled ● Operating decisions are based on quantitative process data
5 Optimized	Improvement fed back into process	● High degree of process control ● Error cause analysis and prevention ● Process data used to improve the process

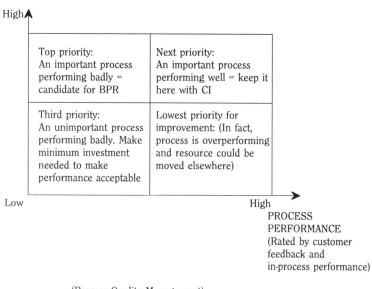

PROCESS IMPORTANCE
(To its customers and
to company goals)

Top priority: An important process performing badly = candidate for BPR	**Next priority:** An important process performing well = keep it here with CI
Third priority: An unimportant process performing badly. Make minimum investment needed to make performance acceptable	Lowest priority for improvement: (In fact, process is overperforming and resource could be moved elsewhere)

High ▲ ... Low ... High →

PROCESS
PERFORMANCE
(Rated by customer
feedback and
in-process performance)

(Process Quality Management)

FIGURE 3.7   Selecting processes for improvement

focus for process improvement should be the customer, and only taking an internal view of how the process is performing will result in any subsequent improvement activity only having an internal focus. The internal assessment of process performance really needs to be combined with a customer view of that process, so that improvement activity also has the essential external perspective which ensures that it really brings benefit to the whole business.

Remember that process improvement is not like baking a cake; just following the recipe will not result in a perfect end-product. Each ingredient is required and each step in the PQM technique needs to be performed, but the outputs of each step only provide information to the management team. It is the quality of the decisions they take based on that information that ultimately determines whether the exercise will be successful!

BUSINESS PROCESS IMPROVEMENT

The activities performed in process quality management are the first steps of business process improvement – establishing the priority for improvement. The next stage is actually to make improvements to the chosen process. Various methodologies exist to help with this stage. They resemble Checkland's soft systems methodology described earlier in that they start with the 'as-is' process (Checkland's real world) and then move into the 'to-be' process (Checkland's ideal world). However, they differ significantly in that none of them take a world view of the process through the eyes of the various people involved or affected by it. Their approach is therefore strictly mechanistic, and because they never considered the world view at the beginning they are generally unable to make the crucial assessment at the end about whether the proposed changes are both *culturally feasible* and *systemically desirable*.

Table 3.3 shows three approaches to process improvement and highlights:

- the unique step of developing the root definition in the soft systems approach
- that process quality management is really a front end to other process improvement methodologies (which tend to start with the assumption that the process to be improved has already been selected).

A fully effective process improvement methodology should be a composite of all three approaches that would cover all the important aspects of business process improvement, as will be seen later.

Many of the tools of process management and improvement have come from the hard systems (engineered systems) areas of business, but are now being applied in the soft systems (human activity system) areas. The hard systems approach is exactly right when dealing with machines and software programs, but not when the role of people within a business process is being addressed. In this circumstance the approach must be modified to bring in some of the aspects of Checkland's soft approach, particularly the use of his 'acid test' – to make sure that the new or improved business process is both systemically desirable and culturally

TABLE 3.3 Process improvement approaches

IBM BUSINESS PROCESS MANAGEMENT	SOFT SYSTEMS METHODOLOGY	PROCESS QUALITY MANAGEMENT
		1 Develop mission statement
		2 Develop CSFs
		3 Identify key processes
1 Get organized		4 Rank processes by importance
2 Talk to your customers		
3 Walk the process		5 Rate process performance
4 Set priorities		6 Compare importance/ performance
	1 Real world – unstructured problems	
	2 Real world – structured problem into issues	
	3 Develop root definition	
5 Benchmark your process	4 Develop conceptual model (ideal world)	
6 Develop solutions	5 Compare real and ideal worlds (as-is and to-be)	
7 Get buy-in	6 Identify feasible, desirable changes	
8 Finalize your improvement plan		
9 Pilot your solution	7 Action to improve the problem situation	
10 Roll out your solution		

feasible (that is, to ensure that from a purely mechanistic view of the process the changes would actually work and would be an improvement, and also to ensure from the human view that the changes would be acceptable to the people involved in the process and would work within the culture of the organization). This extra step would help to overcome the common problem that in many cases the results of the process analysis and improvement do not get implemented.

Detailed process analysis, problem identification, and improvement used to be the domain of the 'Organization and Methods' (O&M) department. Few organizations now have such a department; often it was absorbed into the IS function when that became established with the introduction of the use of business computers. Over time the O&M focus shifted from workflow analysis and improvement towards introducing computer systems to help speed up work activities. The result has been a steady decline in knowledge and understanding of work processes, which is now having to be arrested by relearning many of these old techniques. Webster's *Handbook of O&M Analysis*,[9] published as long ago as 1973, describes the O&M approach, which has many echoes in the various process improvement and 're-engineering' methodologies of today. A summary of the O&M approach (outlined in Table 3.4) and a more detailed explanation of each step follows.

TABLE 3.4 Organization and methods approach to improvement

STEP	ACTIVITY
1	Determine the purpose and scope of the study
2	Obtain facts relating to the existing situation
3	Study the data and form conclusions
4	Formulate proposals
5	Obtain approvals
6	Implement proposals

Determine the purpose and scope of the study
First, gather preliminary data:
- are other departments affected by the study?
- what are the customer's interests and needs?
- what is the current organization?
- work statistics

- quality of work – errors, delays, complaints
- costings of activities
- use of staff – overtime, etc.
- quality control arrangements
- work procedures
- objectives for each main activity.

Next, verify the purpose of the process being examined. At the very beginning of the study the purpose of what is being done must be established, and it must be verified that the work is really necessary and worth doing. As Webster says, 'People become obsessed with the mechanics of the things they are required to do; they elaborate, extend, introduce exceptions and lose a clear sight of the original intention of the activity.'

Obtain facts relating to the existing situation

Data can be collected by using one or more of:

- discussion with management
- examination of the operational, statistical, and financial data
- obtaining written information such as activity lists from those that do the work
- directly observing the flow of work and the working conditions
- random observation using statistical techniques
- asking those who do the work.

An important point, and one that does not come over strongly in many of the process analysis methodologies, is the *movement of work* – how do the papers, materials and people have to move in order for the work to be accomplished; how are machines located to ensure the smooth flow of work? Webster recommends drawing a scale plan, and then drawing lines on it to show where movement occurs, the frequency, and the distances involved, even using string diagrams where necessary. Even with the sophisticated computer simulations available today these simple techniques are still effective in many cases. Also included in this stage of the study is the construction of flowcharts or process charts, using similar techniques to those described earlier. The essential data that needs to be gathered in this stage answers the questions *why, what, who, when, where, how* and *how much.*

Study the data and form conclusions

The basic purpose of this form of study is to identify problems within the work process and their root causes, and also to be able to simplify the process itself. The particular problems that need to be solved should now be focused on, and the data used to uncover the fundamental causes of deficiencies and weaknesses. It is also necessary before starting to formulate proposals, to understand the constraints that may limit action, such as company policy, human factors, the availability of resources, etc.

Process simplification involves not only finding more efficient ways of performing activities, but also establishing whether those activities really need to be done at all. In order to be able to do this, the activities need to be compared to the overall purpose of the process. This can be done by first developing a list of all the things that the process must do in order for it to meet its objective, then deciding what is achieved by each activity that occurs within the process. This can then be compared to the overall purpose of the process in order to decide whether what is achieved by each activity makes a contribution to the purpose and therefore adds value, or makes no contribution to the purpose, and therefore does not add value and should be eliminated.

Formulate proposals

This requires a move from the mechanical world of data gathering and the logic of analysis, into the creative world of ideas generation. The basic rules of brainstorming need to be applied (separating ideas generation from their evaluation). Once ideas have been gathered they can be evaluated and converted into specific, implementable proposals.

These proposals must then be tested with the people who will be affected by their implementation. The people involved in the day-to-day activity within the process may well identify problems or difficulties with the proposal that have been overlooked; with their detailed knowledge of the process they may be able to suggest improvements to the original proposals and, at the end of the exercise, because they have been consulted, involved, and allowed to influence the end results, they will have some 'buy-in' at the implementation stage.

Obtain approvals

Clearly, the manager or executive who sponsored the study needs to approve the recommendations before they are implemented. Others whose agreement should be sought are the managers and owners of processes that interface with the process in question (usually as either a customer or a supplier) to ensure that the proposals that will simplify and improve one process or sub-process do not have the opposite result somewhere else within the organization.

Implement proposals

Now the stage is set for the proposals to be implemented. This should be the responsibility of line management, wherever possible working with teams drawn from the people who operate the process.

REFERENCES

1   Waring, A. (1989). *Systems Methods for Managers*. Blackwell Scientific Publications.
2   Checkland, P. (1981). *Systems Thinking, Systems Practice*. John Wiley, Chichester.
3   Carlzon, J. (1989). *Moments of Truth*. Perennial Library, Harper & Row, New York.
4   Crossfield, R.T. and Dale, B.G. (1990). 'Mapping quality assurance systems: a methodology'. *Quality and Reliability Engineering International*, vol. 6, pp. 167–178.
5   Morgan, G. (1986). *Images of Organization*. Sage Publications.
6   Hardaker, M. and Ward, B. (1987). 'How to make teams work'. *Harvard Business Review*, November/December, vol. 65, no. 6, pp. 112–117.

7   SEI (1991). *A Method of Assessing the Software Engineering Capability of Contractors.* Software Engineering Institute, Carnegie-Mellon University.

8   Crosby, P.B. (1980). *Quality is Free.* Mentor Executive Library, New York.

9   Webster, W.A.R. (1973). *Handbook of O&M Analysis.* Business Books Limited.

RECOMMENDED READING

Beer, S. (1985). *Diagnosing the System for Organisations.* John Wiley, Chichester.

Carlzon, J. (1989). *Moments of Truth.* Perennial Library, Harper & Row, New York.

Checkland, P. (1981). *Systems Thinking, Systems Practice.* John Wiley, Chichester.

Flood, R.L. (1993). *Beyond TQM.* John Wiley, Chichester.

Hardaker, M. and Ward, B. (1987). 'How to make teams work'. *Harvard Business Review,* November/December.

Morgan, G. (1986). *Images of Organization.* Sage Publications.

CHAPTER 4

Benchmarking

Since men for the most part follow in the footsteps and imitate the actions of others, and yet are unable to adhere exactly to those paths which others have taken, or attain to the virtues of those whom they would resemble, the wise man should always follow the roads that have been trodden by the great, and imitate those who have most excelled, so that if he cannot reach their perfection, he may at least acquire something of its savour.
(Niccolo Machiavelli)

According to surveys conducted by the Confederation of British Industries somewhere between 60 and 80 per cent of British industries are now practising benchmarking. However, when asked in another survey what they meant by benchmarking, the huge variation in the answers showed that there is a considerable difference of opinion about what benchmarking is. The exact definition should be expected to vary from company to company as each expresses it in words that they feel a corporate ownership for, but each should contain certain key words, and should position it as a step in business process improvement. Used in this context, benchmarking is a very effective method of driving performance improvement in an organization. The power of benchmarking is that it provides an external view of what is achievable, which helps to answer the three fundamental questions of business improvement:

- Where are we now?
- Where do we want to get to?
- How do we get there?

Because of the way that 'benchmarking' has evolved, the term can be taken to mean anything from competitive product performance comparisons, manufacturing cost comparisons, strategic benchmarking, through to business process benchmarking – which is what is generally meant today by the term. This evolution can be illustrated by looking at how benchmarking has developed in major international companies.

IBM, for example, has a long history of benchmarking, starting at the beginning of the electronic computer era with benchmarking in its original business sense – measuring the computing power of its product running a standard suite of programs (measured in MIPs or millions of instructions per second) and then comparing that to the performance of competitors' products.

The next step in the benchmarking journey was to move from pure product performance comparison to 'reverse engineering' competitors' products. This involved purchasing the competitor product, disassembling it, understanding the parts content and assembly techniques used, and then doing manufacturing and service cost estimates on the basis of 'if we were producing this product, how much would it cost us?' Comparing the resultant estimates for competitors' products to those of its own products tells a company a lot about the excellence of its product designs, parts sourcing strategies and assembly methods. It is then a natural next step to compare the total manufacturing process to those used by other companies, and then to compare the support processes – orders and schedules, production control, warehousing and distribution. Finally, these process comparison techniques, developed in the pure manufacturing environment, can be applied to all the company's business processes, and 'best practice benchmarking', as it is known today, is born!

Benchmarking is often, quite wrongly, confused with competitive analysis. The critical differences are that competitive analysis focuses primarily on the product whereas benchmarking focuses on a business process; also, competitive analysis concentrates on the competition whereas benchmarking spreads a wider net. The limitations of competitive analysis are:[1]

- Lack of direction – competitive analysis quantifies performance gaps but does not offer insights into how superior performance is achieved.
- Industry myopia – competitive analysis limits thinking to what competitors have already achieved rather than what could be achieved.
- The rabbit in the headlights – revealing massive competitive deficiencies can actually paralyze an organization.

These limitations confirm that although competitive analysis is an essential market development activity, it is a separate activity from benchmarking. Commercial organizations must perform competitive analysis, but they must also use the methodical approach provided by benchmarking to look beyond their products to the processes that are the real cause of performance differences, and to look outside of their immediate industry to see what can be learned from others.

TYPES OF BENCHMARKING

Much of the confusion surrounding the term 'benchmarking' stems from its 'flavour of the month' usage as a synonym for 'comparing'. Figure 4.1 shows the relationship between the various types of benchmarking and the related activities of competitive comparisons and market research. It is worthwhile describing these peripheral forms of benchmarking before concentrating on benchmarking as an integral part of process improvement.

Product benchmarking

Product benchmarking is as described in the preceding IBM example. It is the comparison of product performance, features and costs, using techniques such as laboratory performance tests and reverse engineering. This approach is used by all major manufacturers including automobile, electronic, information technology and defence industries. The focus is on

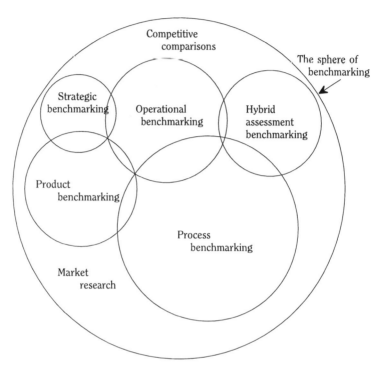

FIGURE 4.1 Benchmarking positioned

the product itself, and conclusions are drawn in directly about the production process used, on the basis of hypothetical cost estimates.

Strategic benchmarking

Before improvement activity (of which benchmarking is a part) can commence, it is necessary to have a clear understanding of what the improvement priorities are within the organization. Failure to prioritize improvement efforts results in either trying to improve everything (trying to boil the ocean) and consequently dissipating all the improvement energy achieving nothing, or going to the other extreme and focusing on the things that are easy to fix, but which can result in an organization performing the trivial things exceptionally well while continuing to do the important things poorly.

Strategic benchmarking has many similarities to competitive benchmarking – comparing the organization to the leaders in the specific industry on a series of parameters[2] such as profitability, market share, return on capital, shareholder return, etc. Data for these comparisons can be derived from an analysis of company reports, or the commissioning of special studies by specialist research organizations. This analysis allows the organization to be ranked against its key competitors in the same industry, and helps the process of identifying where within its operations the problems might be. However, problems cannot be resolved at this macro level – it is necessary to go down to the root cause at the operational process level in order to make genuine improvement.

Operational benchmarking

Operational benchmarking makes comparisons one level down from the strategic, focusing on productivity and direct costs. This comparison will then indicate the problem areas to be investigated at the process level, which is the level that detailed work can be done to identify and implement the improvements required to close the performance gaps. This linkage of strategic, to operational, to business process ensures that the improvements implemented make a real contribution to achieving the organization's strategic goals.

A characteristic of both strategic and operational benchmarking is that they are concerned with the comparison of end results – neither is able to give the complete answer to both *what* the difference is, and *why* that difference exists. In order to answer both of these questions it is necessary to work at the process level.

Hybrid assessment benchmarking

One of the practical difficulties experienced when benchmarking is how to make a real 'apples to apples' comparison between performance in one organization and that in another. One effective way to overcome this is to use a hybrid approach created from the assessment methodology introduced by the quality awards such as Baldrige and the European

Quality Award, combined with a set of criteria developed from the initial process analysis, which identifies the critical parameters that need to be compared with those from the other organizations in a benchmarking study. This allows an objective assessment of all the parties involved in the benchmarking study using a common set of assessment criteria and a common assessment method. The result of this is that valid comparisons can be made which point to areas of superior performance, and which allow the underlying process differences that cause them to be identified.

Process benchmarking

Most benchmarking activity, and most benefits, come from benchmarking at the business process level, because it is only at this level that both the *what* and the *how* question can be answered. Each organization needs to develop its own precise definition of benchmarking – what benchmarking means to them in their own particular business environment. However, a generic definition of process benchmarking that can be used as a starting point is:

> *The continuous, systematic search for and implementation of best practices which improve business processes and lead to superior performance.*

The key words within this definition are:

- *Continuous*
  Benchmarking should not be treated as a 'one-off' exercise; it should be incorporated into the regular planning cycle of the organization.
- *Systematic*
  There is a methodology associated with benchmarking. Several exist, and mostly share the same general approach. The important thing is to ensure that a consistent methodology is adopted by the organization, that process improvement teams are trained in its use, and that it is actually followed.
- *Implementation*
  Benchmarking helps to identify the gaps that exist between current performance and 'best practice', and also how that best practice

performance has been achieved. However, by itself this does not give improved performance – that comes from taking the lessons learned during the benchmarking study and then developing and implementing a process improvement plan based on them. If improvement does not result from the benchmarking exercise then it has been a waste of time! The end result of successful benchmarking is the implementation of change; therefore a precondition for success is that the organization has adopted a philosophy or culture that welcomes change, particularly among supervisors and middle managers who are usually most threatened by these changes.

- *Best practice*
  It is not necessary to identify the absolute 'best practice' in the world in order for benchmarking to be successful. Firstly, it is never certain that what is found is absolute best practice – there will always be someone, somewhere, who is doing better. Secondly, even if the absolute best is found, the gap between current performance and the best may be too big to bridge is one go. (A recent study by Ernst and Young and the American Quality Foundation[3] suggests that 'novices that try to match the techniques used by world-class performers may actually make things worse by trying to do too much, too soon'. Instead, they suggest making gradual progress towards excellence.)
  Thirdly, benchmarking should be a continuous activity – each time through the cycle new and better performing partners should be found.
- *Business processes*
  Benchmarking itself is a fact finding exercise. In order for any benefit to result from the exercise, the data must be analysed and turned into improvement to the business process.

TYPES OF PROCESS BENCHMARKING

There are four generally accepted types of benchmarking partner, as described below. In most circumstances real innovation is found by looking at organizations other than your direct competitors.

Internal

In most larger organizations it is possible to benchmark against other sites or divisions within the same organization. When this is possible it is recommended that initial benchmarking studies are conducted internally – it firstly ensures that all parts of the organization are brought up to the same standard of internal best practice before external parties are approached, and secondly a degree of proficiency with the benchmarking methodology can be developed before third parties are involved; thirdly it ensures that a thorough analysis of the subject process has been conducted prior to the involvement of third parties.

Competitive

This is concerned with the activities of direct competitors and is often conducted through third party research. The reason for this is that a direct approach to competitors to participate in a benchmarking study is likely to be met with suspicion – they are not likely to want to share *what* and *how* with their competitors. The exception is when the process concerned is not directly involved in the areas of competition, when both partners can see a clear benefit to the study, and when they have obtained clearance from their respective legal departments that no law is being breached. Examples[4] of how effective this form of benchmarking can be are:

- Rover halved its test times after benchmarking with Honda.
- British Rail cut the time it took to clean a train to eight minutes after benchmarking against British Airways.

Functional

(Note: in this case the term 'functional' is not referring to a function like 'finance' or 'procurement', but to the basic function performed by the process in question.)

This is conducted with non-competitors and compares processes in organizations performing a similar functional activity. This is usually the easiest approach to collecting data and often yields the most innovative practices. An example here could be a hospital that is looking to improve its ward management process, and realizing that as well as benchmarking against other hospitals, the function of ward management is similar to guest room management in the hotel industry; therefore a hotel chain may be a good benchmarking partner that could yield significant innovation. Other examples[4] are:

- Rank Xerox benchmarking its call handling process against the RAC and British Gas.
- British Airways benchmarking its frequent flyer programme against the Oriental Hotel in Bangkok.

Generic

This is similar to functional benchmarking, but is focused on the processes that are common to any business. Any business has inputs (and therefore a procurement process), employs people to perform value added activity (and therefore has human resource processes), and provides some output (and therefore has marketing, sales and distribution processes).

SUCCESSFUL BENCHMARKING

There are two critical ingredients to successful benchmarking:

1 The methodology employed.
2 The management/coordination approach employed.

The methodology is important in ensuring that individual benchmarking projects are conducted effectively; management/coordination is important in ensuring that benchmarking projects are not *ad hoc* individual events but are part of a systematic company-wide approach.

PROCESS BENCHMARKING METHODOLOGIES

Benchmarking in itself is not a complex operation and the basic steps common to all the various available methodologies are:

1 Understand which processes the improvement effort should be focused on; whatever the type of organization, the most important consideration

when prioritizing processes for improvement should be their importance in meeting customer requirements.

2 Develop a thorough understanding of how that process actually works; identify what is critical to the success of the process; and put performance measurements in place for each of those critical success factors so that a performance baseline can be established.

3 Compare these performance measurements to those achieved by others who are considered to be the best at this particular activity; this establishes the benchmark.

4 From this comparison, identify where the major gaps exist between current performance and the performance of the best, and then investigate the process used to achieve these results.

5 Based on this analysis, develop an improvement plan that will bring the performance of the subject process up to, or better than, the 'best practice' process.

Performance measures indicate what can be achieved. Process comparison establishes *how* it is achieved.

In order for benchmarking efforts to be effective, a consistent methodology should be adopted across the organization. All benchmarking activity in the organization should be conducted using that methodology, and benchmarking team members should be trained in its use. Not surprisingly, all the recognized benchmarking methodologies are similar; they may have a different number of steps, but their parentage can easily be traced back to Camp's original methodology,[5] which in turn uses the structured approach to problem solving introduced to the world as the Deming or Shewhart cycle[6] of **P**lan, **D**o, **C**heck, **A**ct (Fig. 4.2). This cycle is the basic building block of business improvement and many organizations have adopted it, either directly or after making minor changes to make it 'their' improvement tool. It is so fundamental to improvement that *all employees* should be trained in its use (and in the basic analysis tools that it utilizes). The ultimate objective is for this approach of PDCA to become ingrained in the approach all employees bring to problem-solving.

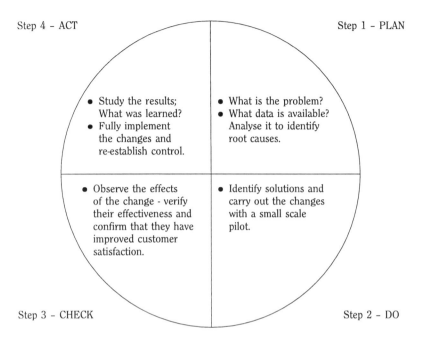

Step 4 - ACT

Step 1 - PLAN

- Study the results;
  What was learned?
- Fully implement
  the changes and
  re-establish control.

- What is the problem?
- What data is available?
  Analyse it to identify
  root causes.

- Observe the effects
  of the change - verify
  their effectiveness and
  confirm that they have
  improved customer
  satisfaction.

- Identify solutions and
  carry out the changes
  with a small scale
  pilot.

Step 3 - CHECK

Step 2 - DO

FIGURE 4.2   The Deming, or Shewhart cycle
Source: Deming, W.E. (1990). *Out of the Crisis*, Cambridge University Press

A GENERIC BENCHMARKING METHODOLOGY

A generic benchmarking methodology, based on IBM's (itself developed after a benchmarking exercise with Xerox among others) is shown in Figure 4.3. This is a sound approach which will be used as an example with which to explore the steps involved in benchmarking.

Planning

Focus the benchmarking study

Establish a sponsor for the project, someone senior enough in the organization and able to overcome any obstacles to the project. Define the problem, issue or requirement that is driving the benchmarking activity, appoint a project leader, and develop a project plan which includes:

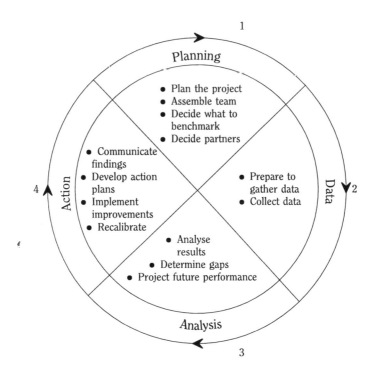

FIGURE 4.3   A generic benchmarking methodology

- process name and owner
- overview of the process
- rationale for what will be benchmarked
- planned approach, including use of internal and external benchmarks
- team members and their roles
- schedule and milestones.

During this step the decision on which process is to be benchmarked is taken. Considerations that influence this decision are the importance of the process in delivering the organization's goals, its importance to delivering delighted customers, its importance to delivering other stakeholder needs, and finally, its effectiveness – what problems does it have?

Establish the benchmarking team

Benchmarking is most effective when performed by a team. The team members should be a project leader and a facilitator who has a thorough knowledge of the benchmarking methodology and related subjects such as process analysis. The other members of the team should be people who are directly involved in the process to be benchmarked – the process owner, designer and operators. The reason for this is firstly that it will encourage their buy-in, their active cooperation in implementing the improvements identified. Secondly, a significant amount of learning occurs during a benchmarking study which does not necessarily find its way into the final report; learning from doing the process analysis, from doing the research, and from seeing first-hand how other organizations perform the same process differently. This learning can be as important as the improvement recommendations that are contained in the final report, and it is a waste if it benefits consultants or central staff groups rather than the people actually performing the process.

Decide what to benchmark

The first step of the methodology included deciding which process was to be benchmarked. This third step then analyses that process to decide exactly what aspects need to be benchmarked. The starting point for this analysis is the initial process assessment that identified a series of problems from various perspectives. These are now broken down into a set of possible causes using simple techniques such as cause and effect diagrams (sometimes known as fishbone or Ishikawa diagrams). The causes thus identified can then be ranked ɪ the order of their impact on customer satisfaction and process performance, so that the exercise focuses on the few critical areas that should be investigated. This list is then used to develop the questionnaires and interview guides that will be used in data collection.

Identify potential benchmarking partners

This is the research step. Potential partners can be identified from many sources:

- award winners
- top-rated companies in industry surveys
- articles in business journals
- internal experts, business partners, suppliers and customers
- industrial and professional associations
- universities
- consultants.

This research can result in a good list of potential partners, but there are two provisos that need to be considered before proceeding further. Firstly, just because an organization has won a prestigious award does not necessarily mean that it is world class at everything it does; in fact some of its business processes may be quite poor. Use reputation as a pointer, but follow up with further research to try to confirm whether they really are best practice in the specific area of interest. Secondly, this step can be quite difficult. Don't give up and settle for a few partners chosen for no other reason than that they are accessible and willing partners; remember that the objective of the exercise is to learn from best practice, not to get through a tedious step as quickly as possible.

Select the benchmarking partners

This step takes the list of potential partners and evaluates them to allow the selection of partners that will provide a good mix of best practice process data. An effective way of performing this evaluation is to use the following matrix. The companies with the highest scores are the ones to be selected as benchmarking partners. The original list of potential partners should be as long as possible; brainstorm a list which includes potential partners from all four categories, and then refine the list by evaluating each partner in turn against the selection criteria. The selection criteria shown in this table can be considered the basic set; others can be added depending on the needs of the group performing the benchmarking project. (For instance, if time is of the essence they may want to add an extra criterion that partner companies have already mapped and analysed their process). The three basic criteria are:

1 How easy will it be to obtain data from this potential partner? Score 0 for impossible, 3 for difficult, 6 for moderate, and 9 for easy.

2 How relevant will the data be once it is obtained? Score 0 for totally irrelevant, 3 for requires major manipulation, 6 for reasonably relevant, and 9 for directly relevant.

3 How high is the potential for innovation from this partner? Score 0 for none, 3 for little, 6 for medium, and 9 for high.

Add the score for each potential partner; the highest scorers are the ones to be approached first. Try to keep at least one partner in each category of internal, competitor, functional, and generic (see Table 4.1), so that the base of data gathered is as broad as possible.

TABLE 4.1 Partner selection matrix

	EASE OF COLLECTING DATA	RELEVANCE OF THE DATA	INNOVATION POTENTIAL	TOTAL SCORE
Internal				
Division A	6	6	3	15
Division B	9	3	6	18
Competitive				
Company C	3	9	6	18
Company D	6	6	3	15
Functional				
Company E	9	3	9	21
Company F	6	6	6	18
Generic				
Company G	6	9	9	24
Company H	9	6	6	21

(Based on Camp, R.C. (1989). *Benchmarking: The Search for Industry Best Practices that Lead to Superior Performance.* ASQC Quality Press)

Data

Preparation

The data that needs to be gathered from the benchmarking partner has to be both quantitative and qualitative. Quantitative data are the in-process performance data and measures of the product produced by the process. These data are compared to the same data from each partner's process. The differences indicate areas in which one partner's process is delivering superior performance. Qualitative data includes items such as a process overview, how the process is maintained, the tools used in the process, use of information systems, education and training, introduction of technology improvements, the practices employed, and the organization required to carry out the process. (At the data analysis stage, it is essential that the root cause of superior performance is identified; is it really due to a process difference or to a difference in organization, or even regulatory environment?)

The other aspect that needs to be addressed at this point is how the data will be collected. Various methods can be employed; the questionnaire developed during the 'determine what to benchmark' step can be sent to the selected partners and then answered by mail, telephone, fax, video conference or site visit.

Collection

Before sending out complex questionnaires or making telephone calls, they should be pre-tested in-house. This will help ensure that the questionnaire is practical – that the questions can actually be answered. It also provides the data to be compared with the benchmarking partner's.

When organizing a site visit (in which the whole team should participate to maximize the learning), make sure that the agenda has been agreed in advance with the partner so that they have had a chance to gather the required data prior to the meeting. Remind them of the ethical and legal requirements of the code of conduct (see Chapter 11). Finally, have at least two people involved in each discussion, one to conduct the interview and one to take notes.

Analysis

Analyse results

Hold a team debriefing session as soon as possible after the visit so that the information gathered can be distilled while it is still fresh in the mind. Points to be considered are:

- Is this partner really achieving better results?
- Why is this partner better?
- What best practice is the partner using?
- How can it be adopted for our business?

Determine performance gaps

At this point the performance gap needs to be understood. To start with, it is essential that the performance measurements from each of the processes are truly comparable. All the data, both quantitative and qualitative, should be analysed to understand where performance gaps exist. Before taking action based on this gap analysis, the size of each gap and the reasons for it need to be understood. It is important to be able to differentiate between performance gaps that are genuinely attributable to process differences, and those that are due to the environment in which the process operates, such as organizational and regulatory constraints, etc.

Project future performance

The philosophy of benchmarking is *adopt, adapt, improve*. The partner's superior practices have to be adopted and then adapted to function within the new organization but effort also has to be made to improve them, to 'aim ahead of the ducks'. Benchmarking partners, competitors and others in the industry are continually improving their processes. If, as a result of a benchmarking study, only parity is achieved then by the time that the actions taken are actually having the desired effect on your performance the others will have moved ahead again. Based on the data gathered during the benchmarking study, project the step improvement that will be made as a result of the process changes that will be made, and then compare that to a

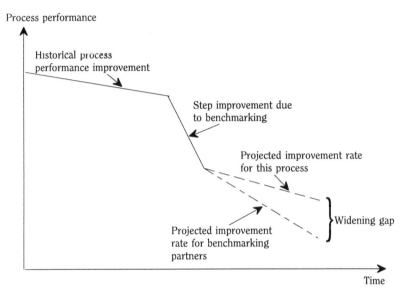

FIGURE 4.4   Gap projection

projection of the likely improvement rate of the partner and others in the industry (see Fig. 4.4 for an example). If this indicates that the gap will widen further in the future, then clearly additional action is required; could continuous improvement programmes increase the subsequent rate of improvement to match that of the best, or is it time to start afresh and completely re-engineer the process?

Action

One of the accusations levelled at benchmarking is that the end result is all too often a report that just gathers dust on a shelf. This can be due to the failure of any one of the steps within the methodology, in particular:

- selecting a process for improvement that is not strategically important
- selecting the wrong partners to compare with
- conducting an analysis based on an incomplete understanding of the subject process

However, the failure to implement the findings of the benchmarking study can also be due to failure at this, the action stage.

Communication
The results of the benchmarking study need to be clearly communicated to all involved parties – management, staff employed in this process, and also the staff involved in peripheral processes that might be affected. The benchmarking report itself is primarily the vehicle for documenting the findings, not communicating them. Effective communication requires face-to-face discussions with the affected parties.

Define action plans
Action plans need to show the resources required to implement the improvement, the timescales involved, the risks (both the 'hard' risks of process or system problems, and the 'soft' risks involving people, such as fear of losing their jobs, fear that they will not be capable of operating the new process, and fear that hard-won skills are being made redundant), and the projected benefits (using techniques such as internal rate of return or payback period). Each action must have an owner who is accountable for its successful completion.

Implementation and monitoring
The best way to manage and monitor progress is to use the existing management system: bring benchmarking actions into the mainstream of management review and do not treat it as a special programme. Use process improvement teams to implement the improvements. These should be cross-functional teams where appropriate, and involve the people who operate the process as well as the necessary specialists.

Repeat
Benchmarking is an ongoing, continuous process. The improvements made as a result of this benchmarking exercise are now incorporated into the business process. It is time to repeat the cycle, selecting new and better

partners in the continuing search for genuine world-class best practice, rather than waiting for some future crisis to stimulate it.

MANAGEMENT AND COORDINATION

Benchmarking, as they say, is not rocket science! The basic principles of the methodology can be taught in a one- or two-day workshop. The real difference between success and failure is in the way in which benchmarking is managed and integrated into the organization. There are several points that need to be considered:

1 Benchmarking must be clearly understood to be a part of business process management, and not an independent activity. The processes selected for improvement must, as discussed earlier, be those that are critical to the success of the organization.

2 Benchmarking activity needs to be coordinated across the organization, not to provide a bureaucratic overhead but to provide clear value-adding such as:
   - provide education for benchmarking team members
   - provide advice and guidance and facilitators to benchmarking teams
   - ensure that the chosen methodology is used consistently by all units
   - provide a single interface to external bodies such as benchmarking clubs
   - provide a single point of contact for 'popular' benchmarking partners
   - provide a clearing house to ensure that best practice is shared internally
   - ensure that there is no undue duplication of benchmarking projects.

3 Although implementation was addressed in the develop and implement action steps of the methodology, it is so critical to success that management attention is required in order to set the scene for success. Benchmarking exercises, like any other form of innovation, often fail at the implementation stage, and the fundamental reasons for these failures are common to other types of innovation which have been thoroughly researched by Professor Rothwell and others (see Chapter 2).

TABLE 4.2   Benchmarking success and failure factors

REASONS FOR NOT BENCHMARKING	KEYS TO SUCCESSFUL BENCHMARKING
It takes too much staff time	Management commitment
The company had not considered it	Clear objectives and plans
Low management interest	Strong benchmarking partnerships
Current performance levels are satisfactory	Consistent, accurate data
	Egos left in the office
Benchmarking is too costly	Implementation and follow-through
Not ready to benchmark	

A recent survey conducted by The Conference Board[7] that focused specifically on benchmarking highlighted the success and failure factors shown in Table 4.2.

CURRENT BENCHMARKING STATUS

The current state of benchmarking in the UK has been established by the 1994 survey commissioned by the Confederation of British Industries,[8] which built on the results of their 1993 survey. Some of the results give cause for optimism and echo the recommendations of experienced benchmarkers elsewhere. These results also serve as a useful summary of some of the key points of benchmarking. For example:

- The focus of best practice process benchmarking is on understanding the process and on discovering how superior performance is achieved by others.
- The greatest benefits are achieved by focusing on the areas of the business that are critical to its success.
- The most profitable learning points are often found in companies outside the immediate industry.
- Only focusing on performance measures leads to frustration – because it

is not clear how the leading companies have achieved superior performance.

● Comparing performance measures helps to diagnose the areas where performance gaps exist, and also the size of them, but superior performance can only be achieved by understanding the underlying process differences that cause the performance gap.

● Respondents identified the following benefits of benchmarking:
  - sets realistic targets (93%)
  - improves productivity (92%)
  - helps to gain new insights (87%)
  - gains early warning of competitive disadvantage (87%)
  - motivates staff by showing them what is possible (81%).

REFERENCES

1   Graff, M. (1991). 'How learning from the leaders pays off'. *Management Consultancy*, July/August, pp. 31–32.

2   Schmidt, J. (1992). 'The link between benchmarking and shareholder value'. *Journal of Business Strategy*, May/June, pp. 7–13.

3   Port, O., Carey, J., Kelly, K. and Forest, S. (1992). 'Special report – quality'. *Business Week*, 20 November.

4   Houlder, V. (1994). 'Measuring up to success'. *Financial Times*, 1 August.

5   Camp, R. (1989). *Benchmarking: The Search for Industry Best Practices That Lead to Superior Performance*, ASQC Quality Press.

6   Deming, W.E. (1990). *Out of the Crisis*. Cambridge University Press, Cambridge.

7   Greene, C. (1993). *Benchmarking the Information Technology Function*. The Conference Board, London.

8   CBI (1994). *Survey of Benchmarking in the UK 1994*. Coopers and Lybrand, with the Confederation of British Industries.

RECOMMENDED READING

Bendell, T., Boulter, L. and Kelly, J. (1993). *Benchmarking for Competitive Advantage*. Pitman Publishing, London.

Camp, R. (1989). *Benchmarking: The Search for Industry Best Practices that Lead to Superior Performance*. ASQC Quality Press, Milwaukee, Wisconsin.

Zairi, M. and Leonard, P. (1994). *Practical Benchmarking: The Complete Guide*. Chapman & Hall, London.

Self-assessment

God grant me the serenity to accept things I cannot change, courage to change the things I can, and the wisdom to know the difference.
(R. Niebuhr)

There are two basic types of self-assessment in common use today. The first is based on ISO 9000, and here the assessment is in the form of a regular audit to confirm that all of the requirements of the standard are being met, and that all processes are properly documented and maintained in a quality management system (say what you do; do what you say). The ISO standard has suffered a lot from the accusation that it is nothing more than a bureaucratic overhead that contributes little to the organization adopting it. There may have been some truth in this in the past for organizations that already had processes and systems that were broadly in line with the ISO 9000 requirements; in this situation the act of obtaining ISO registration may just have added a level of bureaucracy. These organizations often applied for registration because their customers and potential customers demand it from all their suppliers, and therefore rather than using it as a vehicle for improvement they did the minimum possible to maintain compliance and viewed it as a necessary evil. The changes to the standard made in 1994 have gone some way to addressing this 'bureaucracy' concern and have placed the emphasis on problem prevention as well as resolution. However, at the other end of the spectrum from organizations that already broadly comply with the standard there are organizations that live from day to day, with plenty of firefighting and a reliance on individuals rather than systematic approaches; these organizations can benefit greatly from adopting the disciplined approaches demanded by the ISO 9000 standards. ISO 9000 helps them to break the vicious circle and lays the foundations of good practice that can then be built upon with the use of self-assessment methodologies based on Baldrige or the European Quality Award (EQA).

The second type of self-assessment is based on requirements contained in either the US (Baldrige) or EQA models, and it is this type of self-assessment that will now be explored in detail because of their proven track records as continuous improvement vehicles. There is growing evidence that the advent of the US National Quality Award (named after Malcolm Baldrige, the US Secretary of Commerce at the time, who met an untimely end in a rodeo accident) has achieved exactly what its designers intended. It has stimulated US industry to make dramatic improvements in business performance. In the few years since the award was instigated evidence has been accumulated[1] which clearly shows the link between achieving high assessment scores and an improvement in business performance. Some observers point to the reduction in the number of companies applying each year for the award as evidence of a decline in the use of TQM. They miss the point that there is a world of difference between applying for an award and using the award framework internally as a self-assessment vehicle to drive continuous improvement. (The top two reasons given for adopting self-assessment within UK organizations[2] were: to find opportunities for improvement, and to direct the improvement process. Applying for an award came in 11th place.)

In Europe, the EQA has been introduced by the European Foundation for Quality Management (EFQM), and now individual states and countries in the US and Europe are modelling their own quality awards on one or other of these original quality awards. These two are the most influential quality awards commonly used as a basis for self-assessment. The Baldrige was the first to be introduced, and was designed specifically for use as an in-company improvement methodology; it has now found favour in many countries and organizations as a vehicle for driving business improvement. (The Malcolm Baldrige National Quality Improvement Act of 1987, Background and Purposes,[3] states that a national quality award programme of this kind in the United States would help to improve quality and productivity by establishing guidelines and criteria that can be used by business, industrial, governmental and other organizations in evaluating their own quality improvement efforts.) The result is that the Baldrige guidelines contain detailed criteria that describe a world-class total quality organization. When performing self-assessment an organization compares itself to this ideal, identifies the areas for improvement, and then develops plans to implement the required improvements. (This is, in effect, a benchmarking exercise, comparing the organization on a broad range of criteria against best practice, in this case encapsulated within the award framework, identifying the gaps and then developing action plans to close them.) The criteria are reviewed each year and both their wording and their relative scoring weights updated in the light of experience.

A 1994 survey[4] sponsored by the European Committee showed that 37 per cent of respondents claimed a positive relationship between self-assessment and business results. They also identified that one of the major strengths of these forms of self-assessment is the written assessment feedback report. Written assessments are taken much more seriously than verbal feedback by both the assessors and the assessed, and provide a basis for subsequent internal benchmarking and improvement planning. The following points were identified as the most important benefits from self-assessment:

- Line management gains a better understanding of TQM and its importance.
- There are improvements in defect levels, cost of quality, and customer complaints.

The Baldrige award criteria[5] have three objectives in strengthening US competitiveness and are built upon a set of core values and concepts, as shown in Table 5.1.

TABLE 5.1   Baldrige objectives and core values

OBJECTIVES	CORE VALUES
To help raise quality performance practices and expectations	Customer-driven quality
	Leadership
To facilitate communication and sharing among and within organizations of all types based upon a common understanding of key quality and operational performance requirements	Continuous improvement
	Employee participation and development
	Fast response
	Design quality and defect prevention
	Long-range outlook
	Management by fact
To serve as a working tool for planning, training, assessment, and other uses	Partnership development
	Corporate responsibility and citizenship

Although these award frameworks are proving invaluable in improving the business performance of organizations that use them as a basis for self-assessment, they can prove quite counter-productive if used naïvely by organizations that are just beginning on the path towards 'world class'. This is because the emphasis can be placed on the mechanics of performing the assessment by training large numbers of staff as assessors in the chosen framework and putting together teams to assemble data and write long, elegant reports which are then assessed and scored. The emphasis must not be on data gathering and report writing, but on using the results of self-assessment to drive improvement. Therefore the mechanics of performing the assessment should be restricted to the bare minimum needed to produce meaningful improvement plans. The fully fledged use of award frameworks is entirely appropriate for organizations that are already some way down the path towards world class, but in the case of the beginner it can:

- Divert attention towards creating elegant documents rather than making improvement.
- Create a new specialist class of employees who have acquired a detailed understanding of the award criteria.

- Restrict involvement in the self-assessment to the specialists who write and assess the application document, and the managers who receive the feedback, leaving the majority of employees with no benefit or learning from the exercise.
- Encourage management to focus action plans on the areas where the biggest score improvements can be made without regard for the natural sequence in which these improvements should occur.

The full self-assessment process is shown in Fig. 5.1. An important point is that self-assessment needs to be conducted regularly, so that:

- The successive scores can be used to measure progress towards the 'world class' ideal contained in the model.
- As the improvements from the first assessment are implemented and become effective, the next group of improvements can be identified so that the momentum towards 'world class' is maintained.

An analysis of the detailed award criteria reveals an approach that can be used by the beginner. The models expect certain fundamentals to be in place, so the beginner, rather than starting with a full-blown assessment, can identify the fundamental deficiencies of their organization by answering the following questions derived from the core values on which the models are built:

1 Do you know who your customers are?
2 Do you know what their requirements are?
3 Do you use them as a base to design/deliver your products or services?
4 Do you set your goals based on the best that is being achieved externally?
5 Do you know how your operation compares in its practices and approaches to your competitors and to the industry leaders?
6 Do you implement improvements based on these comparisons?
7 Do you, by your words and actions, act as a role model and lead the way?
8 Do you involve your entire workforce in making improvements?
9 Do you operate your organization with seamless processes that flow from customer requirement to delivery with no unmanaged 'white spaces'?

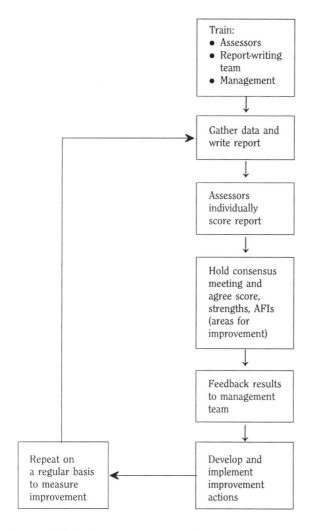

FIGURE 5.1 The self-assessment process

When beginners can answer all of these questions with an unequivocal 'yes', then they are no longer beginners, but are well down the road towards world class, ready to cope with the demands of a full assessment and able to take full advantage of the resultant outputs.

TYPES OF SELF-ASSESSMENT

Organizations have adopted the self-assessment frameworks in a variety of different ways. Some of the more effective variations are described below.

Pure award criteria and methodology

This is the approach adopted by many organizations. They use both the full award criteria and the full assessment methodology from either Baldrige or the EQA, in effect producing an award application that addresses each of the award criteria in a report of approximately 75 pages. The application is then examined by a team of trained assessors (usually from other units within the same company), who score the application and identify its strengths and areas for improvement. These are then reported back to the management team and used by them as a basis for formulating their improvement plans.

An example of this is the approach taken by IBM. All IBM operating units have to produce an annual report describing how they perform against a set of detailed criteria contained in IBM's version of the Baldrige criteria. The report is assessed by a group of independent examiners from other IBM units, who review the document and identify the operating unit's strengths, areas for improvement, and score out of a maximum 1000 points. The unit then takes the areas for improvement and develops plans to address them. The primary purpose of the score is to be able to measure progress by comparing the scores achieved by successive assessments. (A design requirement of the Baldrige award[3] was to design a scoring system which, together with the examination, created a new basis for diagnosis. A score of 500 out of the 1000 points was set as a benchmark in scoring and represents an organization that has put into place a quality system capable of moving it towards world-class quality if its improvement effort is sustained.) After several years of experience with the use of the full Baldrige assessment approach, changes are being made to reduce the bureaucratic overhead involved in writing large application documents and to ensure that the assessment effort is firmly focused on identifying areas for improvement and not in producing elegant applications.

Results have been impressive. A comparison of the business results of the units that have scored at least 500 points against the other units shows that the high scorers have significantly better results in the areas of customer satisfaction, employee morale, market share, revenue and profit. These in-company results mirror the findings of a study undertaken by the General Accounting Office in the US[1] which looked at the results of 20 companies that had achieved high scores with their Baldrige award applications. The GAO concluded that there was a cause and effect relationship between the total quality management practices embodied in the Baldrige criteria and corporate performance.

Questionnaire-style assessments

Using the pure award criteria and assessment methodology creates a significant workload for any organization which can divert management attention away from the real purpose of the identification and implementation of improvements, towards the mechanics of the assessment process itself. In order to overcome this some organizations have developed approaches that try to remain faithful to the intent of the original award criteria but which convert them from examination questions that require a written answer to a format of questions or statements that can be answered with a simple yes/no, or on a graduated scale. This very practical approach to self-assessment is examined in detail in Chapter 9.

Customized to specific company requirements

A company, its management team and all of its employees, have to feel ownership for its quality programme – ownership in the sense that they feel that it is their programme, designed to meet their specific needs which they have had the opportunity to contribute, and not a general purpose programme developed by an external body.

An example of how this customization can be accomplished is the case of a British company that took the Baldrige criteria and those from the European award and developed a composite model based on the best of both of them. The company then added additional criteria to this composite model to place emphasis on other factors that had been identified as critical to its success, and also to make the criteria easier to use. This was accomplished by adding an extra category to emphasize the concept of the internal customer, and then the detailed criteria were reworded to reflect company terminology and also to make the criteria easier to understand. (This last action addressed one of the criticisms levelled at Baldrige: that the wording of the criteria can make them difficult to understand, which in turn encourages the establishment of the professional who can interpret the criteria for others. This is actually one of the key differences between the US and European award models. The US criteria are at a level of detail which is almost prescriptive, whereas the European model describes the general principle and leaves its interpretation to the individual organization.)

Some quality consultants advise against modifying the original award criteria, which were developed by a combination of the best from the business world, together with management consultants and academics. This should be kept in mind if a company does decide to change the criteria; the original authors took great care with the wording of each criterion, and they deserve to be taken seriously. However, it may be that what is lost in the purity of the criteria is more than compensated for by the buy-in obtained within the company.

Finally, the amount of work involved in customizing the criteria should not be underestimated; it is very time-consuming and requires in-depth knowledge of the organization and its strategies, and also of the requirements and thinking behind the criteria contained in the original award frameworks. However, with this warning in mind, customizing the criteria is a very effective approach if it facilitates the buy-in and enthusiasm of the staff involved in the assessment programme.

Using the structured assessment approach with a different set of criteria

This is the approach used by a UK hospital, which used the criteria contained in the UK Government's Chartermark award and Patients'

Charter requirements, coupled with the assessment approach of the quality awards. One of the great strengths of these awards is the robust nature of the assessment process itself; the process is just as effective if a completely different set of criteria are used as the basis of the assessment. In this particular case the criteria were those contained in the Patients' Charter and the Chartermark award. The requirements were extracted from the material published by the Cabinet Office. A workbook was then designed that allowed the hospital's Chartermark application to be independently assessed for evidence of approach, deployment and results in a similar manner to that used by both major quality awards.

EXPERIENCES OF SELF-ASSESSMENT

A group of companies working under the auspices of the EFQM published a report[6] detailing their experiences of performing self-assessments. Their conclusions are summarized in Table 5.2, which clearly shows the benefits that can be obtained from the use of self-assessment.

QUALITY AWARD FRAMEWORKS

New quality awards, often based on the US or European models, are being established in countries around the world. When evaluating these award frameworks for possible adoption as an in-company self-assessment framework, there are two points to be considered:

1 The model itself, and the criteria for 'world-class' performance which it contains.

2 The presentation of the criteria in a 'user friendly' manner.

The latter point is very important as the major benefit of such an award scheme is not the winning of the award itself but in its adoption as an in-company assessment and improvement methodology. Companies that implement a self-assessment approach based on an award model are finding it to be the missing ingredient that is helping them to put the continuous into improvement. Continuous improvement is achieved by performing the

TABLE 5.2   Lessons learned from self-assessment

LESSONS LEARNED	BENEFITS
Do not run self-assessments as a separate activity; integrate them into the business planning process.	It has generated a real sense of ownership for quality among the senior managers.
Keep the process simple and allow local variation in individual countries, but be demanding about requiring significant improvements.	Management teams are setting the agenda for improvement activity.
Self-assessment can be applied to any size of business unit within a company.	Enthusiasm is generated in the managers.
Self-assessments help to develop a more balanced score card.	The actual improvement opportunities are identified.
The feedback report provided as a result of a formal award application is a major learning opportunity.	A deeper awareness is gained of what a true quality company is.
Senior management must be seen to drive the self-assessment process.	Self-assessments give extra impetus to continuous improvement.
Self-assessments need to be correctly positioned as part of an overall management process.	The model forces managers to find out who is better than them, and how they do it (benchmarking).
The focus on customer satisfaction is paramount.	It measures the effectiveness of improvements implemented.
There is only one chance to make a first impression, so the roll-out of self-assessment needs to be carefully managed.	It covers all aspects of the business.
The self-assessment approach selected has to take account of the organization's maturity, culture, environment and strategic issues.	It measures current performance and identifies areas for improvement.
	It builds team spirit.
The self-assessment process has to be clearly positioned against other activities.	The process strongly reinforces 'customer first' within the company.
Scoring can be a little subjective – the emphasis is placed on identifying areas for improvement rather than on a score.	
Improvement will only occur when actions are implemented.	

self-assessment on a regular, probably annual, basis and comparing each new score with the previous one to ensure that improvement really is being made, and by identifying new priority areas for improvement after each self-assessment.

The US and European award criteria also provide an umbrella framework (Fig. 5.2) in which to position the major business improvement initiatives. For companies that already have some of these initiatives under way, the self-assessment framework brings what were individual initiatives together into a cohesive whole. For companies that do not have any initiatives under way, then the self-assessment helps them to identify what is required and how they should be used.

Figure 5.2 shows that there should be two key drivers for business improvement: self-assessment, and the customer. Information from both of these sources is used to:
- create a process approach to the business
- manage the business by fact
- set stretch goals
- use the full potential of the workforce
- re-engineer where necessary

The foremost thought in each of these areas must be, 'what do our customers want, and how well are we delivering that?' Leadership provides the 'constancy of purpose' demanded by Deming.[7] Meeting and exceeding customer expectations, and using self-assessment to measure progress and identify areas for improvement, must be constant goals of the organization, not just passing management whims.

It is obvious that the effectiveness of self-assessments is heavily influenced by the criteria incorporated into the self-assessment framework. The two major sources for these criteria are the US and European awards. The composition of the two models is shown in Figs 5.3 and 5.4.[5, 8]

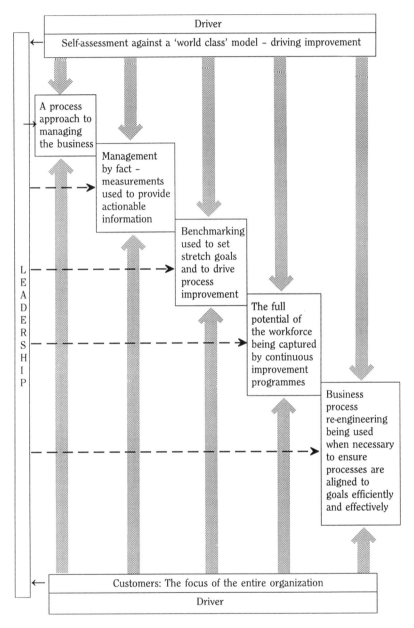

FIGURE 5.2 Self-assessments and business improvement

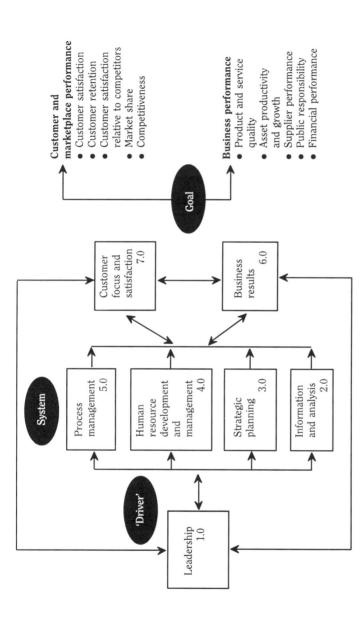

FIGURE 5.3 Baldrige Award criteria framework – dynamic relationships

Source: MBNQA (1996). *Malcolm Baldrige National Quality Award 1996 Criteria*, Washington, DC

Customer and marketplace performance
- Customer satisfaction
- Customer retention
- Customer satisfaction relative to competitors
- Market share
- Competitiveness

Business performance
- Product and service quality
- Asset productivity and growth
- Supplier performance
- Public responsibility
- Financial performance

Goal

System

'Driver'

Customer focus and satisfaction 7.0

Business results 6.0

Process management 5.0

Human resource development and management 4.0

Strategic planning 3.0

Information and analysis 2.0

Leadership 1.0

107

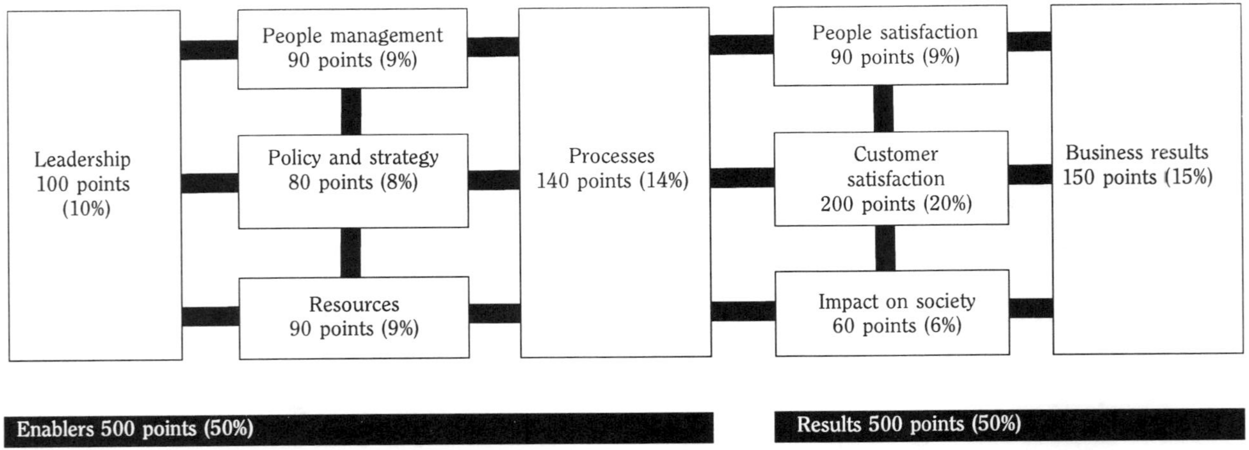
Leadership
100 points
(10%)
People management
90 points (9%)
Policy and strategy
80 points (8%)
Resources
90 points (9%)
Processes
140 points (14%)
People satisfaction
90 points (9%)
Customer
satisfaction
200 points (20%)
Impact on society
60 points (6%)
Business results
150 points (15%)
Enablers 500 points (50%)
Results 500 points (50%)

FIGURE 5.4 European Model for Total Quality Management

Source: *European Quality Award Application Brochure,* European Foundation Quality Management (1996).[8]

Within these models there is a strong emphasis on having systems and approaches that encourage process improvement and the use of benchmarking. They show how the entire business system has to be energized if process improvement is to occur and for the results of those improvements to be apparent in the business performance. Their common themes are:

- *Leadership*
  driving cultural and behavioural change by a combination of acting as role model and realigning reward and recognition systems.
- Processes
  being designed with improvement feedback loops.
- *Benchmarking*
  being used to set stretch goals.
- *People*
  throughout the organization (both horizontally and vertically) being actively involved in focused performance improvement.

INTEGRATING QUALITY ASSESSMENTS INTO THE STRATEGIC PLANNING PROCESS

To be effective, the output from the self-assessment must be linked into the organization's strategic planning process so that the areas for improvement are turned into actions that are implemented. Table 5.3 shows a matrix that can be used to link the self-assessment results to the critical success factors of the business (and therefore to its strategic goals). This approach can be used both as a vehicle for the planning and deployment of improvement actions, and as a scorecard for reporting and tracking purposes. The improvements identified by the assessment are prioritized according to their importance to achieving CSFs, thus ensuring that any improvement actions are for the strategic benefit of the organization as well as improving the self-assessment score.

TABLE 5.3 Improvement planning matrix

CATEGORY	Score from Self-assessment				Areas for Improvement from Feedback Report	Critical Success Factors Affected by Each AFI					Priority for Improvement Action
	93 Act	94 Act	95 Act	96 Plan		CSF1	CSF2	CSF3	CSF4	CSF5	
1											
2											
3											
4											
5											
6											
7											

QUALITY AWARD FRAMEWORKS AND BUSINESS PROCESSES

The US and European quality award frameworks place a heavy emphasis on business processes, both implicitly and explicitly. Explicitly in that they both have a category devoted to process management that asks basic questions on process control, root cause determination, benchmarking, and continuous improvement; implicitly in that throughout each of the models the question *how* is asked. Most low-scoring organizations attempt to answer the *how* by providing a few anecdotal examples of *what* they do, rather than describing a systematic process that addresses the *how*.

Organizations may map their processes to the award framework so that they understand which section each of their processes relates to, but what they often do not do is the reverse; mapping from the framework to their processes to ensure that each *how* has a corresponding process that performs that activity. Not doing this process mapping from the framework to the organization can result in serious process gaps that will hinder the organization's progress towards 'world class'.

The list of *hows* contained in the award frameworks can be used to construct a generic high-level business process model of an organization that meets all the process requirements of either the Baldrige or the EQA frameworks, as shown in Fig. 5.5. This generic process model can provide invaluable assistance to any organization struggling to identify its own business processes.

PROVIDE LEADERSHIP:	Demonstrate personal commitment Reinforce customer focus
COMMUNICATE WITH PEOPLE:	Communicate with employees Communicate externally
MANAGE HUMAN RESOURCES:	Plan human resources Develop employee skills Measure employee satisfaction Provide reward and recognition Encourage employee involvement Manage employee performance
PLAN THE BUSINESS:	Measure business performance Develop performance plan Assess the business Improve business performance Analyse customer related data
FULFIL PUBLIC OBLIGATIONS:	Perform societal impact assessment Provide corporate leadership
MANAGE BUSINESS INFORMATION:	Establish information requirements Provide business information
MANAGE BUSINESS PROCESSES:	Gather competitive and benchmark data Continuously improve business processes Establish performance objectives Control business process performance

MANAGE SUPPLIERS	MANAGE MARKETS	SOLUTION DESIGN	SOLUTION DELIVERY	MANAGE CUSTOMER RELATIONSHIPS
Define and communicate quality requirements	Develop segmentation plan	Integrate customer requirements	Integrate customer requirements	Measure customer satisfaction
Improve supplier performance	Identify opportunities	Design production processes	Design delivery processes	Resolve complaints
Measure supplier performance	Determine customer requirements	Quality assure processes	Quality assure processes	Establish communications plan
				Provide service and support

FIGURE 5.5   Generic business process model

REFERENCES

1 Garvin, D. (1991). How the Baldrige Award really works. *Harvard Business Review*, November/December pp. 80–93.

2 Coulambidou, L. and Dale, B. (1995). *The Use of Quality Management Self-Assessment in the UK: A State of the Art Study.* QWTS.

3 US Department of Commerce (1991). *Interim Report to the President and Congress on the MBNQA.* April.

4 van der Wiele, T., Dale, B., Williams, R., Kolb, F., Moreno Luzon, D., Schmidt, A. and Wallace, M., 'State of the art study on self-assessment'. *The TQM Magazine*, **7**(4).

5 ASQC (1996). *Malcolm Baldrige National Quality Award Criteria.* American Society for Quality Control.

6 EFQM (1994). *Business Improvement through Self-assessment.* European Foundation for Quality Management.

7 Deming, W.E. (1990). *Out of the Crisis.* Cambridge University Press, Cambridge.

8 EFQM (1996). *The European Quality Award Application Brochure.* European Foundation for Quality Management.

RECOMMENDED READING

ASQC (1996). *Malcolm Baldrige National Quality Award Criteria.* American Society for Quality Control.

EFQM (1996). *The European Quality Award Application Brochure.* The European Foundation for Quality Management.

Lascelles, D. and Peacock, R. (1996). *Self-Assessment for Business Excellence.* McGraw-Hill, London.

Measurement

Progress, far from consisting in change, depends on
retentiveness ... Those who cannot remember the past
are condemned to repeat it.
(G. Santayana)

Measurement is fundamental to business improvement. The statement,
'What gets measured gets managed', has now become something of a
cliché, but that does not alter the fact that it is true. The availability of
accurate measurements enables management by fact rather than by gut
feeling or 'management judgement'; decisions are made on the basis of
factual data rather than from assumptions and supposition. The use of
measurement is encapsulated in the Baldrige award, where the preamble to
the award criteria states:[1]

> A modern business management system needs to be built upon a framework of
> measurement, data, and analysis. Measurements must derive from the
> company's strategy and encompass all the key processes and the outputs of
> those processes...

Measurements are used to provide data, which are analysed to provide
information, and information in turn forms the basis for management
decision making and action planning. It therefore follows that the things
that should be measured are the things that are of the most importance to
the organization, that is, important to it achieving its goals. This may seem
obvious, but in many companies what gets measured is either what has

always been measured, or what is actually easy to measure; the linkage of the item being measured to achieving a goal is often not a real consideration. This has been confirmed by Monkhouse[2] in a survey of 200 small and medium-sized enterprises (SMEs) in the UK which showed that there are some significant gaps between what companies measure and what they believe to be important (Table 6.1). The only factors for which the rating of importance matches their measurement are the financials – overall financial performance and price. All the others have a clear gap between their importance and their being measured.

If measurements are to be derived from the company's strategy, then there should be a cascade of measurements from the strategic level, down through the business processes, to each individual. This cascade produces a hierarchy of measurements.

TABLE 6.1 What companies measure and what is considered to be important.

	IMPORTANT (%)	MEASURED (%)
Financial performance	93	97
Customer satisfaction	94	63
Quality	91	79
Price	63	61
Employee development	85	45
Flexibility	69	9
Innovation performance	82	9

THE HIERARCHY OF MEASUREMENT

The hierarchy of business performance measurements is illustrated in Fig. 6.1. Correctly chosen measurements at each point in the hierarchy enable the activities that are most important to the organization to be managed effectively, and to provide a clear linkage between what is measured at each level and the strategic goals of the company.

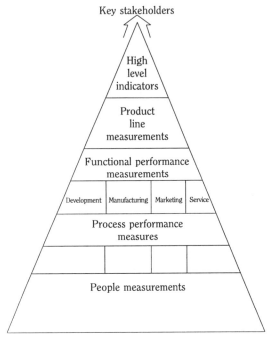

Key stakeholders

High level indicators — Mainly financial measures that indicate overall organization 'health'

Product line measurements — Measures of the contribution made by each product and service

Functional performance measurements — Measures that indicate whether each function is meeting its commitments

Development | Manufacturing | Marketing | Service

Process performance measures — Measures that show that the processes operated by each function are performing correctly

People measurements — Measures that indicate whether each individual in the organization is meeting their objectives

FIGURE 6.1   The measurement hierarchy

This hierarchy of measurements closely parallels the actual hierarchy of the organization and reflects the differing information needs of the people at the various levels; it forms the basis of the management (or executive) information systems (MIS) that are now available. These systems speed up the availability of data throughout the management hierarchy, but in themselves do nothing to address the two fundamental problems of measurement; deciding what to measure, and then gathering valid data. If these are not adequately addressed, then all that an MIS achieves is to make misleading, poor quality data available more quickly throughout the organization than it was before (and probably to make it even more misleading than it was before, because it now masquerades as 'official numbers from the computer', presented as coloured charts at the terminal on the manager's desk).

High-level indicators

At the top of the hierarchy are the high-level indicators. These show the organization's overall performance and are usually a mix of financial and non-financial performance indicators such as return on assets, profit, cash flow, market share, customer satisfaction, employee satisfaction – indicators that show to key stakeholders how well the overall organization is doing. An organization's high-level indicators should measure performance from several viewpoints simultaneously. If only one or two financial performance measures are used at the top level, then that is all that will be managed – at the expense of other facets of organizational performance that may be of equal importance. This was addressed by Kaplan and Norton[3] in their discussion of the balanced score card, which broadened the scope of business measurements beyond just short-term financial performance. Financial perspectives ('how do we look to our shareholders?') and customer perspective ('how do we provide better value to them than our competitors?') feed into the internal business perspective ('what we must excel at') and thus point to the processes that need to be improved.

There needs to be a balance of measures if all the goals are to be achieved. Concentrating on only one performance indicator is rather like squeezing a balloon – it goes in where you squeeze, but pops out elsewhere. In order to compress the whole balloon you have to exert pressure on many points. Exactly the same thing happens with performance measurement: monitor and measure (and therefore manage) only one point and it will end up performing as required, but at the expense of other facets of business performance.

Product line measurements

The next level of measurement within the hierarchy concerns the measuring of the contribution of each product and service. It is the volume of sales of each product and service, and the profit margin achieved by each of them, which, when aggregated, produces the high-level indicators. Each product and service must be accurately measured against plan to indicate that it is meeting planned targets for each major indicator, such as:

- volume
- revenue
- cost
- profit
- quality
- reliability
- customer satisfaction.

The perception of cost, and therefore the profit of a product or service is often distorted by the method of measurement. Overheads and fixed costs throughout the organization's value chain (development, production, marketing, service) are often allocated to products in a purely arbitrary fashion which does not reflect the amount of cost actually absorbed by the product. A solution to this problem is to use activity-based costing, which is discussed later in this chapter.

Functional performance measurements

Performance measures become a lever for change within an organization. The key question for an organization's leaders is whether they are achieving their strategic goals or not. The answer is to deploy these goals throughout the organization via performance measures. The organization's strategies are decomposed into goals and critical success factors (CSFs) for each function in the organization, and then each CSF is further decomposed into a set of measurements that will indicate if it is being achieved. For example, many organizations will have a strategic goal of achieving a certain level of customer satisfaction. Research with their customers will reveal that this goal is comprised of several CSFs that relate to ease of doing business, product quality, reliability, delivery time, after-sales support, etc. Each one of these CSFs is then converted to performance measurements that must be achieved by the functions, departments and individuals within the organization.

Process performance measurements

Regular process measurement is essential. Measurement enables the process to be controlled, to be improved, and its performance to be compared with that of other similar processes. Some performance measures monitor activities within a process (in-process measures) while others (output measures) monitor the results of the process. The basic process flow takes inputs, then performs a series of activities on them to transform them into an output. Without any form of feedback from the output back into the process (Fig. 6.2a) the process will be unstable and unpredictable. The minimum level of process control is to provide a feedback loop so that the output can be used to control the process by comparing the actual output to the planned output and then taking action within the process to bring actual and planned outputs together (Fig. 6.2b). However, output measurement alone is not sufficient (it can be likened to steering a ship by looking at its wake). Output measurement, by definition, is measurement after the event; the process has already produced the product or service before there is any information about whether it is any good or not. A prime example of this approach is the measurement of customer satisfaction; waiting for the result of the bi-annual customer survey to know whether the products and services provided to them were satisfactory or not inevitably results in a pipeline of dissatisfaction when the survey result is unfavourable. The output measure of customer satisfaction should be used as a correlation to the real-time in-process measures, so that these can be used both to control the process and as a predictor of customer satisfaction (Fig. 6.2c).

In-process measures indicate the performance of the process in 'real-time' and can be used both to control the process and to predict the final outcome – the performance of the products produced by the process. The parameters selected to be measured and controlled will be a mixture of product-specific measurements such as conformance to dimensional and performance specifications, and non product-specific measurements such as on-time delivery, cycle time, scrap and rework, work-in-process, etc. The basic in-process measurements of performance are:

- cycle time
- quality
- cost.

(a) Basic process

Input → [Activities] → Output

(b) Process with feedback loop

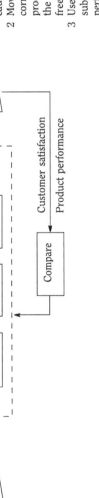

Plan/required output → [Compare] → Feedback measurements

↓ Correct

Input → [Activities] → Output

The objectives of this measurement system are:

1 Detect and correct problems at the point where they are caused.
2 Move the detection and correction back through the process to the suppliers so that the inputs are ultimately defect free.
3 Use process measures to predict subsequent product performance and customer satisfaction.

(c) A controlled and predictable process

Measure   Measure   Measure   Final quality assurance

Suppliers — Inputs → [Activity 1] → [Activity 2] → [Activity 3] → Output → Customer

[Compare] — Customer satisfaction
           Product performance

FIGURE 6.2 Process measurement: (a) basic process; (b) process with feedback loop; (c) controlled and predictable process

Process output measurements show the performance of the product or service produced by the process and are used both as a feedback into the management of the process and, because of their influence on customer satisfaction, they can also be used as a predictor of customer satisfaction. These measurements are typically related to the performance of the product or service produced by the process, such as defect-free delivery, reliability, warranty cost, etc. In general, output measures should be used to confirm what has already been established with in-process measures in order to improve the effectiveness of those measures for process control and as performance predictors. For example, consider the situation of a computer manufacturer measuring the reliability of its product. The traditional way would be to make some measurement of how often the products failed in the customers' offices, then to analyse that failure data to point to areas in the manufacturing process or product design that need correcting. This is wrong for many reasons:

- A complex reporting system is required to gather failure data from the service engineers.
- The time delay between failure at the customer and the product leaving the factory can be long – hundreds or thousands of products may have been shipped in the interim with the same problem.
- The customer is being used as the final tester.
- The items measured are those of importance to the organization, not to its customers.

The right approach is to have in-process controls and measurements that allow for early detection of defects (moving the detection point back through the supply chain so that defects ultimately get detected and corrected at the point where they are caused), using statistical process control to be sure that the process is tightly controlled and producing at a consistent quality level. Test and inspection should be a final verification that the process is in control and not used as the last in-house opportunity to detect and correct defects before shipping the product to the customer (Fig. 6.2c).

If the factors that collectively comprise customer satisfaction are properly understood, then a company should not have to wait for the results of the latest customer satisfaction survey to know whether satisfaction has improved or not. Customer satisfaction is a *lagging* indicator – it is dependent on the performance of other factors. These other factors are *leading* indicators – in other words, if they show performance improvement they indicate that customer satisfaction will improve as a result. For example, if customer focus groups and surveys show that customer satisfaction is the result of a combination of on-time delivery, fast response times and product quality; thus each of these factors can be accurately measured and controlled with in-process measures, allowing the organization to predict the subsequent customer satisfaction based on the performance of these indicators. This allows the organization to be proactive in its management of customer satisfaction – it does not have to wait until the result of its bi-annual survey shows a dip in customer satisfaction before it takes action.

The principal use of measurements is control; either of the overall business or of one of its constituent processes. This is the fundamental reason for having a system of measurements at all. The basic model[4] is the cybernetic control model:

- Specify target standards of performance.
- Measure actual performance.
- Report deviations from planned performance.
- Take action to get back on target.
- Revise plans to accommodate changing circumstances.

The key to this approach is that action must be taken on the basis of the result, so when implementing a new system of measurements the acid test is to ask the question 'What will I do as a result of knowing this?' If the answer is vague or evasive, then the measurement is not the right one!

Another use of performance measurement is emerging with the growing popularity of benchmarking, in which measurements are used to compare the performance of an activity or process in one organization with that performed in another. It is this initial comparison that identifies performance gaps, which are then investigated by detailed process comparisons to understand what causes such gaps. However, because the measures used to control a process are normally measures of the product or service it produces, these may not be an appropriate basis for comparing process performance between organizations when it is the process that is similar, not the product being produced. (For example, when performing internal benchmarking the process and the product are often the same, and in this circumstance direct process measurements can be used to make comparisons. However, when conducting functional or generic benchmarking, the process is similar but the product invariably is not. This process performance comparison usually needs a different approach, as described in Chapter 11.)

People measurements

It is the measurement of each individual's performance that is most fundamental to driving sustained and continuous improvement, because change and improvement are ultimately dependent on the behaviour and efforts of all the employees. The creativity must be encouraged, their participation in problem solving and improvement activity must be stimulated, and their own personal performance must improve continuously. These objectives can only be met with a system of measurements and performance appraisal at the individual level. For example, if an organization considers that its quality performance is of paramount importance to its competitive position, it should use that as one of the criteria for assessing senior management performance and compensating it. (The acid test for effective personal performance measurements is 'what is the individual's pay based on?') This helps to stimulate senior managers to take the leadership role in improvement activities that is essential for success. It also means that they will set similar objectives for their reportees and therefore send a clear message throughout the organization about what is important to the organization and what must be achieved. In a similar way, the activities that all employees are asked to perform by their management, and the level of performance required of them, must be clearly linked, through the hierarchy of measurement, to the strategies, goals and critical success factors of the organization. The final point on individual performance measurements comes from Deming, who emphasized that no one should be blamed or punished for a level of performance over which they have no influence (and conversely, neither should they be rewarded for apparently high levels of performance over which they have no control).[5]

A MEASUREMENT FRAMEWORK

Clues about the types of measurement requirement to manage a 'world-class' organization can be obtained by examining the data requirements contained in the Baldrige and EQA models. Table 6.2 gives examples of the types of measurement that each model expects.

Zairi[6] identifies the critical success factors associated with the selection of effective measurements. They must:

- eliminate deficiencies from the process
- reflect customer requirements
- point out areas for improvement
- relate to leverage points
- give feedback for driving improvement effort
- evaluate performance accurately
- be designed, developed, and maintained by the process owner.

CASE STUDY: THE USE OF PROCESS MEASUREMENT

This process improvement exercise took place within a hospital radiology department. The reporting process was selected as the highest priority for improvement because of the general perception within the department that there were many problems associated with it, and because it was a large consumer of the department's resources. The reporting process starts with the X-ray examination of the patient being performed, and finishes with the consultant radiologist's report being received by the requesting doctor. It includes examining the film on a light box, dictating a diagnostic report,

TABLE 6.2   Measurements implied by the quality award models

BALDRIGE	EQA
Public responsibility, sanctions under law, regulation, contract.	Customer satisfaction, such as: reliability, quality, delivery, responsiveness, support, complaint handling.
The effectiveness and extent of employee involvement.	People satisfaction, such as: working environment, training, communications, awareness, reward and recognition.
The effectiveness and extent of education and training.	Impact on society such as: quality of life, environment, global resource preservation, infringements, complaints.
The effectiveness and extent of employee reward and recognition.	Business results – financial and non-financial measure of success such as: cycle times, cost of quality, waste, defects.
Employee well-being and satisfaction.	
Product and service quality, such as: accuracy, timeliness, reliability, performance, behaviour, delivery, after-sales service, documentation, effective complaints management.	
Company operational performance, such as: manpower, materials, energy efficiency, cycle time reduction, environmental.	
Business and support service, such as: quality, productivity, cycle time, cost.	
Supplier performance.	
Customer satisfaction.	
All measurements must have targets and be compared to industry averages, industry leaders, and benchmarks.	Each measure should be compared to own company targets, competitors, and best-in-class benchmarks.

typing the report, and mailing it to the requesting doctor. A quality improvement team was formed, trained in the basics of process management and problem solving, and then facilitated by an experienced practitioner throughout the improvement project.

The first thing the group did was to map the process. This stimulated discussion about who the real customer of the process was. Once this was agreed to by the requesting doctor, the next question was 'What are the customer's requirements?' Further discussion revealed that a contract existed with some of the doctors which committed the radiology department to a five-day turnaround time from the day the examination was performed to the day the report was received by the doctor. It was then decided that achieving this five-day process cycle time was the real problem to be addressed. The next step was to establish how long the process was actually taking. From the limited data available it was established that the average was actually around five days. The initial reaction from the group was that, in this case, the target was being achieved and that they should investigate some other problem. However, the next question was 'If five days is the average, how often is that exceeded, and what is the maximum that is achieved?' The answers were: quite often, and 14 days!

It was then agreed that this was a genuine problem that needed to be resolved. The action plan agreed was basically a three-step plan, as shown in Fig. 6.3. There was an option of a fourth step – to benchmark against other organizations that performed functionally similar processes (for example, insurance companies that have processes requiring the fast turnaround of documents, such as claim forms or quote requests, to their customers). This option was held in reserve because the department manager was not sure that the resource involved in such an exercise would produce a result that could not be achieved by other means. (*Message*: adapt the improvement methodology to the environment in which it is to be used. Improvement methodologies are not cookbooks; they provide a framework for gathering information and guiding management thinking. Slavishly following a methodology in inappropriate circumstances will not guarantee success.)

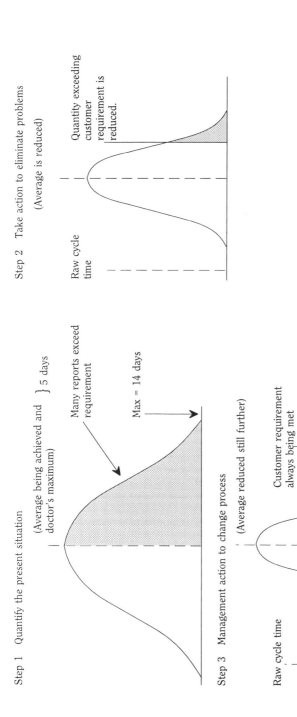

FIGURE 6.3 Process cycle time reduction

Action plan

Step 1

Plans were made to gather real performance data by implementing a system of in-process measurements, and by conducting a customer survey of doctors to gather their perceptions. The 'raw cycle time' was also established. The raw cycle time is the theoretical time it would take to process a report from start to finish without any processing delays or errors. This is often an excellent 'paradigm buster', opening people's eyes to the fact that dramatic process performance improvement should be possible. In this case the raw cycle time was a matter of a few hours, whereas what was being routinely achieved was five or more days!

Step 2

Detailed process mapping and analysis identified many problems, often individually minor, but when these were resolved they collectively reduced the average cycle time considerably and tightened the distribution, so that far fewer reports were exceeding customer requirements. The process was now under control, although still not capable of always meeting the customer requirement. (Deming's *special causes* had been removed.) Customer satisfaction started to improve.

Step 3

Further action was required to improve the process further to ensure that it was capable of always meeting the customer requirement. This required management action to make fundamental changes to the process, rather than just eliminating special causes as in the previous step. The management actions taken (to address Deming's *common causes*, that is, faults with the system) included using technology to distribute the reports via e-mail, using voice recognition to eliminate typing, etc. The process was now in control and capable of meeting its customer requirements.

Although cycle time reduction had been the focus of the improvement project throughout, the identification and elimination of problems and the management initiated changes to the process also had the very desirable side-effect of reducing the time spent on rework, checking, and error recovery, and thus improving quality and reducing cost.

ACTIVITY-BASED COSTING

Activity-based costing[7,8] developed out of the perceived shortcomings of the traditional absorption costing methods used by most manufacturers. Absorption costing is based on the premise that most of the costs associated with the manufacture of a product are the direct costs of the shop-floor workers who built and tested the product. These costs, together with other direct product costs such as the cost of materials, could be easily allocated to products or product families. Indirect labour costs such as engineering, procurement, finance and production control, which had traditionally made up a small amount of the total cost, were simply allocated to the products on the basis of the direct headcount or some other arbitrary method. This approach was acceptable when direct labour cost was the major portion of total cost, but this is no longer the case. Modern manufacturing strategies and technologies have reduced the percentage of product cost that corresponds to direct labour quite significantly, resulting in the indirect costs being an accordingly higher percentage. Allocating these costs on the basis of direct labour is no longer valid, and new ways of cost allocation had to be devised.

This led to a complete rethink about the way to allocate fixed costs based on two key principles:

- The cost accounting system needs to reflect the true cost drivers.
- The cost management system needs to provide the information that management wants, rather than what the accountants can provide.

The basic principle of activity-based costing (ABC) is that it is activities that drive costs. Therefore ABC aims to identify the major activities involved in a business, establish their cost, and then to establish the linkage between activities and products. The activities should be analysed to identify which are value-add and which are non value-add, that is, those that either do, or do not add value as perceived by the customer. The approach is to focus on the activities performed by the support departments, and to relate the activities they perform to the product that they were performed for, then to use these cost drivers to allocate cost to products. Activity-based costing often uncovers uncomfortable truths that apparently profitable products have actually been subsidized by others because of the vagaries of absorption costing.

Activity based costing also has a role to play in the management of suppliers and customers; in the case of suppliers, it allows a company to differentiate between the low-price supplier and the low-cost one. In general, the low-cost (that is, the total cost of doing business) is preferable to the low-price one, which is generally achieved at the expense of other important aspects of the customer/supplier relationship. ABC's role in the customer relationship is in enabling the organization to calculate and attribute costs correctly between those customers who want limited product, low cost and low service, and other customers who want high variety and support.

Although originally developed for the manufacturing industry, ABC is now used as a process analysis tool in many industries, where it has been found to be effective in establishing which activities are causing high cost, and in identifying which are the value-add and non value-add activities in a process (which is a series of activities that transform inputs into outputs). It therefore provides an excellent way of evaluating the process as a starting point for process improvement. The use of ABC as an integral part of business process analysis and improvement is shown in Fig. 6.4.

This shows that ABC in the process improvement context serves two purposes – it first helps in the selection of the process to focus on, because it enables costs to be attributes to activities, which together form processes; secondly, because it enables each activity to be costed, it points to the high-resource consumers within the selected process where attention needs to be paid.

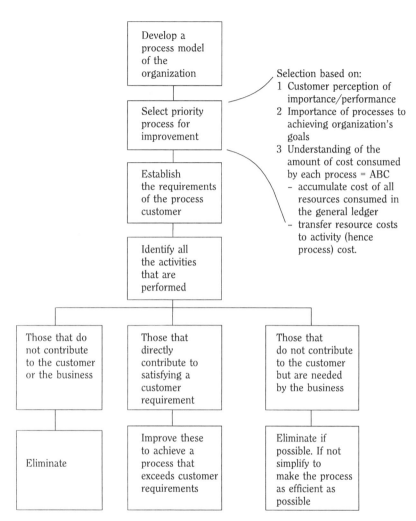

FIGURE 6.4 Integrating activity-based costing into process improvement

DEPARTMENT PURPOSE ANALYSIS

The reason for using ABC as a tool for business process improvement is to identify the cost drivers and the value-add/non value-add activities within the process. A simpler approach, and one that can be used by the people involved in the process rather than of having to use someone with specialist knowledge, is department purpose analysis (DPA). Because the analysis is performed by the people directly involved rather than by an outsider, they become directly involved in the improvement activity and therefore 'buy-in' to the changes that result from the analysis.

DPA also helps with the transformation from a vertical, functional organization to a horizontal, process-oriented one. Referring back to Fig. 1.4, in a functional organization there are usually many departments involved in the total process that starts with identifying the customer's requirements and ends with fulfilling them. Each department involved along the process actually has a supplier and a customer, and also is a supplier and a customer itself. A department's supplier and customer may be external to the organization, or they may be other departments upstream and downstream to them in the process. In essence, DPA (Fig. 6.5) is a method that first identifies the purpose of the department, based on its customer's requirements, then analyses the activities that take place in the department to establish the resource consumed by each activity. It also identifies whether each activity adds value for the customer or not, and then uses improvement teams to eliminate non value-add activities and improve the value-add ones.

The steps in DPA are:

1 To align all the departments involved in the process; each has to define their customers and suppliers. Next, agree with them what the customer's requirements are and how they will be measured. This is then formalized into a service level agreement (SLA) between each customer and supplier in the process chain. At the conclusion of this step each department knows exactly what its inputs and outputs are and is ready for the next step.

2 To analyse all the activities that take place within the department and

Step 1: Negotiate service level agreements

Department:		
Customer:		
Outputs:		
Measurement:		
Supplier:		
Inputs:		
Measurements:		

Step 2: Record department activities

Date Activity	09.00 09.30	09.30 10.00	10.00 10.30	10.30 11.00	11.00 11.30	11.30 12.00
1 Filing						
2 Typing						
3 Scheduling						
4 Manag't reports						
5 Resolve complaints						
6 Find notes						
7						

Step 3: Analyse into value/non value-add

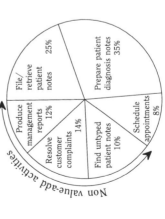

Step 4: Eliminate non value-add activity

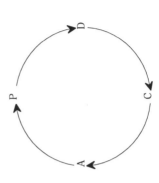

FIGURE 6.5 Department purpose analysis

identify which of those really do add value (that is, they are directly involved in providing the required customer output), and those that are not. This is accomplished by getting the department members to identify the major activities that they perform. This list is then used to create a simple time recording sheet on which all department members record their activity (in half-hour blocks) for a month.

3 The activity data can then be aggregated and used to create a pie chart showing what proportion of the total available time was spent on each activity. The activities can then be separated into those that add value and those that do not.

4 The final step is to form problem-solving teams (trained in a structured problem-solving method, usually based on Deming's PDCA cycle) and have them work on eliminating each of the non value-add activities which regularly occur within the department, and to enhance those activities that do add value.

REFERENCES

1   ASQC (1996). *Malcolm Baldrige National Quality Award Criteria.* American Society for Quality Control.

2   Monkhouse, E. (1994). 'The strategic use of non-fictional measures in small and medium-sized organisations'. *British Academy of Management Annual Conference.*

3   Kaplan, R. and Norton, D. (1992). 'The balanced scorecard – Measures that drive performance'. *Harvard Business Review*, January/February, pp. 71–79.

4   Adnum, D. (1993). 'Using performance indicators for effective public sector management'. *Management Accounting*, January, pp. 48–52.

5   Deming, W.E. (1990). *Out of the Crisis.* Cambridge University Press, Cambridge.

6   Zairi, M. (1992). *TQM-Based Performance Measurement.* Technical Communications (Publishing) Ltd.

7   Armitage, H. and Russell, G. (1993). 'Activity-based measurement

information: TQM's missing link'. *CMA Magazine*, March, p. 7.

8   Scott, P. and Morrow, M. (1989). 'Easy as ABC'. *AA Magazine*, September, pp. 44–49.

RECOMMENDED READING

Deming, W.E. (1990). *Out of the Crisis*. Cambridge University Press, Cambridge.

Kaplan, R. and Norton, D. (1992). 'The balanced scorecard – measures that drive performance'. *Harvard Business Review*, January/February.

Continuous improvement

Every day, in every way, I am getting better and better

(Emile Coué)

Companies that have won the US National Quality Award (Baldrige) have summed up what continuous improvement means to them. Their common starting point has been to make the assumption that market standards or expectations are rising at a faster rate than their companies' normal rate of improvement.[1] This gives them a real business context for their continuous improvement efforts, as even a market leader will soon be overtaken by the others in the market if they do not continuously strive to improve themselves.

It is often stated that continuous improvement is a Japanese business invention uniquely suited to their national culture, and that its tools and techniques are unsuccessful when applied by Western organizations. While it is certainly true that Japanese companies outperform their Western counterparts, it has also been clearly demonstrated that Japanese-owned companies operating in Europe also outperform their locally owned counterparts,[2] even though they are both operating in the same cultural environment with the same labour pool. Japanese-owned companies are on average 15 per cent better than domestically owned companies in both practice and performance on a whole range of factors including: quality, lean production, logistics and concurrent engineering. These results point to the fact that it is management practice that drives performance, with 'local culture' making a secondary contribution.

Continuous improvement is now slowly reawakening in the West after being allowed to become dormant, but surprisingly it actually has its roots firmly in Western culture. There is little evidence to support the existence of a strong continuous improvement movement in Japan prior to the end of the Second World War. The techniques that Japanese industry developed into *kaizen* were previously established as standard practice by American industry in order for it to be able to meet the demands placed upon it by wartime production requirements. These techniques were then introduced into post-war Japan by a US administration that needed to rebuild Japanese industry after the devastation of the war.

The start of the continuous improvement movement can be traced back to 19th-century Scotland.[3] From there it migrated to the United States, but just as US industry was beginning to get to grips with the concepts of continuous improvement, it was overtaken by the conflicting requirements of the mass production techniques developed by Ford and Taylor in the early days of the 20th century. It took the demands placed on industry by the Second World War to re-awaken the use of some of the continuous improvement techniques in order to boost productivity and quality, and in fact one of the factors that influenced the outcome of the war was the ability of the allies' industries to make quantum leaps in yields, quality and cycle time.

Unfortunately the post-war period brought a time of complacency for Western industry; demand for goods far outstripped manufacturers' abilities to supply and there was a ready market for anything, regardless of its quality. The spell was only broken in the 1970s when the Japanese 'suddenly' started to produce better quality products, more quickly and more cheaply. This forced the West to respond to the new competitive threat by relearning its own lessons. However, the problem faced by Western industry trying to reintroduce continuous improvement long after their first attempts was that the attitudes of both management and employees had been affected by the extensive use of mass production techniques. These required that managers and engineers kept a monopoly on control and innovation, with workers and their supervisors being confined to just doing what they were told. Continuous improvement needed to break down these stereotypes by getting the workers involved in problem solving and improvement.

An early example of a scheme to encourage employees to offer improvement ideas is the one introduced by a Dumbarton shipbuilder in 1871.[3] This was a suggestion scheme that gave workers awards for improving existing tools or machines, inventing new ones, reducing accidents, reducing waste, reducing cost or improving quality. A few years later, the NCR company in the United States introduced a similar suggestion scheme, but added the refinement of worker education to encourage them to develop additional skills that would make them more eligible for advancement.[3] NCR-style suggestion schemes were gradually adopted by many major US companies and, indeed, are still used in many companies today. However, with the introduction of other employee involvement initiatives as part of their continuous improvement programmes, these companies are beginning to realize that schemes that only reward employees on the value of the cost savings achieved are becoming counter-productive, and that different reward and recognition schemes are required to reinforce the types of employee behaviour required in a continuous improvement environment.

The principles of continuous improvement were captured in a wartime education programme for American industry which was aimed at delivering the productivity improvements required to feed the war machine. There were three elements to this education programme:

1 *Job instruction training* taught supervisors the value of training and how to provide it.
2 *Job methods training* taught supervisors how to generate improvement ideas and how to ensure that they were implemented.
3 *Job relations training* provided the human relations training supervisors needed to make them more effective.

It was these training programmes that the US occupational forces introduced to Japanese industry after the war, and which they developed into the *kaizen* approach.

REQUIREMENTS OF CONTINUOUS IMPROVEMENT

Research into continuous improvement programmes[3] has identified some of the requirements for successful implementation:

- It must be clearly understood that improvements at first cause dislocation and almost always require time before they prove worthwhile.
- Operating practices that restrict the flow of ideas must be eliminated.
- Employees must continuously be trained and developed, particularly in techniques of improvements methods.
- A continuous improvement effort needs an efficient mechanism to handle improvement ideas.

These requirements are at the heart of the conflict between 'traditional' mass production systems and continuous improvement. Fordist-style mass production systems actively discourage their process workers from making changes, or thinking of improvements and taking the initiative. The job of the workers is do precisely what they are told to do. Any improvement, change or deviation from that is for the management and professional engineers to decide. This conflict between mass production and continuous improvement is discussed by Imai in his book *Kaizen*,[4] but rather than being characterized as the difference between Eastern and Western approaches, the differences should really be considered to be those between two conflicting production systems. In the *mass production* system it is the role of management and the professional engineer to improve the system and the role of the process worker to operate, control and maintain the existing system. In the *continuous improvement* system everybody is involved in improving and maintaining the system, although the ratio of improvement to maintenance changes depending on the individual's position in the organizational hierarchy. The difference between the two approaches is shown in Fig. 7.1.

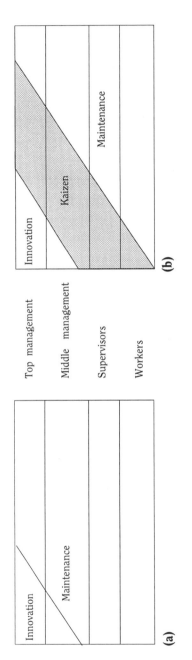

(a)

Top management

Middle management

Supervisors

Workers

(b)

Maintenance = Maintaining current technological, managerial and operating standards.
Improvement = Activities that improve current standards: there are two components to improvement.
● *Kaizen* = Small improvements made to the status quo
● Innovation = Drastic improvement made to the status quo

FIGURE 7.1   Mass production (Western) and continuous improvement (Japanese) systems: (a) Western and (b) Japanese perception of job functions

Source: Iamai, M. (1986). *Kaizen: The Key to Japan's Competitive Success*, Reproduced with permission of McGraw-Hill, Inc.

In the mass production approach improvement is via innovation – infrequent but radical changes controlled by management. In the continuous improvement system there is another dimension to improvement – incremental improvement as well as innovation. Incremental improvement is the responsibility of everybody.

KAIZEN

The Japanese term *kaizen* is often used as a synonym for 'continuous improvement'. However, although the objective is continuous improvement, *kaizen* actually encompasses far more than the activities usually recognized in the West as those that directly contribute to continuous improvement. The following list shows the separate elements of *kaizen*, which really comprise a total production management system (indeed, many echoes of *kaizen* can be found in the total quality management system models used in Baldrige and EQA) rather than just an approach to continuous improvement.

- Customer orientation
- Total quality control
- Robotics
- Quality control circles
- Suggestion system
- Automation
- Discipline in the workplace
- Total productive maintenance
- *Kanban*
- Quality improvement
- Just-in-time
- Zero defects
- Small group activities
- Co-operative labour and management relationships
- Productivity improvement
- New-product development.

Some of these *Kaizen* activities, such as quality control circles, suggestion systems, and quality and productivity improvement are recognized as elements of continuous improvement, while others such as robotics, automation, total productive maintenance and just-in-time, are generally considered to be separate strategies that need continuous improvement as a prerequisite for their successful implementation – that is, continuous improvement is an enabler for them. For example, just-in-time (JIT) and continuous improvement fit together like hand-in-glove. JIT requires the elimination of the buffer stocks of work in progress that characterize traditional manufacturing methods (the buffer stocks are there to protect continued production when problems occur – interrupted shipments from suppliers, malfunctions in the manufacturing process that stop production while they are corrected, etc.). This in turn requires that the causes of all these problems are eliminated rather than tolerated as a part of life's rich tapestry, and the way to eliminate them once and for all is to get the process workers themselves to do it: train them in problem-solving techniques, form them into problem-solving teams, and get them to solve the problems that keep interrupting production. Thus, JIT needs the techniques of continuous improvement for it to become established, and JIT gives continuous improvement a strategic context in which to flourish.

A basic principle of *kaizen*, continuous improvement and of total quality management is the empowerment of the employee. If the employees are going to make the improvements that were once reserved for management, they must be empowered to make those changes. They must be given the tools that allow them properly to analyse the situation so that they can make genuine improvements that contribute to the overall success of the organization. The most important of these tools is the use of a structured problem-solving approach such as the Deming wheel, combined with the use of analysis tools such as Pareto charts, run charts, fishbone charts, control charts, scattergrams, flowcharts and histograms (often referred to as the seven basic tools of quality). All employees should be trained in their use and be expected to use them in their everyday work; these tools should not be kept back for use only in formal problem-solving or improvement teams. Another basic principle is that everybody is involved in *kaizen*, managers and non-managers, both individually and in teams. Although everybody should be involved in continuous improvement there are differences in the approach, focus, scope and effect of continuous improvement, as shown in Table 7.1.

TABLE 7.1   Differences between continuous improvement approaches

	Management Kaizen	Team Kaizen	Individual Kaizen
Tools	7 statistical tools New 7 tools Professional skills	7 statistical tools New 7 tools	7 statistical tools Common sense
Involvement	Managers and professionals	QC circle	Everybody
Target	Systems and procedures	Within the same department	Own area of work
Cycle	Duration of the project	4–5 months	Anytime
Achievements	As many as management choose	2 or 3 per year	Many
Support	Line and staff Project team	Small group activities QC circles Suggestion system	Suggestion system
Implementation cost	Sometimes requires small investments	Mostly inexpensive	Inexpensive
Result	New/improved systems	Improved work procedures Revised work standards	On the spot improvement
Booster	Improvement in management performance	Morale improvement Participation Learning experience	Morale improvement Kaizen awareness Self-development
Direction	Gradual and visible improvement	Gradual and visible improvement	Gradual and visible improvement

Source: Imai, M. (1986). *Kaizen, The Key to Japan's Competitive Success.*
McGraw-Hill. Reproduced with permission of McGraw-Hill, Inc.

An example of the Japanese approach to quality and continuous improvement was provided by an engineer from IBM Japan while he was working at one of IBM's UK factories. Although this is only a single anecdotal example (Table 7.2), it does provide some insight into the Japanese approach at the working level.

WHAT IS CONTINUOUS IMPROVEMENT?

The following statements encapsulating some of the ideals of continuous improvement were made by speakers at a continuous improvement conference in London†:

> *Releasing the creative potential of the workforce*
> 'Everybody at Rover has two jobs – do the work, and improve the work.'
> 'With every pair of hands you get a free brain'.

> *Creating an atmosphere of trust*
> 'People will never improve themselves out of a job.'
> 'Make money with people, not out of people.'
> 'Manage things – lead people.'

> *Who assesses value-add/non value-add?*
> 'It has to be the customer.'

Continuous improvement has two themes: first encouraging the involvement of the entire workforce both as individuals and in teams, to identify and solve problems that are affecting their work; second, encouraging the entire workforce to use their creativity in offering suggestions for improvement, making use of their understanding of the way work is conducted, and their intellectual ability to solve problems in a structured manner. Feigenbaum[5] identified 10 principles that are required to be in

† Continuous Improvement Conference, Church House, Westminster, London, 26 January 1994.

TABLE 7.2 Example of the Japanese approach to continuous improvement

Simultaneous engineering	Teamwork (production, contractors, vendors, engineering, designers, procurement, production control)	Human spirit quality control	Japanese-style Circles	Quality Control assessment	Salary	Innovation
Quality depends on the design: Japanese companies periodically swap designers and manufacturing staff – designers should know their customers' needs.	Total team meetings – share the product's functions and applications, review problems and instigate improvement to ensure there is no recurrence, think of potential problems.	Don't divide job assignments completely for each person – it will lead to 'leaked' jobs that nobody is covering.	Cleanliness Make quality visible Prevent recurrence Prevent potential problems	Continuous quality improvement activities.	Improve the motivation of individuals by changing from a *demerit* system which punishes failure to a *merit* system which rewards success.	Study other companies to discover new ideas for your own company.

place if employee involvement programmes are to be successful:

1 Genuine, not superficial, management involvement.
2 All employee ideas have to be given serious consideration.
3 The programme has a long-term continuity.
4 The improvement programme is applicable to all areas of a business.
5 Organization must be clear and simple.
6 Emphasis should be placed on voluntary participation.
7 Group meetings must be seen to have a clear value to the participants.
8 Involvement sessions and the programme itself must be kept fresh.
9 Leadership should be from line rather than staff functions.
10 Involvement programmes are an important part of a total quality or improvement strategy; they are not the substitute for one.

CONTINUOUS IMPROVEMENT AND BUSINESS PROCESS RE-ENGINEERING

Continuous improvement and business process re-engineering need not be mutually exclusive. They do have different approaches and philosophies, but they can exist side by side, and a business needs to use both approaches to achieve its full performance potential, as shown in Fig. 7.2.

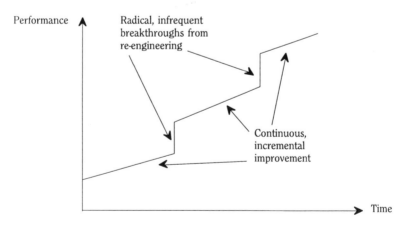

FIGURE 7.2   Continuous improvement and re-engineering

The occasional leaps in performance improvement that can be brought about by major innovation techniques like business process re-engineering must be interspersed with an ongoing programme of continuous improvement. Continuous improvement needs to be treated as a basic principle of process management because without it process performance will quickly fall behind that being achieved by others.

Continuous improvement is based on the premise that the particular process is required by the business; it does not question the need for the process or its output, but concentrates on making it more efficient and effective. Continuous improvement requires:

- Releasing the creativity of members of the workforce, which requires approaches that will help and encourage them to offer up improvement ideas.
- Harnessing their knowledge of their jobs and related processes to identify and solve problems that adversely affect them.

To do this successfully requires the effective use of a combination of the 'hard' things, the tools or methods that are used by employees in their involvement and problem-solving efforts, and the 'soft' things, the vehicles that are used to encourage and promote continuous improvement activities. More attention is usually given to the 'hard' things, but in fact these tools and techniques are simple to learn and use and are not generally the reason for failure. Failure is more often due to the 'soft' issues such as reward, recognition, empowerment and, most importantly, a lack of strategy and leadership. The establishment of new recognition practices can alter the company's values and thereby positively change the company culture.[6] Public recognitic n is an effective way of recognizing the individual or team but, equally important, it gives a powerful message to all other employees about what is important to the organization and what its priorities are.

CIRCA (Continuous Improvement Research for Competitive Advantage)

Continuous improvement is becoming acknowledged as a powerful approach for maximizing the potential of any organization, but its theory and practice have, until now, been poorly understood by the majority of Western industry. For this reason, a detailed research programme into continuous improvement has been conducted in the UK under the direction of Professor Bessant,[7,8] funded by the UK government. This research programme looked at a whole range of questions relating to continuous improvement, such as how to start it, how to maintain momentum, and how to apply it to a wide range of business processes.

The research has established that successful continuous improvement requires a system of five interlocking components, as shown in Fig. 7.3. Each component is required in order to implement and sustain a successful continuous improvement programme. The components of the system are:

1 *Strategy*

Continuous improvement needs to be integrated into the organization's overall strategy. It must be focused on making improvements that ultimately contribute to the organization achieving its strategic goals. Commitment to continuous improvement should be clear in mission and vision statements. Top management must be committed to continuous improvement, and demonstrate that commitment by words and deeds. There must be a clear strategic commitment to continuous improvement, which is understood by all employees.

2 *Infrastructure*

Continuous improvement requires effective communications channels, trained facilitators, and the ability to enable and manage the process of continuous improvement using the appropriate vehicles such as company-wide task forces, project teams, problem-solving groups and individual activities.

3 *Process*

Continuous improvement relies on the use of a structured problem-solving approach, generally based on the Deming wheel of Plan, Do, Check, Act (see Fig. 4.2). It also requires the ability to communicate and capture the results so as to avoid making the same mistakes twice; that is, to be a learning organization. The use of reward and recognition systems that reinforce the types of behaviour required in a continuous improvement environment and of feedback loops so that the continuous improvement process itself is constantly improved and rejuvenated, are also required.

4 *Tools and techniques*

The full range of tools must be available, from the simple to the most complex, and employees must be trained in their use, with advice, guidance and facilitation available when needed.

5 *Culture*

The organization must have core values and beliefs that support continuous improvement, and which are shared throughout the entire employee population. Management must recognize that the small steps matter, and that it is all right to fail, provided that the individual and the organization learn from the failure.

The research has also identified the four stages that continuous improvement programmes go through from infancy to maturity (Table 7.3), as well as the major inhibitors to success.

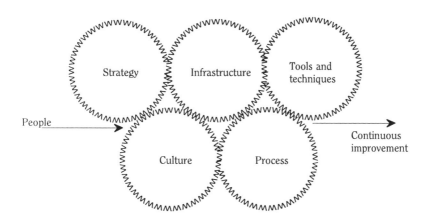

FIGURE 7.3 The continuous improvement engine

Source: Based on a presentation given by Professor Bessant to the CIRCA network

TABLE 7.3 The stages of continuous improvement and its inhibitors

Continuous improvement stages	The major inhibitors
1 Treat symptoms and fight fires	Lack of top-level commitment Afraid to take risks Reward fire-fighting rather than prevention
2 Systemize, anticipate and prevent; get processes under control	Company culture – preference for the radical and the quick fix Inappropriate measurement systems Poor communications No time or resources Improvements are not fixed into performance standards and do not last
3 Eliminate problems and root causes; put emphasis on understanding and improving processes	
4 Find new ways of doing things	

EMPLOYEE RECOGNITION

The concept of releasing the creative potential of the entire workforce is fundamental to effective continuous improvement. In order to encourage this initiative from employees, they need to feel that this type of behaviour is important to their organization.

Recognition does not have to be the presentation of a large money award to an individual or group. Indeed, there is a real danger in this approach when employees begin to believe that monetary awards are a part of their total payment package. The danger is that rather than fostering an open, team-based culture, large cash awards do the opposite – they encourage employees not to share their ideas with their colleagues so that they do not have to share the award either. Often the most effective forms of recognition are the simplest ones: public praise for a job well done; a mention in the company journal for a suggestion made, or a team photograph on the notice board.

Employees must also be sure that recognition is not based on either luck or favouritism. Recognition based on luck was demonstrated perfectly by Deming with his famous red and white bead experiments.[9] (Members of the audience were invited to participate in this experiment. They were each in turn given a large jar full of red (20 per cent) and white (80 per cent) beads and told that their job was to draw 50 beads out of the jar while blindfolded, and that they were to extract only white ones. Of course, each pulled out handfuls of beans with various combinations of red and white. Those that were closest to meeting Deming's demand were rewarded, those furthest from it were punished – but rewarded or punished because of an event for which the outcome was totally random and over which they had absolutely no control!) Employees are not fools – poorly conducted recognition quickly breeds cynicism, which is very difficult to eliminate once it has taken hold.[6]

COMMUNICATION

Deming's 10th point[9] is 'Eliminate slogans, exhortations and targets for the workforce'. His reason for this is that they are based on the assumption that poor quality is totally the fault of the worker, and if only they would take a pride in their work and do their jobs properly, there would be no problems. He believed that the truth is that most problems are the fault of the system, which is management's responsibility. Such exhortations and misguided posters breed resentment and frustration, and ultimately lead the workers to conclude that the whole thing is a management hoax! If exhortations and posters are the wrong forms of communication, what are the right ones?

The reason for communicating is to stimulate learning. Management need to communicate to the workforce the values that they subscribe to, so that the workers will learn to adopt the required behaviour patterns; when a worker discovers the solution to a problem, that solution needs to be communicated to all other workers, so that they can learn from the experience. The CIRCA research identified two categories of communication: those forms that exist as part of the organization's infrastructure and those forms introduced specifically as part of their continuous improvement programme. Clearly, all the communication media that are part of the infrastructure can be used for continuous improvement related communications. Examples of both categories are shown in Table 7.4.

TABLE 7.4 Continuous improvement related communications

Communications that are part of the infrastructure	Communications that are specific to continuous improvement
Team briefings Company newsletters Electronic mail Videos Memos Training programmes Performance appraisals 'All hands' meetings	Process performance charts displayed Improvement team photographs displayed Videos of improvement projects Published minutes of CI steering group meetings

In summary, CIRCA found that the key ingredients for mobilizing and managing continuous improvement are:

1 *Train and develop all employees.* All employees need to be given training in the use of structured problem solving and the quality tools that accompany it. They also need to understand the concepts of business processes, their analysis and improvement. Training needs should be established for each individual and personalized education and training programmes developed for them.

2 *Develop a continuous improvement process.* There needs to be a repeated cycle of action, experience and review. Most continuous improvement processes are based, either directly or indirectly, on

Deming's Plan, Do, Check, Act. This process needs to be embedded in the organization's culture so that it does not require a conscious decision on behalf of an individual or group to use it; they use it in their day-to-day work to solve problems and do not reserve it specially for 'formal' continuous improvement exercises.

3 *Measure the effect of continuous improvement.* Measurement is the key. It allows the organization to establish exactly where it is at any given point in time, and most importantly, allows 'before and after' comparisons to be made to ensure that genuine improvements are made and not just cosmetic changes. If the anticipated performance improvement does not occur, having a sound system of measurements in place allows that fact to be detected and corrective action taken.

It is also necessary to be able to differentiate between performance improvement that is due to fundamental change to the process, and performance improvement due to the 'Hawthorne effect'. (This is the effect first noted by researchers at Western Electric's Hawthorne plant in the 1930s when investigating productivity in the relay assembly area. They noted that when they increased the lighting level to make it easier for the assemblers to see, their productivity increased. Later they reduced the lighting back to its original level, explaining to the operators that this would make their work easier, and surprisingly saw a further increase in productivity. This led to the conclusion that the productivity improvement was not due to any real improvement to the work environment or the process, but was in fact due to the morale improvement of the workers caused by others taking an interest in them and their working environment.)

4 *Document continuous improvement experiences.* Achieving some degree of improvement in one small part of the organization is all well and good, but if the entire organization is to benefit, each improvement needs to be documented and communicated to the rest of the organization so that they can implement it as well, where appropriate. Improvements can be documented and shared via electronic databases, internal papers, company newsletters, or formal process change notices

(treating change to a business process in the same way that an engineering change to a product is treated).

5 *Encourage experiments and do not punish failure.* Continuous improvement (encouraging employees to use their creativity and knowledge to make suggestions and solve problems) will not get established in any organization that punishes mistakes. Punishing mistakes encourages a safety-first approach where people will not take any risks; instead they will only do exactly what they are told by their supervisors so that any problem that does occur is not their fault.

6 *Display the progress made by continuous improvement teams.* Displays of the progress being made are powerful motivators, both to the team actually involved in the particular exercise, which will get a sense of pride by seeing the results of their efforts on public display, but also to the rest of the workforce who are not directly involved –they will start to perceive participation in continuous improvement activity as a good thing for them as well.

7 *Challenge the system and go looking for problems.* Initial activity in organizations new to continuous improvement tends to focus on firefighting. As the more obvious problems are solved momentum can be lost if new targets for continuous improvement cannot be identified. A systematic challenging of the status quo is required to continually drive performance improvement.

8 *Bring different perspectives to bear.* We often cannot see the wood for the trees. People become so familiar with the process and the environment in which they work that it needs someone with a fresh pair of eyes to point out problems that have been overlooked. This different perspective can be achieved by job rotation, secondments, and cross-functional teams.

REFERENCES

1   Porter, A.M. (1993). 'Baldrige winners discuss continuous improvement path'. *Purchasing,* January, pp. 55–58.

2   Hanson, P. Voss, C. Blackmon, K. and Oak, B. (1994). *Made in Europe: A Four Nations Best Practice Study*. IBM Consulting Group.

3   Schroeder, D.M. and Robinson, A.G. (1991). 'America's most successful export to Japan: continuous improvement programs'. *Sloan Management Review*, 67, Spring.

4   Imai, M. (1986). *Kaizen: The Key to Japan's Competitive Success*. McGraw-Hill, New York.

5   Feigenbaum, A.V. (1991). *Total Quality Control*. McGraw-Hill, New York.

6   Carder, B. and Clark, J.D. (1992). 'Employee recognition'. *Quality Progress*, December, pp. 25–30.

7   Bessant, J. Burnell, J. Harding, R. and Webb S. (1992). 'Helping industry towards continuous improvement, The UK CIRCA project'. *Industry & Higher Education*, September, pp. 185–189.

8   Bessant, J. Harding, R. Webb, S. Gilbert, J. and Caffyn, S. (1994). 'Rediscovering continuous improvement'. *Technovation*, February.

9   Deming, W.E. (1990). *Out of the Crisis*. Cambridge University Press, Cambridge.

RECOMMENDED READING

Imai, M. (1986). *Kaizen: The Key to Japan's Competitive Success*. McGraw-Hill, New York.

CHAPTER

8

Business process re-engineering

> **The reasonable man adapts himself to the world: the unreasonable one persists in trying to adapt the world to himself. Therefore all progress depends on the unreasonable man.**
> (George Bernard Shaw)

Business process re-engineering (BPR) is really a new title for an old activity – that of designing a completely new process rather than trying to improve the existing one. In essence, business process re-engineering challenges the status quo; instead of asking the continuous improvement question 'How can we improve what we are doing?', it asks a more fundamental question, 'Do we really need to do what we are currently doing?' Of course, this question itself is not new. What is new is that the answer is now more frequently 'No! The process does not need to be performed that way any longer', either because the requirement for the process output has changed, or because the rapid progress of information technology (IT) innovation that is occurring now has allowed a fundamentally different approach to achieving the required output. The availability of new IT is not by itself an essential precondition for business process re-engineering but radical change does require some form of new capability, which is often, but not exclusively provided by IT. For example, the new capability that enabled a manufacturer of cash issue machines to re-engineer their transatlantic product distribution process was the availability of cheap, volume air freight that allowed them to cut a week out of the distribution cycle by shipping by air instead of by sea, and the emergence of specialist door-to-door distribution organizations that could use their own high-speed, high-volume delivery networks instead of the manufacturer's.

The fundamental difference between business process re-engineering and continuous improvement (CI) is, according to Hammer and Champy,[1] that BPR is *starting over* – it is not *tinkering* with what already exists, or making incremental changes. An important tool that helps in making the decision between BPR and CI is benchmarking, which enables the gap between current performance and what best practice is achieving to be understood. Knowing the size and nature of the gap helps with the decision about whether continuous improvement by itself can close it, or whether more radical BPR approaches are needed.

Figure 8.1 shows that CI and BPR mark the extremes of a process improvement continuum. Any process improvement methodology can be positioned somewhere along this continuum, depending on the degree to which it exhibits the characteristics that mark the extremes.

Both BPR and CI share some common themes; for instance, they both recognize the importance of processes that start by considering the needs of the customer. However, they differ fundamentally in that continuous improvement operates within the framework of a company's existing processes and seeks to improve them by continuous incremental improvements – carry on with what is done, but do it better. Business process re-engineering seeks breakthroughs, not by enhancing what is done, but by discarding the approach completely and replacing it with an entirely new one. Another key difference is that continuous improvement is essentially a 'bottom-up' activity that is driven by the people involved in the process who are seeking ways of making it perform better, whereas BPR is a 'top-down' approach that must have the active drive that only the CEO can provide.[2] First, because it requires that the organization has a process rather than a functional orientation – something that only a person sitting above the functional structure can impose. Second, because it requires

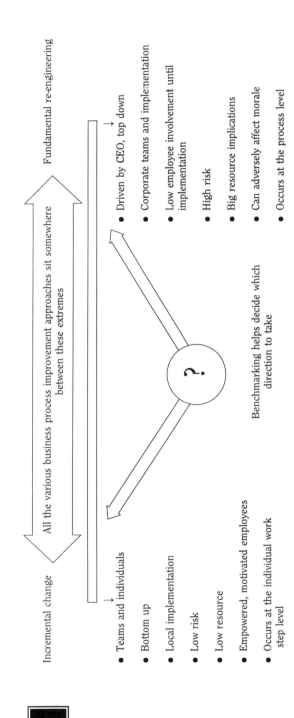

Incremental change

All the various business process improvement approaches sit somewhere between these extremes

Fundamental re-engineering

- Teams and individuals
- Bottom up
- Local implementation
- Low risk
- Low resource
- Empowered, motivated employees
- Occurs at the individual work step level

- Driven by CEO, top down
- Corporate teams and implementation
- Low employee involvement until implementation
- High risk
- Big resource implications
- Can adversely affect morale
- Occurs at the process level

Benchmarking helps decide which direction to take

FIGURE 8.1   The process improvement continuum

someone able to force change through the organization and not accept the 'push-back' of middle managers who are trying to resist fundamental change.

Recognizing that organizations often do not have the resources to address the improvement of all their business processes at the same time, some method for prioritizing processes for improvement has to be used (see Fig. 3.7). However, as well as needing to set the priorities for process improvement, it is also important to decide which processes need the radical change of BPR and which can accept the incremental changes of CI. As mentioned previously, benchmarking can help make this decision, which is based on comparing internal and external performance indicators as shown in Fig. 8.2.

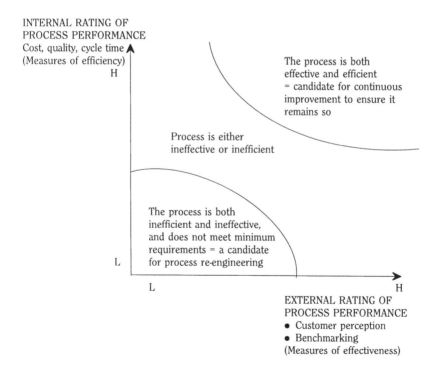

INTERNAL RATING OF
PROCESS PERFORMANCE
Cost, quality, cycle time
(Measures of efficiency)
H

The process is both
effective and efficient
= candidate for continuous
improvement to ensure it
remains so

Process is either
ineffective or inefficient

The process is both
inefficient and ineffective,
and does not meet minimum
requirements = a candidate
for process re-engineering

L

L   H
EXTERNAL RATING OF
PROCESS PERFORMANCE
● Customer perception
● Benchmarking
(Measures of effectiveness)

FIGURE 8.2   Radical or incremental change?

Performing this internal/external assessment will show that some processes are clearly both ineffective and inefficient and should be re-engineered, while others are both efficient and effective, and should be continuously improved to ensure that they continue to do so. For processes that fall into these areas the decision is black or white: either BPR or CI. The problem comes with the grey area in the middle where the process has problems with either effectiveness or efficiency. Here benchmarking can identify what external best practice are achieving and helps with the decision to adopt BPR or CI (and of course, the continual comparison to best practice provided by benchmarking brings in a flow of ideas that fuel both CI and BPR.

EFFECTS OF BUSINESS PROCESS RE-ENGINEERING

Business process re-engineering affects far more than just the particular process being addressed and touches the whole organization – the way it is structured, its personnel policies, and its leadership practices. Hammer and Champy[1] identified the following effects:

- Work units change from functional departments to process teams.
- Jobs change from simple tasks to multi-dimensional work.
- People's roles change from controlled to empowered.
- Job preparation changes from training to education.
- Advancement criteria change from performance to ability.
- Focus of performance measures and compensation shifts from activity to results.
- Values change from protective to productive.
- Organizational structures change from hierarchical to flat.
- Executives change from scorekeepers to leaders.

They also identified two preconditions for effective process re-engineering:

- The first is that the CEO must make a compelling argument for change. He must convey a forceful message that re-engineering is essential for an organization's survival – *a case for action*.
- The second precondition is that the CEO must convey a clear message

about what the company needs to become, in order to give the employees a goal to aim at. If people are going to accept the need for re-engineering, they first have to accept a vision of what the organization will be like in the future, which will sustain them through the painful period of change. The message should also make management think clearly about the extent of the change required – *a vision statement.*

DECIDING BETWEEN CI AND BPR

Many organizations now understand that continuous improvement is an essential strategy for continued business success. The aims of continuous improvement are to improve quality and to reduce the waste, cycle time and cost of all the processes operated by the business. However, there must always come a point where further improvement to the existing process is futile because:

1 The law of diminishing return operates, resulting in more and more effort being put into achieving less and less improvement.

2 The realization that the existing process, even when totally optimized and operating perfectly, can no longer achieve the results required of it.

In the less mature organization this decision point is not consciously reached – some form of crisis is required to force radical change. In the more mature organization there will be a regular review of process capabilities against requirements, with the requirements based on benchmarking, a clear understanding of the customers' needs, and on reviewing the organization's goals and critical success factors. These regular reviews provide an answer to the question 'Can this process be developed by continuous improvement approaches so that it continues to achieve all that is required of it?' If the answer is 'yes', then the continuous improvement path is still appropriate. If the answer is 'no', then it is 'time for discontinuous thinking ... a time to break away from the outdated rules and assumptions that underlie operations ... time to re-engineer the process'.[1]

Business process re-engineering and continuous improvement have a common driving force provided by the assessment of the business needs, from which they may conclude that the process is either redundant, in need of total redesign from a base zero, or a candidate for CI. In order for either approach to succeed, the organization requires both the technical competence to redesign or improve the process, but more importantly it requires a culture that gives it the ability to accept the resultant change. Although BPR and CI share the same driving force, they have some fundamental differences:

- Continuous improvement is conducted by the people who actually manage and operate the process, whereas business process re-engineering is typically conducted by a full team of experts including process experts, IT experts, and 'external' consultants (at least external to the process, possibly from a central support group, or possibly engaged from an external consulting firm).
- Continuous improvement is based on the existing process and improving it by process analysis and simplification. Business process re-engineering starts with a fundamental review of the business and its goals, establishing first what outputs are required by the customer, and then what processes are required to create those outputs.
- Business process re-engineering is often accompanied by the introduction of new IT which enables the desired output to be achieved in ways that were unknown when the process was first established. IT also has a part to play in CI by making the existing process more efficient, but only after process analysis and simplification has been completed. If new IT is introduced before process simplification, then instead of it improving efficiency, it will only result in achieving a state of muddle and chaos quicker than could be achieved without it.

The mature organization will approach BPR by the rational assessment of all its processes (possibly using the business process excellence index described in Chapter 12), whereas the immature tends to follow the 'Darwinian' approach of natural selection – cut the headcount by 20 per cent and the survivors will slowly stop doing anything that is not vital! It is important that for each process under consideration, a conscious choice is made between continuous improvement and business process re-engineering, or employees may spend a lot of time making improvements to a process that ends up being eliminated through re-engineering. It is vital that all employees understand the corporate strategy towards process improvement in order to avoid the twin evils of either inactivity or duplication of effort.

DIFFERING APPROACHES TO BPR

As a result of assessing the capabilities of each process, some will be considered to be candidates for re-engineering, and others for continuous improvement. This is the second of four possible approaches to BPR identified by Davenport.[3] His four possible approaches are shown in Table 8.1. Examination of the four approaches shows that they are not actually a series of alternatives; it is possible to use all four, and it is certainly common (and effective) to use a combination of the first two; each process should be managed by a combination of continuous improvement interspersed with the occasional radical step changes; and the priority for radical re-engineering should be decided regularly by going through the exercise of creating a portfolio of process change programmes.

As previously described, an organization should assess all of its processes to decide which of those require re-engineering and which require incremental or continuous improvement (approach 2). Approach 4, using the savings from the quick fixes to fund the more fundamental changes, is often favoured by organizations that engage external consultants because it means that their work is largely self funding. A basic requirement of the re-engineered process is that it has the capability for continuous improvement designed into it from the beginning (approach 1) – it needs to have a 'robust' design trajectory capable, with the use of continuous improvement, of meeting not only today's requirements but also those of the foreseeable future. Once the point is reached that the new process can no longer meet requirements, then it is time to re-engineer again (applying continuous improvement approaches to a process which

TABLE 8.1 Davenport's approaches to business process re-engineering

APPROACH	DESCRIPTION
1 Sequencing change initiatives	This approach alternates radical, innovative step changes with periods of incremental improvement.
2 Creating a portfolio of process change programmes	This involves mapping all processes, then ranking them according to a set of criteria as candidates for either incremental (continuous) improvement or total re-engineering.
3 Limiting the scope of work redesign	This is a relatively untried approach and requires the re-engineering team to design only the top-level process and then lets the process workers design the detailed parts of their work process.
4 Undertaking improvement through innovation	This is the 'low hanging fruit' approach. Choose the quick fixes first, and use the savings to fund the bigger, longer-term improvements that need to be made.

really needs to be re-engineered in order to meet its objectives has been described by Davenport as 'tidying up the room while the bulldozer waits outside').

PROCESS LIFE CYCLE

It is clear that processes have a definite life cycle, and that approaches to process management and improvement that may be appropriate at one stage in the life cycle may be completely inappropriate at other stages. A business process is a living thing, a human activity system designed in response to some business need, and which will wither and die when either the need changes or when the process is no longer capable of satisfying that need. The business process life cycle goes through four stages (Fig. 8.3):

1 *Infancy*

Any new process will have teething troubles when first introduced. When these are resolved the process will meet all the requirements expected of it, but management must not expect it to be perfect from the start and prematurely write it off as a disaster just because it has some early problems – they have to persevere through the early difficulties.

2 *Youth*

All the early problems have been resolved, the process is stable, meets all requirements and is capable of being continually improved.

3 *Middle age*

The process is beginning to creak at the joints. It can no longer meet all of its customers' requirements and, as customer satisfaction deteriorates, controlled continuous improvement gives way to 'firefighting'.

4 *Senility*

The terminal period of the process life cycle. It is no longer capable of meeting minimum requirements and is actually driving customers away. The senile business process will actually drag the whole business to the death-bed if management allow it.

The essence of good process management is to understand that all processes go through a life cycle (as shown in Fig. 8.3), to be able to sustain the period of youth for as long as possible through continuous improvement, and to be able to recognize when the process is no longer capable and replace it with a re-engineered process *before* its death-rattle causes a crisis within the organization.

BPR METHODOLOGIES

There is a confusing profusion of methodologies available under the general headings of business process re-engineering or redesign. A methodology should be selected because it is considered to be the most appropriate for the organization, not just because it is widely promoted. The

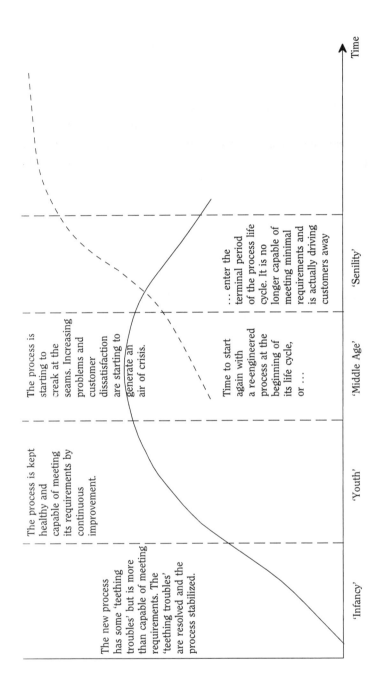

The new process
has some 'teething
troubles' but is more
than capable of meeting
requirements. The
'teething troubles'
are resolved and the
process stabilized.

The process is kept
healthy and
capable of meeting
its requirements by
continuous
improvement.

The process is
starting to
creak at the
seams. Increasing
problems and
customer
dissatisfaction
are starting to
generate an
air of crisis.

Time to start
again with
a re-engineered
process at the
beginning of
its life cycle,
or ...

... enter the
terminal period
of the process life
cycle. It is no
longer capable of
meeting minimal
requirements and
is actually driving
customers away

'Infancy'   'Youth'   'Middle Age'   'Senility'

Time

FIGURE 8.3 Business process life cycle

important thing is that the organization and its employees feel 'ownership' for the methodology, and in order to achieve this it may be appropriate to select the best points from several methodologies to construct a unique 'best of breed' methodology that has been custom-built for the particular organization (see Table 8.4 for an example). Table 8.2 compares a selection of methodologies, and it can be seen from this comparison that they share a similar general approach of:

- understand the requirements (of the customer and the business)
- map the 'as is' process
- design the 'to be' process
- implement.

Whether these approaches are all pure business process re-engineering is a moot point. The term 'business process re-engineering' often gets misused, with all process improvement activity in an organization given that fashionable title. None of the approaches shown in Table 8.2 actually start with a 'clean sheet', but in general start with the existing business processes and then confirm the process customers' requirements. On a continuum that has continuous incremental improvement at one end, and clean sheet process re-engineering at the other (see Fig. 8.1), each of these approaches would fall somewhere around the middle of the continuum, and could be more accurately called 'process redesign'.

Towers[11] sums up this multitude of approaches by confirming that no single foolproof methodology has emerged and that each organization should adopt and adapt in order to implement an approach that suits its own culture. His research has identified 11 general principles that all successful approaches share. It would seem reasonable to expect that if these principles for successful implementation of business process re-engineering are correct, then the reasons for failure would be the absence of these principles. Other research conducted by Manganelli[12] has identified the reasons why re-engineering programmes fail, any in many cases do correlate with Tower's success factors. These success and failure factors are compared in Table 8.3.

TABLE 8.2 Business process re-engineering methodologies compared

	FUREY[4]	HARRISON AND PRATT[5]	POPI[6]	DAVENPORT & SHORT[7]	CPR – KAPLAN & MURDOCK[8]
Step 1	Identify the process's customer driven objectives.	Set direction – decide which processes are to be redesigned, and in what sequence.	Initialize process improvement – identify the business processes and establish process owners.	Develop business vision and process objectives.	Identify core processes, focusing on major strategic directions and customer needs.
Step 2	Map and measure the existing process.	Baseline and benchmark – identify customer requirements and map the 'as is' process.	Analyse customer expectations – use tools such as QFD.*	Identify processes to be redesigned.	Define performance requirements, both customer driven and financial. Identify the gaps between current and required performance.
Step 3	Analyse and modify the existing process.	Create the vision – visualize the future process.	Analyse process flow.	Understand and measure existing processes.	Pinpoint problems. Map process and information flows. Do root cause analysis and prioritize problems.
Step 4	Benchmark for innovative, proven alternatives.	Launch problem-solving projects.	Measurement for process effectiveness – use tools such as SPC.†	Identify IT levers.	Develop a vision. Brainstorm and identify options. Set stretch goals. Evaluate alternatives and develop action plans.
Step 5	Re-engineer the process.	Design improvements.	Measurement for process efficiency.	Design and build a prototype of the process.	Make it happen. Roll out the changes.

Step 6	Roll out the new process.	Implement change.	Improve process effectiveness – use tools such as DPP.‡	Success requires strong leadership, cross functional teams, single accountability.
Step 7		Embed continuous improvement.	Improve process efficiency.	
Step 8			Improve process flow.	
Step 9			Measure supplier performance.	
Step 10			Ensure supplier improvements.	

* QFD (Quality Function Deployment),[9] a graphical technique for taking information on customer wants and needs and translating them into product and process requirements through the successive decomposition of 'what' into 'how'.

† SPC (Statistical Process Control),[10] using statistical techniques to measure critical process parameters that are both useful indicators of output quality and also provide the ability to assign variations to special and common cause, so that appropriate actions can be taken.

‡ DPP (Defect Prevention Process), is a structured methodology for converting corrected problems into preventable ones.

TABLE 8.3   The causes of success and failure

PRINCIPLES FOR SUCCESSFUL RE-ENGINEERING PROGRAMMES (TOWER)	REASONS WHY RE-ENGINEERING PROGRAMMES FAIL (MANGANELLI)
1 A BPR programme will take strong leadership, substantial time, and real commitment.	Many re-engineering programmes lack senior executive sponsorship.
2 Begin with a baseline assessment of your processes today.	Many organizations select the wrong processes to re-engineer.
3 Consultants are extremely useful in moving a BPR programme forward.	
4 Define BPR in quantitative terms, and set up a BPR directorate.	
5 BPR should be institutionalized through structural changes including 'working groups' and through the development of formal procedures.	Very few organizations follow a detailed re-engineering methodology.
6 BPR means revised and revamped technology.	
7 Successful BPR begins internally, within the organization, before it moves out to your business partners and customers.	Some organizations are trying to re-engineer functions rather than processes.
8 The organization's training budget will increase 30 to 50 per cent; but it is worth it because BPR rests on the shoulders of your staff.	Many companies' re-engineering efforts are under-financed and under-staffed.
9 Staff motivation remains the most difficult aspect to get right.	The term re-engineering is imprecisely defined – it is used as a euphemism for downsizing or is confused with TQM.
10 Expect that 40 per cent of staff will not be able to measure up.	
11 Evaluate the risks, but do not let them become deterrents.	

THE BEST WAY TO RE-ENGINEER

There is a reasonable correlation between the principles for success and the reasons for failure, so these factors can be used as a sanity test of the several different approaches to business process re-engineering. But at the same time it should be realized that all of these approaches are very mechanistic in nature and have the same failings as the hard systems approach described in Chapter 3. *None of them, in their early stages, make an effort to gather the views of all the people involved or affected by the process*, so that the purpose of the process can be understood from all perspectives which will allow the critical test to be performed at the action planning stage: 'Is this change *both* systemically desirable and culturally feasible?' If the answer to this question is not 'yes' to both, then that change will not succeed. The fault with most of the business process re-engineering methodologies is that they never gather the data that allows this test to be made.

In order to counter this failing the principles of soft systems methodology need to be incorporated with business process re-engineering so that a 'best of breed' BPR methodology can be developed that adopts and adapts the best of the various known approaches. Table 8.4 gives an example of such a 'best-of-breed' methodology that incorporates the key elements from the soft systems methodology with the best from the various BPR methodologies, and which has been 'sanity' checked against the success and failure factors in Table 8.3. This best-of-breed methodology could be adopted by any organization as it is, or the approach used to construct this methodology could be used to create one that is uniquely suited to their own organization. The most significant changes/additions to the 'sample' methodologies are shown in the table in italics.

1 *Get the CEO to personally drive the BPR efforts.* Does the CEO really need to be involved? Absolutely! Particularly so when the corporation is being re-engineered with new organization structures, new computer systems and new business processes. The amount of change and risk dictates not only that the CEO is personally leading the effort but also how much of his or her time is taken up with it. With the truly large

TABLE 8.4   A 'best-of-breed' re-engineering methodology

STEP	DESCRIPTION
1	Get the CEO to personally drive the business process re-engineering efforts.
2	Analyse all the organization's processes and select the ones for re-engineering.
3	Train staff in the organization's approach to re-engineering and form re-engineering teams.
4	*Develop a root definition of each process being re-engineered.*
5	Map and analyse each 'as is' or real world process being re-engineered.
6	Develop a conceptual 'to be' model of the process that meets the requirements of the root definition (re-engineer the process).
7	Compare the 'as is' and 'to be' processes and identify all the changes that need to be made.
8	*Test that each required change is both culturally feasible and systemically desirable.* *– conduct walk-throughs with affected staff* *– run simulations and pilot tests.*
9	Develop action plans.
10	Train staff in the new processes.
11	Roll out the new process, ensure that it meets all its requirements and is stable.
12	*Implement continuous improvement based process management with the new process.*
13	Regularly assess each process using the business process excellence index (Chapter 12).
14	Re-engineer the process again when it is no longer able to meet requirements – do not get stuck in a paradigm.

changes he or she is actually betting the survival of the corporation on the re-engineering being successful.

2 *Analyse all the organization's processes and select the ones for re-engineering.* It is just not practical (in fact it could be downright suicidal) to try and re-engineer all an organization's processes at the

same time. Each process needs to be assessed using the methods described earlier, to first decide which can go down the continuous improvement path and which really must be re-engineered. Then the candidates for re-engineering must be prioritized into the sequence in which they will be tackled.

3 *Train staff in process management and the organization's approach to re-engineering and form re-engineering teams.* Each process should be owned by a manager with sufficient authority to be able to make decisions on changes and improvements wherever they may be required within the 'seamless' process that could span several departments, functions or even countries. They must select their team, train them in the tools and techniques of process re-engineering, and then actively lead them through the entire re-engineering project.

4 *Develop a root definition of each process being re-engineered.* The process must be defined from the perspective of all the people affected by it, rather than just from a purely mechanistic point of view. The process objective needs to be worked into a root definition by using the CATWOE mnemonic, as seen in Chapter 3. In this way the process can be seen from many perspectives which can then be used to test the viability of alternative solutions.

5 *Map and analyse each 'as is' or real-world process being re-engineered.* Mapping the 'as is' process is performed in order to gain a clear understanding of how and why the process operates the way it does. This gives the re-engineer the knowledge of what activities are essential in order to meet the process objectives/root definition, and what activities can be eliminated in the new process. It also enables the planning of the changes required to move from the present process to the re-engineered one.

6 *Develop a conceptual 'to be' model of the process that meets the requirements of the root definition (re-engineer the process).* This is where the creative design work takes place. As part of the redesign, a thorough research of new capabilities provided by emerging new technologies needs to be conducted, so that the redesign considers both

the objectives of the process and the novel ways of achieving those objectives based on new technology capability and robust, simplified process designs. This research for novel approaches should include benchmarking – looking at the approaches used by other organizations operating the same process to see what can be learned from them. Not benchmarking as a part of process improvement or re-engineering can lead to a 'fool's paradise' because the lack of outside perspective leads management to think that things are a lot better than they really are.

7 *Compare the 'as is' and 'to be' processes and identify all the changes that need to be made.* Detailed implementation and training plans need to be developed. This can only be done if the implications of each and every change are understood.

8 *Test that each required change is both culturally feasible and systemically desirable. Conduct walk-throughs with affected staff and run simulations and pilot tests.* The perception data gathered at the root definition stage can be used as an initial sanity check of the proposed changes to test that each is both feasible and desirable. Those that pass this test can then be reviewed with the affected staff (from both this process and other business processes that interact with it).

Simulations and pilot tests should be run to ensure that the planned changes will produce the desired outcomes and to identify any problems with implementation.

9 *Develop action plans.* The testing done at the previous stage will provide good input on the problems that can be anticipated during the implementation phase. The key to good action planning is to ensure that every action has a clearly defined owner who knows that he or she will be held accountable for its success, that the schedule is clearly understood and the criteria for success as defined. There must be no ambiguity in action plans.

10 *Train staff in the new processes.* One of the key ingredients for success is training; all affected members of staff must understand how to perform their new roles in the new process, and also how to operate the new computer systems that will probably be introduced at the same time.

The effects of fear should not be underestimated. People who have grown into their present roles over a period of years will have many fears, such as their ability to cope in the new environment and with new technology, their possible loss of status and career path, and the potential de-skilling of their job and loss of job satisfaction. Fear is removed by familiarization and training.

11 *Roll out the new process, ensure that it meets all its requirements and is stable.* This means that the requirements have been defined in quantifiable terms and that a measurement system has been put in place that allows management to confirm that both the requirements are being fully met and that the process is stable; consistently meeting requirements without constant interference or firefighting.

12 *Implement CI-based process management to the new process.* Now is not the time to relax and take the focus off the new process. Now is the time for putting continuous improvement programmes in place to make the small, incremental improvements that will keep the process vital and responsive to changing needs.

13 *Regularly assess each process using the business process excellence index (Chapter 12).* Emotional attachment to the new process is out of place. All processes must be regularly assessed so that the organization can detect the moment when it is no longer capable of meeting the requirements, which will change over time as new customers are acquired and existing ones identify new requirements.

14 *Re-engineer the process again when it is no longer able to meet requirements – do not get stuck in a paradigm.* Do not wait for the crisis this time!

REFERENCES

1   Hammer, M. and Champy, J. (1993). *Re-engineering The Corporation: A Manifesto For Business Revolution.* Nicholas Brealey, London.

2   Cover Story – A Word With Michael Hammer. *Datamation,* August 1, 1993.

3   Davenport, T.H. (1993). 'Need radical innovation and continuous improvement? Integrate process, re-engineering and TQM'. *Planning Review*, May/June, pp. 7–12.

4   Furey, T.R. (1993). 'A six-step guide to process re-engineering'. *Planning Review*, March/April, pp. 20–23.

5   Harrison, D.B. and Pratt, M.D. (1993). 'A methodology for re-engineering businesses'. *Planning Review*, March/April, pp. 7–11.

6   Abbott, R. (1991). *The Process of Process Improvement: Your Total Quality Management Tool Bag*. IBM Technical Report, April.

7   Davenport, T.H. and Short, J.E. (1990). 'The new industrial engineering: Information technology and business process redesign. *Sloan Management Review*, Summer, Vol. 31, pp. 11–27.

8   Kaplan, R.B. and Murdock, L. (1991). 'Core process redesign'. *The McKinsey Quarterly*, 2.

9   Hauser, J. and Clausing, D. (1988). 'The house of quality'. *Harvard Business Review*, May/June.

10 Deming, W.E. (1990). *Out of the Crisis*. Cambridge University Press, Cambridge.

11 Towers, S. (1993). 'Business process re-engineering – lessons for success'. *Management Services*, August, pp. 10–12.

12 Manganelli, R.L. (1993). 'It's not a silver bullet'. *Journal of Business Strategy*, November/December, Vol. 14, p. 45.

RECOMMENDED READING

Hammer, M. and Champy, J. (1993). *Re-engineering the Corporation: A Manifesto for Business Revolution*. Nicholas Brealey, London.

PART

3

Implementation

INTRODUCTION TO PART 3

Part 3 explores the practical issues of implementation, using case study examples where appropriate. The case studies have been carefully chosen to highlight specific learning points, rather than just to provide some passing interest to the reader as is often the case in books of this type. All the case studies are real, but in many instances the identity of the organization concerned has been concealed in order to avoid causing any embarrassment.

The four major components of continuous business improvement that are explored in-depth in Part 3 are:

● the use of self-assessment to drive improvement
● continuous improvement
● benchmarking techniques
● business process re-engineering (or more accurately, process redesign).

The key issues associated with each of these are shown in Figure 3A, a fishbone, or cause-and-effect diagram.

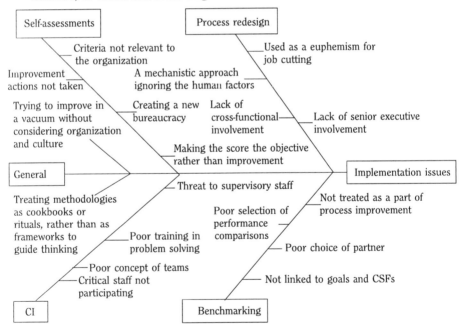

FIGURE 3A   The principal issues of implementation

CHAPTER 9

Self-assessment to drive business improvement

The secret of success is constancy of purpose.
(Disraeli)

The growing use of quality award models as the basis for internal self-assessment programmes across industry is proving to be *the* key driving force in making improvement happen. As was seen earlier in Chapter 5, there are various quality award models that, although they have some differences, also share some common themes, such as the essential need to manage any organization through its processes; the need to be continuously improving processes using approaches such as benchmarking; the need for active, participatory executives; the need for all employees to be involved in continuous improvement; and the overriding need to put the customer first. As well as sharing some common characteristics in their content, they also share some common characteristics in their approach which involves the organization writing a detailed report describing how they meet each award criterion; this is then examined by trained and experienced assessors who identify the strengths and areas for improvement, and award a points score. This approach, when used on a regular self-assessment basis, gives a regular measure of progress as the score improves, a regular update on the organization's areas for improvement, and also provides a world-class framework in which to position all the improvement strategies that an organization may adopt.

However, although the general body of evidence is beginning to show the clear link between a high score in a quality award assessment and improving business results, there are still many problems associated with the use of these award models as internal self-assessment frameworks that need to be understood and avoided if an organization is to gain real benefit from implementing self-assessment.

WHAT ARE THE KEY ISSUES?

The key issues can be grouped into four areas:
- improvement actions not taken
- criteria not relevant to the organization
- making the score the objective rather than improvement
- creating a new bureaucracy.

Improvement actions not taken

Implementation is a common failure point of all methodologies. Whether the methodology in question is continuous improvement, re-engineering, benchmarking or self-assessment, the report and recommendations are often put on one side and not acted upon until the next assessment is due! Just as the effect (lack of action) is common to the various methodologies, so are the causes of failure.

These common causes have been described in detail in previous chapters, and in summary are as shown in Table 9.1.

Criteria not relevant to the organization

An organization has to feel comfortable that the criteria contained within the self-assessment framework are actually relevant to it. This applies both to the organization as a whole, and to each of its units who will be performing self-assessments. An enormous amount of energy can be put

TABLE 9.1 Common causes of failure in implementation

CAUSE	EFFECT
1 Lack of senior executive commitment and involvement	The CEO delegates driving improvement to someone else. Senior management seen as paying lip service to improvement while really focusing on schedules and costs.
2 Lack of resources	The headcount has been cut by 20% and there is nobody to do this. Improvement activity imposed on staff in addition to all their other work.
3 Poor communication	The project team expect the final report to generate action itself, instead of having face-to-face meetings with all interested parties.
4 Cynicism and apathy	This initiative seen as just another flavour of the month. These sorts of things have been tried before and nothing happened, so what is going to be different this time?
5 Lack of strategic focus	Management will not commit the resources required for implementation because they do not see the proposed improvement as a priority.
6 Poor organization for improvement	Implementation is given to a person or team who do not have the authority to make the required changes. Monitoring implementation is not included in the normal management system so it fails due to lack of attention.
7 Viewing improvement mechanistically and not getting buy-in	Employees resent being treated like parts of a machine. They will ignore, resist, sabotage changes imposed on them in these circumstances.

into understanding the detailed requirements of the award criteria. Staff are sent on assessor training courses so that they understand the assessment process and the requirements of the award criteria. When they get back to the office they then have to start trying to interpret the requirements for their own parts of the organization, becoming embroiled in long debates with their local management teams about how each individual criterion could be applied to their own particular area, and what data are required for the application report.

A way of avoiding this problem is to customize the award criteria for the organization concerned, as described in Chapter 5. The customization should be done by a team drawn from the central quality group together with line management, to ensure that the revised assessment criteria are as faithful to the intent of the original criteria as possible while being pragmatic; that they can be understood and applied by line managers and their staff who can see that the criteria really are relevant to their areas.

Making the score the objective rather than improvement

The point of self-assessment can easily be lost. The reason for doing it is to drive improvement through the organization, with the assessment score only being used to measure and confirm that progress really is being made towards the ideal contained within the assessment framework. However, as soon as some element of incentive is introduced (for example, by the use of an internal award scheme or bonus payments) then the attention of middle management becomes focused on achieving a better score than their peers in other functions or units and any real improvement in performance becomes almost coincidental, a side-effect rather than the objective.

This obsession with a score also directs management effort towards trying to present their data in the best possible light, consuming man-years of effort in creating lengthy reports that describe how they perform (or like to think that they perform) against each criterion, with once again the report and the score derived from it being the subject of the management focus, rather than the driving of improvement efforts.

The use of mini-assessments is an effective way of overcoming this problem, and they are described later in this chapter.

Creating a new bureaucracy

The detailed requirements of the criteria, particularly with the Baldrige model, quickly breed a new professional specialist: the person who has in-depth knowledge of the assessment methodology and the criteria, who is able to interpret the criteria and provide, 'what the assessor is really looking for here is ...', guidance to the people gathering data and writing sections to go into the final report. They also often form the editorial team that puts together the report for their unit, and participate in the assessment of reports from other units.

Other groups of specialist staff spring up around the corporation whose sole purpose is the administration and organization of the self-assessment programme; making sure that each unit submits its assessment report on schedule, organizing teams of assessors to examine the report and to conduct site visits.

These problems of excessive resource demands can be overcome by using self-assessment criteria that are relevant (customized) to the organization and do not require continual interpretation, together with an assessment methodology that enables all the available resource to concentrate on identifying and implementing improvements.

MINI-ASSESSMENTS

A way of avoiding the worst of the excesses described above is to implement a self-assessment programme based on a subset of the award criteria; capturing the essence of the criteria and then using that to develop a questionnaire that can either be completed by the individual manager, or groups of managers, who can then come together in a consensus meeting to discuss and agree their individual assessments of the organization, or by interview with an experienced assessor.

There are various forms that self-assessment can take. The assessment may be conducted either in discussion with the experienced assessor or by genuine self-assessment.

- The criteria can be converted into statements of world-class behaviour that the individual can compare themselves against and rate themselves on a graduated scale that measures how close they come to that ideal.
- The criteria can be converted into a series of binary, yes/no questions that can be answered by an individual.

The necessary caution is that self-assessment without any kind of external check and balance can quickly become an exercise in self-delusion. The first time that the self-assessment is conducted the result may be fairly accurate, but the second time around, after the manager and his team have made a real effort to implement improvements that address the 'areas for improvement' from the first assessment, they will have a mindset that improvement must have occurred and that therefore the self-assessment score must have improved significantly. For this reason the use of an independent assessor to conduct the interviews and facilitate the consensus meeting must be recommended.

The self-assessment may be conducted by an individual (a department manager for example) or by a group (an entire management team or a manager and staff). When conducted by a single individual it is best to remove as much subjectivity as possible from the exercise by giving the manager a series of binary yes/no questions to answer. At the end, the assessment workbook should guide the manager through an analysis of the answers in order to develop his improvement plan. This form of self-assessment is improved by having the manager perform the assessment together with an independent assessor.

A better form of self-assessment, which is not only likely to be more accurate but which also encourages the development of team spirit, is to rate the organization against a series of world-class statements developed from the award criteria, with the rating first being conducted by the individual members of the team (either a management team or a manager and staff). After completing the individual rating, the team all meet together to form a consensus of the score and the organization's strengths and areas for improvement for each of the criteria. Once consensus has been reached they can work together to develop and implement improvement actions.

Examples of the way in which the European and Baldrige criteria can be rewritten for use in self-assessments are shown in Figs 9.1 and 9.2.

Note: item 1.2 carries 25 points out of a possible 1000, therefore it should merit approximately 2 full pages in an 80 page report. There are four areas to address and this example (1.2.a) would merit approximately 250 words with possible diagrams and tables in a full written assessment.

1.2 Management for Quality Describe how the company's customer focus and quality values are integrated into day-to-day leadership, management, and supervision of all company units.	a. How the company's customer focus and quality values are translated into requirements for all managers and supervisors. Describe: (1) their principal roles and responsibilities within their units; and (2) their roles and responsibilities in fostering co-operation with other units.

(a)

1.2 Management for Quality How are customer focus and quality values integrated into day-to-day leadership, management, and supervision of all units?	In the following boxes, tick the statements that most closely agree with the way in which you manage for quality.

There is little customer focus	Some managers have customer related objectives	All managers have customer related objectives	Managers participate and encourage cross-functional teams	All departments have internal customer/ supplier agreements
0%	10%	30%	30%	30%

(b)

FIGURE 9.1   A Baldrige based example of the questionnaire approach. (a) The original Baldrige criteria (using category 1 as an example); (b) a questionnaire version of the same criterion

Note: category 1 carries 100 points out of a possible 1000, therefore it should merit approximately 7 full pages in a 75 page report. There are six parts to this criterion, this example (a) would merit approximately 1 page in a full written report.

| 1. Leadership
The behaviour of all managers in driving the company towards Total Quality. | 1a. How the executive team and all other managers inspire and drive Total Quality as the company's fundamental process for continuous improvement.
Evidence is needed of visible involvement in leading Total Quality.
Areas to address could include how managers take positive steps to:
● communicate with staff
● act as role models leading by example
● make themselves accessible and listen to staff
● give and receive training
● demonstrate commitment to Total Quality |

(a)

A self-assessment version	
1. Leadership The behaviour of all managers in driving the company towards Total Quality	In the following boxes, tick the statements that most closely agree with the way in which you manage for quality.

Total Quality and continuous improvement are not practised.	Managers hold regular communication meetings with their staff with CI and quality as the prime topics.	Managers and executives actively participate in and lead CI activity.	All quality and improvement education is introduced and closed by senior managers.	Quality and improvement progress is always the first topic at managers meetings.
0%	10%	30%	30%	30%

(b)

FIGURE 9.2   A European quality award based example of the questionnaire approach. (a) The original EQA criteria (using category 1 as an example); (b) a questionnaire version of the same criterion.

Other variations of self-assessment, all aimed at avoiding the bureaucratic overhead of full assessments, have been developed which focus on the true objective of assessments – the continuous improvement of the organization. Brown[1] identifies four possible approaches to conducting Baldrige-based assessments: surveys, mock applications, real applications, audits. The EFQM[2,3] further amplifies these and offers organizations the following approaches:

1 *The simulated award approach.* The organization being assessed writes a full 75-page submission as if it were actually applying for the award. This is then assessed internally using a team of trained assessors who identify strengths, areas for improvement, and score, and then feed this back to the management team. This approach enables the most accurate assessment to be made, but is also the most labour intensive.

2 *The pro forma approach.* One page per criterion is suggested. The criterion is described, and space left for the assessor to write the organization's strengths, areas for improvements, score and the evidence which supports the assessment.

3 *The matrix chart approach.* This uses the EFQM framework as a base, but translates the criteria into statements of behaviour and results that the organization would expect, graduated in increments of, say, 10 per cent. The assessor then reads the statements in the matrix until he finds the one that most closely fits the organization for approach, and then notes the score associated with that score. The same is then done for results.

4 *The workshop approach.* The management team gather the data required by the EFQM criteria, and then present it to their peers in a workshop. The presentations are followed by discussion to reach a consensus on score, strengths and areas for improvement.

5 *The peer involvement approach.* This is similar in some ways to the simulated award approach but, rather than write a full submission, working documents, reports and graphs are used, thus avoiding any unnecessary work.

6 *The questionnaire approach.* This approach takes each criterion and

converts it into a question. The question can be phrased to require either a yes/no answer, or a graduated response on a scale of 1 to 5, for example, depending on how closely the organization fits the behaviour described in the question.

There are obviously pros and cons for each of these approaches, and the organization must choose the one that it considers to be most appropriate to its own particular needs. The common characteristic of all of these approaches is that they require trained assessors to facilitate the consensus discussion. They are all enhanced by the use of the site visit, where the assessors actually visit the site being assessed and talk to the managers and employees. The site visit allows the assessors to test deployment; for example, communication vehicles can be well described in a submission, and managers conducting a self-assessment can score themselves quite highly, but the real test is to actually ask the employees: what do they think are the organization's goals, strategy, vision, etc.? The site visit also allows the assessors to establish whether a cause-and-effect relationship exists between the results reported and the approaches the organization uses.

VARIOUS COMPANY APPROACHES

Some companies such as Rank Xerox use the full criteria without any modification, but effectively eliminate the wordsmithing that dominates the writing of the full 70–80 page award application by restricting the number of pages to 30. This forces report authors and their managers to abandon any thought of embellishment and to concentrate on short, concise, direct answers to each question. This approach then yields the benefits of the full assessment (a written report that can be used as a benchmark around the company, and honest feedback report by independent examiners, a vehicle for educating new staff, etc.) without unnecessary bureaucracy.

Another excellent approach to self-assessment is that used by the Royal Mail in the UK. It uses the European model as a basis for its self-assessment process, called *Business Excellence Review*. The process is an internal assessment carried out by all business units every two years, with the assessments being conducted by managers trained in the assessment methodology. A particular strength of this approach in the way that the assessment results, and benchmarking, are directly linked into the organization's business planning process.

SELF-ASSESSMENT USING OTHER CRITERIA

Some organizations adopt the principles of self-assessment from the Baldrige or EFQM approaches, but then marry the assessment methodology with criteria to meet their own specific needs. An example of this is the approach taken by a UK hospital applying for the Government's Chartermark award. The Chartermark award involves writing a short (approximately 25 page) report describing how the applicant achieves the requirements contained in the Citizen's and Patient's Charters. In order for the hospital's application team to understand for themselves how well they have performed against each criteria, a hybrid form of self-assessment has been developed using the assessment methodology of Baldrige together with the criteria contained in the various charters. A brief extract is shown in Fig. 9.3.

The written application is assessed against each Chartermark requirement in turn, using exactly the same scoring matrix as used by Baldrige and EQA which assesses each criterion for approach, deployment and results. The score for each criterion is placed in the relevant columns and on an adjoining page the assessor notes the strengths and areas for improvement that influenced the score. These are then used to produce the feedback report and subsequently form the basis for improvement planning.

CHARTERMARK REQUIREMENTS
- Services delivered to the highest standard at present available. (Column A)
- Application is supported with evidence of performance against each Chartermark principle. (Column B)
- Evidence is provided of measurable improvements in the quality of service over the last two years. (Column C)
- Evidence is provided that customer satisfaction has been achieved. (Column D)
- Plans are in place to introduce at least one innovative enhancement to their services without increasing cost to the tax payer or consumer. (Column E)

REQUIREMENT	A	B	C	D	E	AVE %
CHARTERMARK PRINCIPLE: PUBLICATION OF THE STANDARDS OF SERVICE THAT THE CUSTOMER CAN REASONABLY EXPECT, AND OF PERFORMANCE AGAINST THOSE STANDARDS. • Organizations should set and display targets for key areas of performance in a form which the citizen understands and publish information regularly on performance against those targets.						
RELEVANT PATIENT'S CHARTER RIGHTS & STANDARDS: • To be guaranteed admission for treatment by a specific date no later than two years from the day when your consultant places you on a waiting list. • To be given detailed information on local health services, including quality standards and maximum waiting times. • Waiting time for an ambulance service. When you call an emergency ambulance it should arrive within 14 minutes if you live in an urban area, or 19 minutes if you live in a rural area. • Waiting time for initial assessment in accident and emergency departments. You will be seen immediately and your need for treatment assessed. • Waiting time in outpatient clinics. You will be given a specific appointment time and be seen within 30 minutes of that time. • Cancellation of operations. Your operation should not be cancelled on the day you are due to arrive in hospital.						
RELEVANT LOCAL CHARTER STANDARDS • Waiting time for first outpatient appointment.						

FIGURE 9.3   Self-assessment against Citizen's and Patient's Charters

REFERENCES

1   Brown, M.G. (1993). *Baldrige Award Winning Quality*. ASQC Quality Press.

2   EFQM (1994). *Self Assessment 1995 Guidelines*. European Foundation for Quality Management.

3   Lascelles, D. and Peacock, R. (1995). *Self-Assessment for Business Excellence*. McGraw-Hill, London.

RECOMMENDED READING

Brown, M.G. (1995). *The Pocket Guide to Baldrige*. Quality Resources, New York.

CHAPTER 10

Implementing continuous improvement

We are what we repeatedly do. Excellence then, is not an act but a habit.
(Aristotle)

MAINTAINING THE MOMENTUM

In order to increase the understanding of the factors that contribute to successful continuous improvement, the Continuous Improvement Research for Competitive Advantage (CIRCA) programme was initiated by the UK government as a joint venture between industry and academia. The programme first thoroughly investigated the continuous improvement programmes in operation in a core of UK companies, and then from this primary research formulated a detailed model for successful continuous improvement that was then tested and refined in companies that formed a broader network across the UK.

The CIRCA research findings do not point to one single cause of success, but instead show that the successful implementation of continuous improvement is broadly based and is generally the result of a combination of a number of factors associated with the five gears in the continuous improvement engine (see Fig. 7.3): strategy, culture, infrastructure, tools and process.

Strategy

It is a basic tenet of continuous improvement that small improvements matter, that the net result of many small incremental improvements is a measurable improvement to the organization's overall business performance. Although this is true, the perception of many senior managers is different. They see many improvement teams making many 'improvements', but are not able to discern any fundamental improvement to their business. Often this is because the improvements, as well as being individually small and incremental in nature, are focused on trivial areas of activity where even if large improvements were made they would not have a significant impact on business performance. Success in continuous improvement, as in benchmarking and all other types of improvement, needs a top-down direction – there needs to be a strong link between the activities subjected to continuous improvement and the organization's goals and critical success factors. Starting continuous improvement teams by letting them focus on improving their immediate environment by proposing changes, such as rearranging office layouts or workflows to save time and avoid inconvenience, is fine when they are feeling their way and gaining confidence in their ability to contribute to improvement programmes, but once that has been established they need to be directed to what is strategically important to the company. This can be achieved by linking the activity of continuous improvement and problem-solving teams to the kind of process analysis described in Chapter 3. The process analysis work identifies the areas within the business process that need to be improved; continuous improvement teams provides the resource and tools to make the improvements.

Setting clear strategic goals and communicating them across the entire organization is a prerequisite for successful continuous improvement. Without it, continuous improvement efforts will be unfocused, and will result in trivial improvements being suggested, followed by reducing interest from management and employee demotivation as they themselves realize that they are not achieving anything.

Culture

Continuous improvement has to become part of the corporate way of life if it is to take root and flourish. Failure to accomplish this results in the 'flavour of the month' labels often given to corporate quality programmes. In order for it to become part of the corporate way of life it has to feature in the beliefs, values and traditions of the organization. Three core cultural beliefs have been identified:

1 *The belief that small improvements matter.* This belief allows the responsibility for improvement and problem solving to be moved away from specialist engineers and managers, and given to the entire workforce. They may not have the organizational power and knowledge to make the few big changes, but they are the ones with the detailed knowledge of how the organization actually operates at the working level and they experience the operational problems at first hand, and are therefore ideally placed to solve them when given the authority and the requisite training.

2 *The belief that everyone has creative potential.* Just because staff have not in the past taken an active part in problem solving does not mean that they do not have the ability to do so. It is more often an indicator that they have not been allowed to do so; the workers' role has been to operate the process as designed, not to introduce local variation to it by making changes. Change was the prerogative of the specialist. Liberating the staff by encouraging them to propose improvements and giving them the right training invariably unblocks a stream of creative problem solving.

3 *The belief that mistakes are learning opportunities.* Employees will not lift their heads above the parapet of their day-to-day jobs and take the risk of making changes if they are going to be punished by their management every time they make a mistake. A blaming culture is not a continuous improvement culture. Continuous improvement requires a learning organization that accepts that failures will sometimes occur but then uses them positively as learning experiences.

The following story* is told of Tom Watson, the founder of IBM, who was not known for suffering fools gladly. A young manager made a decision that went wrong and ended up costing the company $50 000 to correct. Tom Watson heard of this and sent for the manager. On receiving the summons, the manager thought that he was to be fired, cleared his desk, and then went along to Watson's office:

> 'Well, young man,' said Watson, 'are you the one who just made this mess?'
> 'Yes, sir,' said the young man, 'and I guess that you are going to fire me now?'
> 'What!', said Watson, 'Fire you, after I've just invested $50 000 in your education!!'

Infrastructure

The preceding cultural beliefs affect the way in which a company is structured. A hierarchical, centralized, command-driven structure will not foster continuous improvement, which requires flattened organizational structures, strong vertical and horizontal communications, and employee empowerment. There is not a single 'right' blueprint for the type of organizational design required for successful continuous improvement, but research did conclude that both the organization and the continuous improvement programme have to be adapted until they 'suit' each other. The key areas are the degree of empowerment, the communication and decision-making processes, the level of team working, the development of flexible, multi-skilled workers, the approach to training, and the fostering of inter-functional relationships.

Tools

Although some improvement may occur as a matter of luck, effective, widespread continuous improvement requires the use of a set of tools that the entire workforce has been trained to use. A minimum toolkit, sometimes called the seven quality tools, is:[1,2]

---

* A story often told by Rolf Burgermeister, an inspirational speaker on the management of change.

- Pareto analysis
- run charts
- graphs
- check sheets
- cause-and-effect diagrams
- brainstorming
- flowcharts.

Process

As with other improvement activities, continuous improvement needs to be treated as a process rather than a single activity. The basic process of continuous improvement (based on the Deming wheel) is well known, but unfortunately in many organizations it is not well deployed. Instead of being accepted by everybody as a tool to be used whenever problems are encountered in their day-to-day work, its use is reserved for special occasions when required by management. The result is that instead of structured problem analysis, conclusions are jumped to; and instead of root causes being addressed, symptoms are. The improvement cycle has to be complete and repetitive – a virtuous circle that builds on success to motivate employees to continue with problem solving and improvement activity.

VEHICLES TO DELIVER CONTINUOUS IMPROVEMENT

The CIRCA research identified a number of vehicles that are used to achieve continuous improvement, and found that companies with sustained, successful continuous improvement programmes were using several of these vehicles, ranging from the big corporate drives down to the small local initiatives, rather than trying to concentrate all continuous improvement activity into one or two of them. One reason for this is that small local initiatives by themselves can result in the improvement efforts being focused on what are trivial areas when considered from the total business perspective. Combining the small local initiatives with the big corporate drives gives them a strategic position that helps ensure that their resultant improvements yield something of significance to the total business. There are large, medium and small examples of continuous improvement vehicles.

Large continuous improvement vehicles

These are typically driven by senior management, are company-wide initiatives, have long timescales, have a great impact on the organization, and require significant resource. Examples are:
- suggestion schemes
- self-assessment programmes (usually based on the EQA or Baldrige).

Medium continuous improvement vehicles

Characteristics of these are that they involve cross-functional teams of people, have medium timescales, have variable impact that can be major, and have lower resource requirements than the larger corporate vehicles. Examples are:
- problem-solving teams
- process improvement groups
- quality circles
- task forces.

Small continuous improvement vehicles

Characteristics of these are that they are used by individuals, are focused on local workplace improvements, operate on a short timescale, have relatively low impact, and have low resource requirements to implement. They are often linked to small-scale award schemes that allow them to be rewarded immediately by their department manager with small monetary awards. The basis for these activities is usually a problem-solving methodology based on Deming's PDCA, in which all individuals are trained.

DIAGNOSING THE HEALTH OF CI SYSTEMS

The continuous improvement engine or system needs to be monitored regularly to ensure that all five gears are present and working correctly. The CIRCA team developed a self-assessment tool based on their findings with the core research companies (Table 10.1), and subsequently proved its effectiveness by testing it with many other companies in the research network. The self-assessment helps an organization to identify the strengths and weaknesses of its continuous improvement system by answering a series of questions, and then using these strengths and weaknesses as inputs to their planning process.

Like the other self-assessment frameworks discussed in Chapter 9, this one also works by comparing the actual practices within an organization to a model of best practice. The best practice may be a total management system as contained in the US and European quality awards, the UK Government Chartermark or, as in this case, a best practice model of continuous improvement. As with other self-assessment frameworks:

- The score is only to give a baseline from which to measure future improvement.
- The questions are really aimed at identifying the organization's strengths and areas for improvement (which are then used as a basis for action planning).
- The self-assessment has to be conducted regularly.

The self-assessment approach is to:

1 Perform the assessment.
2 Identify strengths and weaknesses.
3 Plan and implement actions to address the weaknesses.
4 Repeat the self-assessment to measure progress (by comparing scores) and to identify new areas for improvement.

The self-assessment is in five sections, corresponding to the five gears of the continuous improvement engine. Each contains a series of statements of what 'best practice' is. The assessor rates the organization on how closely they match each statement. To maintain a reasonable level of objectivity in situations where the assessment is not being carried out by an independent assessor, the individual performing the assessment should always ask themselves the 'show me' question: 'If I was asked to produce evidence to support my assessment, could I?'

TABLE 10.1 Continuous improvement self-assessment workbook (based on CIRCA research findings)

For each 'best practice statement' in the five areas to be assessed, decide which of the 'examples for rating guidance' most closely matches your organization, and note the associated score, from 1–4, in the rating column.		
STRATEGY		
Best Practice statement	**Examples for rating guidance**	**Rating**
CI is an integral part of the organization's business strategy.	4. There are organizational goals and objectives that support and promote CI. 3. All functions have several objectives that support improvement but these are not linked to the business plan. 2. One or two of the functions have at least one objective that supports improvement, but these are not linked to the business plan. 1. CI is an 'add on' with no links to the overall business strategy.	
Everyone within the organization understands the policy on CI and how it fits in with company strategy.	4. All employees understand the reason for CI, how it will help the organization achieve its goals, and their role in it. 3. Most employees understand why the company has adopted CI, but are not clear about their role in it. 2. There is some understanding of the CI strategy among certain groups. 1. There is a widespread lack of awareness of what the company aims to achieve by adopting CI.	

TABLE 10.1 (STRATEGY) (*continued*)

Best Practice statement	Examples for rating guidance	Rating
There is strong top management commitment to CI.	4. Top managers demonstrate their commitment to CI by enacting CI values (encouraging participation, viewing mistakes as learning opportunities, listening to others, etc.) and are actively involved with CI (as leader, team member, facilitator, coach, giving recognition). 3. Top managers support their subordinates in CI, for example allowing time and money to be spent on CI activities and training. 2. Top managers state their commitment to CI. 1. Top managers do not do or say anything to support CI.	
CI is management strategically.	4. CI was implemented and is developed according to a predetermined plan which is modified in light of changes in the business environment. 3. CI was introduced according to an implementation plan but has since been left to develop at random. 2. There are sporadic interventions to regenerate CI but no strategic planning. 1. Improvement takes place on an ad hoc basis.	

TABLE 10.1 (STRATEGY) (*continued*)

Best Practice statement	Examples for rating guidance	Rating
The organization takes a long-term view of CI.	4. CI values are incorporated into the organization's mission/vision; improvement activity is incorporated into long-term (3/5 years) business plans; the company has altered its structure to support CI in the long term; there is training for future CI needs. 3. CI is viewed in the medium term, for example CI goals and plans extend two years ahead. 2. CI is talked about as being long term, but there are no actions to support this. 1. CI is seen as a quick fix to specific short-term problems.	

Total score for strategy = ... points out of a max. of 20, = ... %

TABLE 10.1 (*continued*)

CULTURE		
Best Practice statement	**Examples for rating guidance**	**Rating**
There is a positive working atmosphere throughout the organization.	4. Everyone in the organization shares a sense of common purpose; there are good working relations throughout. 3. The majority of employees share a sense of common purpose; most of the time relations between the functions are good. 2. There remain some divisions between certain groups of employees; there is some loyalty to the organization but it is not widespread. 1. There is a strong us & them separation between different groups; management/staff; production/non-production; there is little loyalty or pride in the organization.	
There is a common belief in the value of small improvements.	4. At least 90% of employees are actively looking for and are implementing small improvements. Recognition is given to small improvements. 3. A large majority of employees are actively looking for and implementing small improvements. 2. Up to half of employees are actively looking for and implementing small improvements. Some managers encourage this. 1. Very few people are actively looking for and implementing small improvements. The reward/recognition system only acknowledges big gains.	

TABLE 10.1 (CULTURE) (*continued*)

Best Practice statement	Examples for rating guidance	Rating
There is a widely-held belief in the ability of every employee to make a contribution.	4. Throughout the organization people at all levels recognize the value of their own and others' contributions and participate regularly. 3. In most areas of the organization people are given opportunities to contribute and believe in their ability to do so. 2. There are pockets in the organization where people are encouraged to extend themselves. 1. Managers have little confidence in the ability of their staff to contribute beyond the scope of their everyday job. Innovation and change are confined to managers and specialists.	
Failure is regarded as an opportunity for improvement/learning.	4. Mistakes are learning opportunities. Repeated mistakes lead to training. Calculated risk taking is encouraged. The learning from errors is shared with colleagues. 3. A mistake is discussed with the person who made it and sometimes preventative action is taken. 2. People are reprimanded for errors. There is a tendency to hide mistakes/failures or to fix them without anyone else knowing. 1. Individuals are blamed/disciplined for mistakes. Mistakes are rectified by specialists/managers, thus depriving those who made them of a learning opportunity. Mistakes are accepted as part of working life and are not acted upon.	

Total score for culture = ... points out of a max. of 16, = ...%

TABLE 10.1 (*continued*)

INFRASTRUCTURE		
Best Practice statement	**Examples for rating guidance**	**Rating**
The organization has a participative structure.	4. The structure is flat (3 or fewer layers of management); everyone works as a part of a team. 3. There are fewer layers in the hierarchy than previously but there is scope for further reduction. The majority of people are involved in teamworking. 2. Steps are being taken to flatten the organization's hierarchy. Some employees work as part of a team. 1. The organization is hierarchical; there is little or no team working; inter-departmental co-operation is poor.	
The organization and its employees are flexible.	4. The organization is able to respond rapidly to external pressures (for example, those brought about by legislation, competitors, economic situation). Staff are multi-skilled and flexible. 3. Both shop floor and office staff are multi-skilled. There is some job rotation. 2. Multi-skilling of shop floor employees is underway. 1. Employees are specialists in their job function; there is no flexibility.	
The work force is genuinely empowered.	4. Employees work in self-managed teams with control over their day-to-day operations, and have authority to make decisions on things like overtime, holidays, recruitment, etc.; they may have some control of budget. 3. Teams/non-management staff are empowered to take spending decisions that relate to their job function. 2. There is limited empowerment. People can make decisions about certain things but not others such as spending; people are involved in setting local targets. 1. Management style is directive. Employees are not allowed or encouraged to make decisions for themselves.	

TABLE 10.1 (INFRASTRUCTURE) (*continued*)

Best Practice statement	Examples for rating guidance	Rating
There are effective channels of communication.	4. All employees are aware of the latest developments in the company. There are a variety of communication media which operated up, down, and across the organization. 3. There is at least one effective channel for bottom-up communication. Most, but not all, agree that they receive the information they need. 2. Some mechanisms for vertical and horizontal communication have been introduced but they are not effective, for example, there are notice boards that no one reads. 1. The only formal communication channels are top-down. People rely on the grapevine for information. Employees are generally unaware of what other areas/functions of the business do.	
The organization is committed to the training and development of its people.	4. The company supports employees who wish to learn job or non-job related skills. There is a structured development programme for all employees. 3. The company has a training budget, but no structured personal development programme. People usually get the training they ask for but it is up to individuals to instigate it. 2. The company supports some training which has to be job-related. 1. There is no provision of time or money for training.	
There is good provision for CI facilitators.	4. There are trained facilitators in all areas of the organization and in addition, managers act in a facilitator role. 3. There are trained facilitators in all areas of the organization. 2. There are facilitators but they have no training. 1. There are no CI facilitators.	

TABLE 10.1 (INFRASTRUCTURE) (*continued*)

Best Practice statement	Examples for rating guidance	Rating
There is a well-established set of CI vehicles (mechanisms that promote and encourage CI activity).	4. The set of vehicles is well established and has at least one type of large, medium, and small vehicle; these vehicles are widespread throughout the organization. 3. There are two or more types of vehicle in use in most areas of the organization. 2. There is only one type of CI vehicle in use in most areas. 1. There are no CI vehicles.	

Total score for infrastructure = ... points out of a max of 28, = ... %

TABLE 10.1 (*continued*)

PROCESS		
Best Practice statement	**Examples for rating guidance**	**Rating**
There is a formal process for managing CI.	4. A formal process for managing CI, which includes a cycle of monitor, review, act, is followed. 3. There is an informal process which is usually followed, though it is not made explicit by being written down. 2. There is a theoretical process for managing CI, but it is not put into practice. 1. CI is managed on an ad hoc basis, there is no formal process.	
For each vehicle there are clear operating guidelines (how to set it up and run it on a day-to-day basis).	4. Everyone is aware of how each vehicle should be set up, operated, and closed down, and puts this into practice. 3. There are operating guidelines for all the vehicles but they are not widely followed. 2. There are operating guidelines for some, but not all the vehicles. Some of the guidelines are informal or incomplete. 1. There are no operating guidelines for any of the vehicles.	
There is a formal problem solving process or improvement cycle in use throughout the organization.	4. The company has a formal problem solving process which incorporates a feedback loop. Everyone understands this process and applies it methodically in their day-to-day work. 3. There is a problem solving process but it is rarely used outside formal CI activity. 2. There is a problem solving process but it is rarely followed. 1. There is no formal problem solving process.	

TABLE 10.1 (PROCESS) (*continued*)

Best Practice statement	Examples for rating guidance	Rating
The process used to manage CI makes provision for capturing and transferring learning.	4. The process incorporates mechanisms for capturing learning and using it elsewhere. 3. The process captures learning but does not promote its dissemination. 2. The process attempts to capture learning. 1. There is no provision for capturing and transferring learning.	
Total score for process = ... points out of a max. of 16, = ... %		

TABLE 10.1 (*continued*)

TOOLS		
Best Practice statement	**Examples for rating guidance**	**Rating**
A wide range of CI tools are in use in the organization.	4. At least 15 different CI tools are used within the organization. There are several tools to support each stage of the company's problem solving process. 3. Between 8 and 14 different CI tools are used within the organization. There is at least one tool to support each stage of the company's problem solving process. 2. Between 1 and 7 different tools are used within the organization. 1. No CI tools are used within the organization.	
The use of the CI tools is widespread across the organization.	4. All employees (at all levels and in all parts of the organization) use the tools as and when appropriate. 3. The tools are used in all parts of the organization, but not by everybody. 2. There are pockets of tool use, for example among engineers, or in a particular department; many tools are only used by managers. 1. There are only a handful of people using each tool.	
There is a company CI toolkit for which someone has responsibility.	4. There is a company toolkit which is available for everyone, and which has a designated manager. 3. There is a company toolkit available for everyone, but it is not managed. 2. There is information on tools but it is not collected into a formal toolkit that is readily accessible. For example, information on tools may be kept on file, but it is not readily accessible. 1. There is no toolkit in any form.	

TABLE 10.1 (TOOLS) (*continued*)

Best Practice statement	Examples for rating guidance	Rating
There is good provision of training in using the CI tools.	4. Everyone has received training in most of the CI tools in use in the organization. 3. Most people have received training in some of the CI tools. 2. Some people have received some training in some of the tools. 1. There is no formal training in using the CI tools.	

Total score for tools = ... points out of a max. of 16, = ... %

Score summary	Max. points	Actual	Percentage
Strategy	20		
Culture	16		
Infrastructure	28		
Process	16		
Tools	16		
Total	96		

TABLE 10.1 (*concluded*)

| **Rating Rationale and Improvement Plans** |
| For each of the statements rated, note here the factors that influenced the rating you gave. Indicate positive factors (strengths) by a '+', and negative factors (areas for improvement) by a '−'. Then note actions that should be taken to reinforce the strengths and eliminate the areas for improvement. |

Strengths and areas for improvement	**Proposed actions**

REFERENCES

1   Goal/QPC (1988). *The Memory Jogger: A Pocket Guide of Tools for Continuous Improvement*. Methuen.

2   Ishikawa, K. (1982). *Guide to Quality Control*. Asian Productivity Organisation, Tokyo.

FURTHER INFORMATION

For more information about the CIRCA network contact:

Pauline Nissen or Professor Bessant
University of Brighton
CENTRIM
Falmer
Brighton

CHAPTER

11

Benchmarking: from theory to practice

When you meet someone better than yourself, turn your thoughts to becoming his equal. When you meet someone not as good as you are, look within and examine your own self.
(Confucius)

Chapter 4 described the basic principles of benchmarking and explored a generic methodology to explain how to conduct a benchmarking project. It also highlighted that there are two components to benchmarking, the methodology itself and its management and coordination. The methodology is fairly straightforward in principle and can be learned on a one- or two-day course. Newcomers to benchmarking may experience some practical difficulties on their first couple of projects, and they may want to recruit someone experienced in benchmarking (often from an internal or external consulting group) to help and advise them while they gain proficiency. The second component is one that is often overlooked completely; the process of managing and coordinating benchmarking on a company-wide basis.

COORDINATING BENCHMARKING

Without a process for coordinating benchmarking, companies find that the benefits are confined to small isolated parts of their organization because they have no mechanism for sharing the learning from benchmarking, and that they present a fragmented and unprofessional face to the outside world. The answer to these problems is to implement a process for coordinating benchmarking that ensures that:

- When a benchmarking study is completed, the results can be shared across other parts of the organization that operate the same process.
- Learning that results from overcoming the practical problems of benchmarking can be shared across the whole organization.
- Duplication of effort does not occur; various groups in different parts of the same organization do not all benchmark the same process.
- There is a central contact point so that other organizations seeking partners have a defined single point of contact.
- Various teams focusing on different processes do not all approach the same target partner independently.
- All benchmarking teams have been properly trained in the benchmarking methodology and have done the preparatory steps thoroughly before they attempt a site visit.
- Advice, guidance, and support to benchmarking teams is provided when needed.

This problem is more severe in large multi-site, multi-national organizations. Single-site organizations can achieve the above objectives in a fairly straightforward way. A benchmarking coordinator can chair regular meetings of the people actively involved in benchmarking activity on the site, so that experience sharing can be face-to-face. Report summaries can be circulated as hard copy around the management team to promote learning and to stimulate further activity. Successful benchmarking projects can also be presented directly to the management team by the people involved in the project.

However, the larger organizations need to put a more formal structure in place to achieve the same objectives. A successful approach used by companies such as Ericsson and IBM is to:

1 Use the e-mail system, as a communication vehicle to distribute examples of best practice, as a reference database of completed benchmarking

studies, and as a bulletin board so that benchmarking teams can post problems or requests for information that can be answered by other benchmarking practitioners anywhere else in the organization.

2 Appoint a benchmarking coordinator/champion who will:
  - organize training and facilitate sharing
  - provide the link to the organization's business process owners
  - coordinate the activities of the local benchmarking coordinators in the business units
  - provide the interface to outside organizations for receiving requests from other organizations, to represent the company to any benchmarking clubs it may belong to.

COMMONLY ENCOUNTERED BENCHMARKING PROBLEMS

Commonly encountered problems or issues that cause benchmarking efforts to fail are:

- they are not linked to goals and critical success factors
- a poor selection of performance comparisons
- a poor choice of partner
- benchmarking not treated as part of process improvement.

Not linked to goals and critical success factors

One of the causes of ineffective benchmarking is projects being initiated from the bottom up without ensuring that the focus area has any strategic relevance. Successful benchmarking efforts are driven from the top down by the organization's goals and critical success factors. The important initial steps of any effective approach, as discussed in earlier chapters are:

1 Establish the organization's goals and critical success factors.
2 Identify the processes that deliver them.
3 Rate the processes and establish priorities.
4 Map the chosen process(es).
5 Identify the critical process parameters.

6 Put performance measurements in place.

7 Select benchmarking partners who excel at the chosen process (organizations that have this process as their core competence, which gives it its competitive advantage).

The stress for any process improvement must be on satisfying its customer. An excellent example of this is the way that 3M in Germany have developed their benchmarking methodology with a very strong customer linkage at the beginning. Their first step, deciding what to benchmark, consists of three stages: first, identify the customer; second, identify the customer's critical success factors; and third, identify 3M's internal business processes that deliver them.

Poor selection of performance comparisons

Business process benchmarking compares the performance of the chosen process to that of the partner's. The comparison should be based on a detailed analysis of the process in question to identify the parameters that are critical to the process's successful operation, and the problem areas within the process that need to be improved.

The fundamental measures of a process are cost, quality, cycle-time and customer satisfaction, and the benchmarking comparison should be based on these measures, selected primarily on what is important to the customer and other stakeholders. This then ensures that the measures of process performance are linked directly to the organization's goals. The comparison should also be based on a suite of measurements, not just a single indicator. For example, just comparing on cost could ignore the fact the chosen partners may be achieving low cost at the expense of quality or cycle-time.

The problem for benchmarkers is that the process performance measures that already exist were established for purposes such as process monitoring and control, not for comparing the performance of the process against that of a similar process operated by another company. One reason why the measurements used for process control are not suitable for process comparison is that they are often product related; that is, physical aspects of the product are measured (dimensions, functional performance, etc.) throughout the process and then used to control the process. When it comes to 'functional' benchmarking, comparing a process in one industry with that of a functionally similar process in another industry, although the processes are similar, the product, by definition, is not. Therefore product-independent performance measures need to be used as the basis for process comparison.

A useful technique that helps to overcome this problem of being able to compare 'apples to apples' is to use process performance assessment as the basis for comparison rather than trying directly to compare actual in-process measures. An example of this technique is a benchmarking project of the 'New Product Introduction' process:

1 All the benchmarking partners agree as to what are the critical factors of the process on which they want to compare performance.

2 The partners agree on a performance assessment matrix that they can all use (in Table 11.1 a scale of 1 to 5 was used, defined as very poor to world class, with alternative definitions from Baldrige in parentheses). The scale and definitions for each score must be agreed by all partners and be as objective as possible.

3 Each partner completes the matrix for their organization. (Note that it is essential that this is done by the process owner in conjunction with their process improvement team – not by someone from a central staff group or other third party.)

4 The individual process assessments are then consolidated on one chart and the highest scorer for each critical factor identified (Table 11.2).

5 A hypothetical 'best of breed' can now be built up (see the last column in Table 11.2): the ideal company that is the best at each factor. Invariably this hypothetical best of breed is significantly better than the highest scoring individual company, emphasizing that no single company is ever the best at everything – it is always possible to learn from others!

6 Each highest scorer gives a full explanation of their high scoring approach to the particular factor, so that the other partners can learn from their approach. Once again it is essential that this is done by the

TABLE 11.1 Process assessment matrix to be completed by each partner

Factor	Attributes for Performance Assessment				
	1 very poor does not meet any requirements (no systematic approach evident)	**2** meets some requirements (beginning of a systematic approach)	**3** meets requirements (a sound systematic approach)	**4** exceeds some requirements (clear evidence of improvement cycles and analysis)	**5** world class (responsive to all requirements with a strong fact-based improvement process)
Understanding of market trends					
Understanding of current customers					
Understanding of potential customers					
Accepted new product definition					
All requirements considered					
Product meets sales forecasts					
Fast market testing of prototype					
Product flexibility for customization					
Market acceptance					

TABLE 11.2   Process assessment comparison

Factor	Performance Rating for Each Company				
	A	**B**	**C**	**D**	**Best of breed**
Understanding of market trends	2	**3**	**3**	**3**	3
Understanding of current customers	2	3	2	4	4
Understanding of potential customers	2	2	3	2	3
Accepted new product definition	2	1	4	2	4
All requirements considered	**3**	**3**	1	2	3
Product meets sales forecasts	2	**3**	3	2	3
Fast market testing of prototype	2	2	1	**4**	4
Product flexibility for customization	3	3	3	**4**	4
Market acceptance	2	**4**	3	**4**	4
Total rating	**20**	**24**	**23**	**27**	**32**

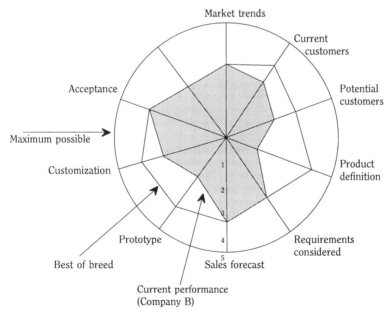

FIGURE 11.1   Polar chart gap analysis

process owner and their team who have the detailed practical knowledge of how the process really works.

7 The partners learn from the approaches used by their high-scoring colleagues and incorporate them into their own process, following the maxim:

$$Adopt \rightarrow Adapt \rightarrow Improve$$

The process comparison data can also be shown graphically, as shown in Fig. 11.1 (page 219). This type of representation using a polar (sometimes also called spider or radar) chart is an excellent method of showing where the gaps exist.

The most important point to remember is that in benchmarking the comparison of performance measures is only used to indicate which areas of process performance the partner's process excels at in comparison to your own process. Once these areas of difference have been pointed to, then the focus of attention should shift away from *what* to *how* – the approaches that the partner employs that yield superior performance.

Poor choice of partner

Identifying the right partner is one of the most difficult steps in benchmarking. The conventional wisdom contained in the various books on the subject suggests focusing on award winners, citations in professional journals, recommendations from customers and business partners, researching business articles, etc. These are all valid sources of information, but what are the indicators of excellence that may point to a particular organization possibly being a paragon of best practice?

The benchmarker's interest is first of all on the organization itself, and then on the processes it operates. Indicators of excellence at the organization level, indicators that the organization may have 'best practice' processes, can be established by examining the core values of the organization. These are described in Table 11.3, together with possible sources of that information. The sources are:

- *Annual reports*
  These often contain information about the company's vision, attitudes to quality and continuous improvement.
- *In-house journals*
  These report/encourage continuous improvement, recognition of improvement teams, new company programmes such as benchmarking and process improvement.
- *Conference agenda*
  Companies that are recognized as being the leaders in TQM, benchmarking, etc., are often asked to speak at conferences. Reviewing lists of conference speakers is therefore a useful pointer.
- *Customers and suppliers*
  If possible, obtain the names of some of the potential partner's customers and suppliers and ask them their opinion of the company in question.
- *Initial discussion with partner*
  Initial research into the company needs to be confirmed during the informal initial discussion with the prospective partner.

TABLE 11.3 Pointers to possible benchmarking partners

HIGH-LEVEL INDICATOR	ANNUAL REPORTS	IN-HOUSE JOURNALS	CONFERENCE AGENDA	CUSTOMERS AND SUPPLIERS	INITIAL DISCUSSION WITH PARTNER
Corporate values: does the organization's vision, mission and goals, provide a focus on the needs of all stakeholders? i.e. customers, employees, suppliers, and shareholders.	X	X		X	
Leadership: do the senior managers in the organization serve as role models for their employees?		X	X		X
Continuous improvement: is continuous improvement embedded into the way that the organization functions? Is improvement driven by actively seeking opportunities to do better as well by the need to eliminate problems?		X	X	X	X
Employee participation: are employees encouraged to offer their ideas on how improvements might be made? Are they encouraged to participate in improvement teams?		X			X
Management by fact: are measurements derived from the organization's strategy and goals, and do they encompass the key processes for achieving those goals?	X				X

TABLE 11.3 (*continued*)

HIGH-LEVEL INDICATOR	ANNUAL REPORTS	IN-HOUSE JOURNALS	CONFERENCE AGENDA	CUSTOMERS AND SUPPLIERS	INITIAL DISCUSSION WITH PARTNER
Business process management: does the organization know which are the key processes that deliver their corporate goals? Have they appointed senior executives as owners of each process? Have the processes been mapped and are they actively being improved?	X	X		X	X
Customer focus: does the organization clearly put a strong emphasis on understanding their customers' requirements and on knowing that their products and services completely satisfy those requirements? Does it have a 'first-class' reputation?	X	X	X	X	X

Benchmarking not treated as part of process improvement

A common failing of newcomers to benchmarking is to treat it as an independent technique divorced from other activities such as business process improvement, business planning and goal setting. The unwary can be encouraged into this pitfall by an over-enthusiastic response to self-assessment feedback. For instance, an organization that has scored fairly low on a Baldrige or EQA-based self-assessment may rightly conclude that one of the more pervasive shortcomings is their general lack of benchmarking. However, a low-scoring organization has some more fundamental areas to address before it starts worrying about benchmarking.

An organization scoring in the 300–400 range is going to have problems with its style of leadership, its involvement of employees in improvement, its lack of focus on its customers, erratic results and unmanaged processes. In terms of priority, these points should be addressed first and then, after the organization's business processes have been identified and process management implemented, benchmarking can be introduced as a way of setting stretch process performance targets and introducing novel approaches into those processes. If the organization falls into the trap of starting benchmarking prematurely, the infrastructure in terms of process, people and management will not be in place to do anything with the findings of the benchmarking studies.

Ensuring that benchmarking is integrated with the other improvement activities, in particular business process improvement, is best accomplished by making it the responsibility of the process owner; the benchmarking coordinator provides expert support, advice and training, but the process owners and their improvement teams actually conduct the benchmarking as part of their process improvement activity.

OTHER BENCHMARKING QUESTIONS AND MISCONCEPTIONS

There are some questions frequently asked by people, of varying experience levels, who attend benchmarking conferences, seminars or education sessions.

Is benchmarking just a way of shedding staff?

If cost cutting (i.e. headcount reduction) is the sole objective, then benchmarking and process improvement are not going to be the most appropriate methods because they need enthusiastic staff involvement – people will not volunteer to 'improve' themselves out of a job! If cost cutting via headcount reduction is the real objective, then that is what should be done. Nothing other than harm is achieved by masquerading it as benchmarking or process improvement, because after the headcount reductions are completed the remaining employees will have no trust at all in any other so-called improvement initiatives – continuous improvement will be dead!

If shedding staff, rather than improving cost, quality, cycle-time and customer satisfaction, is the real objective of the exercise, then it is probably far better to meet that issue head on. If the organization has to reduce headcount by 20 per cent in order to achieve an acceptable level of expense, then reduce heads by that amount and then improve or re-engineer the processes using benchmarking, continuous improvement and re-engineering. This conscious effort to involve employees in the improvement work at this point will result both in improved processes that are able to meet all the customers' requirements with the reduced headcount and will also start rebuilding morale and enthusiasm after the trauma of headcount reductions.

Benchmarking is just copying, so how does it help you get into the lead?

This displays a fundamental lack of understanding of the basic principles of benchmarking. Simple copying will never yield real benefit. First, even though the process being benchmarked is notionally the same, the environment in which it operates will not be identical in two dissimilar organizations (and remember that real learning and innovation comes from comparing organizations that operate the same process in different industries – *functional* benchmarking), therefore straightforward copying will not work. The basic philosophy of benchmarking is to identify the ideas and approaches that enable the other organization to achieve superior performance, then to adopt those practices so that they will be successful within your organization, but then, most importantly, to improve upon them – use some creativity in their implementation which will move you ahead of the game.

What benchmarking clubs are there, and how do they help?

Benchmarking clubs are being established in many countries as vehicles to promote and encourage the use of benchmarking as a means of driving business improvement. They vary in the type of services that they offer to their members, and in whether they are 'for profit', or 'not for profit'. They started in the United States, with the Strategic Planning Institute's Council on Benchmarking, and then the American Productivity and Quality Center's International Benchmarking Clearinghouse. These pioneer organizations formed the model for those that are now emerging in other countries around the world.

As the most basic level, a benchmarking club may be no more than a loose network that provides a listing of contact names and addresses in the member organizations, so that when someone wants to make a request for a benchmarking partner they know the name of someone else with whom to make the initial contact. At the other extreme, there are organizations like the International Benchmarking Clearinghouse in the US and the Benchmarking Centre in the UK that offer a full range of benchmarking services such as: partner introductions, literature research, network meetings, common interest groups, conferences, education and news-letters. More and more organizations are finding that these 'clubs' provide an invaluable support service to their benchmarking efforts.

An important aspect of benchmarking is performing desk research to gather information already in the public domain that is relevant to the project underway. This information may provide useful background reading, it may directly provide examples of best practice, or it may point to organizations that are potential partners for the project. The advent of computerized databases has taken away the need to spend hours in libraries reading business journals and other publications. These can now be accessed via on-line systems; a search of 'key words' will bring to the screen all published articles that contain the key words and that are therefore potentially relevant to the particular benchmarking project. There are general purpose databases, but also some that are specifically targeted at benchmarking. These specialist databases, as well as providing the normal literature search facilities, also provide 'best practice' examples and 'bulletin boards' to post requests for information of partners to other subscribers to the network. At least two benchmarking 'clubs' now make their services available via the Internet. (Some of the benchmarking clubs currently in existence are listed at the end of this chapter.)

BENCHMARKING AWARDS

In order to encourage the use of benchmarking and to recognize benchmarking projects that can be held up as examples of best practice which overcome the major pitfalls related to benchmarking, the European Best Practice Benchmarking Award has been established, and was presented for the first time in 1995 (with Hewlett-Packard winning the award, and IBM the runner up). Its objectives are to:

- identify the best examples of benchmarking in Europe
- facilitate the sharing of best practice in benchmarking
- share real life experiences
- dispel the myths surrounding benchmarking.

The panel of judges are drawn from national benchmarking clubs across Europe, and each application is judged on leadership, process and results.

The Hewlett-Packard application was an excellent illustration that benchmarking projects do not have to be part of major process re-engineering exercises in order to make a contribution to the organization. This study was triggered by customer satisfaction survey results that showed a low satisfaction rating with their contract administration (which provided the strategic link – the need to improve an area of customer dissatisfaction). A small team was formed comprising the process manager, two process workers and a benchmarking advisor, and a clear benchmarking process followed (select partner, gather data, perform gap analysis, identify and implement improvements). This relatively small-scale benchmarking study is probably typical of many that are undertaken, and serves as a good example of its type.

The IBM study also started from customer satisfaction survey results, but in this case the survey showed that customer satisfaction levels were at 98 per cent. Achieving satisfaction levels of this magnitude is often a recipe for complacency but this particular organization decided that they needed to test these results with a benchmarking study, and also to identify further improvements that could be made. (Using customer satisfaction as the driver for process improvement and benchmarking is a key success factor.) A well-defined benchmarking process was used, and all the team members and the management team were trained in its use. Expert help and guidance was brought in from other areas of the company to assist the team when required. This study did confirm the findings of the customer satisfaction survey and placed the organization second only to the emergency services in its call handling but, importantly, the study also identified several incremental improvements that were implemented to help ensure that the organization was able to maintain its high levels of customer satisfaction.

BENCHMARKING CASE STUDY: TEAM RECOGNITION
(Note: the organization's name has been concealed to protect its anonymity.)

Background
The company's business priorities, which collectively constituted their fundamental objective of 'customer satisfaction through total quality', were:
- people involvement
- customer focus
- continuous improvement.

Teams, particularly self-directed work teams, were one of the key initiatives, seen as the future of quality improvement efforts. Team recognition and reward were a necessary part of the expansion of the use of teams, whose reward system allowed for the rewarding of individual contributions but not for the contributions of teams. Improvement was required in this area and benchmarking was seen as a way of learning from what other companies were doing.

(A clear link was established between this particular project and the strategic requirements of the organization, avoiding the pitfall of focusing improvement efforts on areas that are insignificant to the organization.)

Problem analysis

The existing recognition process was analysed and the following problems identified:

- Appraisals and compensation should not be given together.
- Rewards and appraisal systems were centred around individual contributions and competition.
- Continuous improvement, customer satisfaction, and teaming efforts were not recognized, appraised and rewarded.
- Implementation of peer appraisals was difficult and constituted a cultural change.
- Identification of elements and structure for pay for knowledge system was unclear.
- There was no formal recognition award for quality in teaming.

Key measurements were established that allowed these points to be quantified and subsequently compared with the benchmarking partners. These measures were:

- award types and monetary amounts
- pay for knowledge elements/gainsharing
- cycle time for recognition
- appraisal cycle
- training hours per person
- types of teams and how many teams exist.

(A clear agenda was established of exactly what areas needed improvement and what needed to be compared to other organizations – avoiding the common pitfall of lack of preparation, leading to industrial tourism.)

Methodology

There were three stages to this study:

1 A team was formed which met to brainstorm companies they believed to

be leaders in the area of team work. All together, 20 potential partners were identified this way.

2 A literature and database search was performed to gather information on teams and recognition.

3 Possible partners were invited to a 'team recognition and reward process' sharing day. At this meeting, all partners presented their approaches to reward, recognition, appraisal, and pay for knowledge systems. Seven (two of whom were competitors) of the original 20 companies attended this sharing meeting.

(This is the 'classical' approach to establishing benchmarking partners. Start by brainstorming a large group of potential partners, then do the research to find out what data already exists in the public domain to confirm the choice of partners, and then involve several partners in the final benchmarking exchange so that a 'best of breed' can be established from the best practices and performance of the combined group. The final partners were a mix of internal, competitor and functional.)

Data analysis

The information provided by each of the partners was compared and a matrix of best practice developed for each of the aspects of the 'team recognition and reward process' under consideration. In all, 23 best practice learning points were identified. The best practice matrix was as shown in Table 11.4.

TABLE 11.4   Case study best practice matrix

PRACTICE	INTERNAL	COMPETITOR	FUNCTIONAL
Reward		Company A	
Recognition			Company B
Peer appraisals	Division X		Company C
Compensation	Division X		Company C
Awards		Company E	Company B
			Company D

(A basic principle of the benchmarking code of conduct is that information, including the names of the companies that participate in a study, is not divulged to a third party – hence Table 11.4 only identifies participants as companies A, B, etc. Another basic point about benchmarking is that no single company is the best at everything, therefore just comparing to one other company severely restricts the learning opportunity. Performing the comparison in this way allows learning from each company; A is best with its approach to reward, B with its approach to recognition, etc.)

BENCHMARKING ETHICS

The whole concept of benchmarking is built around the free exchange of information to the mutual benefit of all parties. It is not, as is sometimes claimed, either industrial espionage or stealing shamelessly.

The Benchmarking Centre and companies like IBM and the National Health Service have adopted a code of conduct that was developed in the US by the Strategic Planning Institute and the International Benchmarking Clearinghouse. This code of conduct has now become the *de facto* standard that governs benchmarking activity. It defines principles of legality, information exchange, confidentiality, use of information, first and third party contact, and preparation. It is recommended that when contact is first made with a potential benchmarking partner, the prospective partner is provided with a copy of the code of conduct and asked to confirm that it will abide by its principles. (Because of its importance as a fundamental set of ground rules that should govern all benchmarking activity, it is reproduced below in full, with the kind permission of the Strategic Planning Institute's Council on Benchmarking.)

The benchmarking code of conduct

(a) Principles

1 **Principle of Legality**. Avoid discussions or actions that might lead to or imply an interest in restraint of trade, market or customer allocation

231

schemes, price fixing, dealing arrangements, bid rigging, bribery or misappropriation. Do not discuss costs with competitors if costs are an element of pricing.

2 **Principle of Exchange**. Be willing to provide the same level of information that you request, in any benchmarking exchange.

3 **Principle of Confidentiality**. Treat benchmarking interchange as something confidential to the individuals and organizations involved. Information obtained must not be communicated outside the partnering organizations without prior consent of participating benchmarking partners. An organization's participation in a study should not be communicated externally without their permission.

4 **Principle of Use**. Use information obtained through benchmarking partnering only for the purpose of improvement of operations with the partnering companies themselves. External use or communication of a benchmarking partner's name with their data or observed practices requires the permission of that partner. Do not, as a consultant or client, extend one company's benchmarking study findings to another without the first company's permission.

5 **Principle of First Party Contact**. Initiate contacts, whenever possible, through a benchmarking contact designated by the partner company. Obtain mutual agreement with the contact on a transfer of communication or responsibility to other parties.

6 **Principle of Third Party Contact**. Obtain an individual's permission before providing their name in response to a contact request.

7 **Principle of Preparation**. Demonstrate commitment to the efficiency and effectiveness of the benchmarking process with adequate preparation at each process step, particularly at initial partnering contact.

(b) Etiquette and Ethics

In actions between benchmarking partners, the emphasis is on openness and trust. The following guidelines apply to both partners in a benchmarking encounter:

- In benchmarking with competitors, establish specific groundrules up-front, e.g. 'We do not want to talk about those things that will give either of us a competitive advantage, rather we want to see where we can both mutually improve or gain benefit'.
- Do not ask competitors for sensitive data or cause the benchmarking partner to feel that sensitive data must be provided to keep the process going.
- Use an ethical third party to assemble and blind competitive data, with inputs from legal counsel, for direct competitor comparisons.
- Consult with legal counsel if any information gathering procedure is in doubt, e.g. before contacting a direct competitor.
- Any information obtained from a benchmarking partner should be treated as internal privileged information.
- Do not
  - Disparage a competitor's business or operations to a third party
  - Attempt to limit competition or gain business through the benchmarking relationship.

(c) Exchange Protocol

As the benchmarking process proceeds to the exchange of information, benchmarkers are expected to:

- Know and abide by the Benchmarking Code of Conduct.
- Have a basic knowledge of benchmarking and follow a benchmarking process.
- Have determined what to benchmark, identified key performance variables, recognized superior performance companies, and completed a rigorous self-assessment.
- Have developed a questionnaire and interview guide, and will share these in advance if requested.

- Have the authority to share information.
- Work through a specified host and mutually agree on scheduling and meeting arrangements.
- Follow these guidelines in face-to-face site visits:
  1 Provide meeting agenda in advance
  2 Be professional, honest, courteous, and prompt
  3 Introduce all attendees and explain why they are present
  4 Adhere to the agenda. Maintain focus on benchmarking issues
  5 Use language that is universal, not one's own jargon
  6 Do not share proprietary information without prior approval from the proper authorities of both parties
  7 Share information about your process if asked, and consider sharing the study results
  8 Offer to set up a reciprocal visit
  9 Conclude meetings and visits on schedule
  10 Thank the benchmarking partner for the time and for the sharing.

BENCHMARKING CLUBS

United Kingdom
The Benchmarking Centre
Truscon House
11 Station Road
Gerrards Cross
Buckinghamshire
Tel: 44 1753 890070

Sweden
Swedish Institute for Quality Benchmarking Service
Garda Torget 1
S-41250
Goteberg

Italy
Italian Benchmarking Club
Via Isonzo 42/C
00198 Roma

Germany
Information Centre Benchmarking
Fraunhofer Institute
Pascalstrasse 8–9
10587 Berlin
Tel: 49 30 314 214127

USA
The Benchmarking Exchange
1960-B Soquel Drive, Suite 356
Aptos, California 95003
Tel: 1 408 662 9800

The SPI Council on Benchmarking
1030 Massachusetts Avenue
MA 02138
Tel: 1 908 953 9007

American Productivity & Quality Center
123 North Post Oak Lane, Suite 300
Houston, Texas 7024

Redesigning
business processes

**We can easily forgive a child who is afraid of the dark;
the real tragedy of life is when men are afraid of the
light.**
(Plato)

Some of the confusion that surrounds the subject of re-engineering is
caused by the lack of distinction between the two different and separate
types of re-engineering:

- re-engineering a particular business process (better described as *process redesign*)
- re-engineering an entire business

This distinction has been characterized[1] as shown in Table 12.1.

The example of Ford's accounts payable quoted by Hammer[2] is an
example of redesigning a business process, not re-engineering an entire
business. Briefly, he describes how Ford believed they could reduce cost in
their accounts payable department by reducing headcount by 20 per cent
from the 500 then employed in that organization. However, Ford was able
to visit Mazda in Japan where they found that the entire accounts payable
department comprised only five people. Clearly, Ford needed to improve
performance by orders of magnitude, not just by 20 per cent, and to do that
would require a fundamental rethink of the way accounts were managed.
(Incidentally, this also illustrates the power of benchmarking, for it was

**TABLE 12.1 Differences between redesigning a business
process and re-engineering an entire business**

RE-ENGINEERING A BUSINESS	REDESIGNING A BUSINESS PROCESS
'Business re-engineering is the conscious, planned and managed reshaping of an organization behind a new corporate vision. The reshaping is influenced entirely by the clearly defined market place the business is targeting and the customer needs within that market place. It refers to the complete transformation of a whole business from a functional to process oriented management structures.'	'This is the redesign of a specific activity within an organization. Process re-engineering is the low-risk evolutionary alternative to business re-engineering. It allows an organization to attack the problem in bite-sized chunks which, although difficult to chew and swallow, are less likely to cause indigestion.'

benchmarking against Mazda that showed Ford what really could be achieved, and more importantly, *how* to achieve it.)

Ford finally achieved a 75 per cent reduction in headcount, not by making a series of incremental process improvements, but by making the fundamental shift away from matching purchase order to invoice to goods received, and introducing invoiceless processing enabled by the use of an on-line database; that is, by redesigning the total process.

BUSINESS PROCESS REDESIGN: CASE STUDY

Organizations have always attempted to redesign their business processes from time to time, as it becomes obvious that they are no longer able to fulfil the business need. What is new is the increasing ability of new technologies to radically affect the way in which work is done. Some claim that the driver of business process redesign is technology, but this is not really the case; the *driver* always has to be the customer – fulfilling the customer's expectations in the most efficient and effective way possible. However, the *enablers* for the radical change required by process redesign are new technologies and other new capabilities that were not known when the process was first designed.

The following case study illustrates the point.

Redesigning a product supply process

A supplier of computer terminals manufactured them at three separate plants to supply the various markets: one plant in the UK to supply Europe, one plant in the US to supply the Americas, and another in Japan to supply the Far East. During the design phase of a new product it was decided to concentrate all production in one plant to maximize the cost benefits of the economies of scale. The UK plant was given the product mission.

The original process used by the UK plant to supply products to the other countries in Europe (Fig. 12.1) was:

1 The product was highly feature-sensitive, so each was built to a customer order as received by the factory from the country marketing group. The order was transmitted to the factory directly by an order entry system. When the order was received by the factory it was entered into the production scheduling system.

2 The completed products were shipped by truck from the factory to the company's UK distribution centre in London, where they were consolidated with other products for shipment, by country. When a full truck was ready, it was dispatched to the distribution centre in the country concerned, where it was unloaded and all the products booked into stock.

3 The finished products were kept in stock until called for by marketing for delivery to the customer.

Air shipment was only used when specifically requested by the receiving country who had to pay the additional costs.

This process has been in use for many years, with minor improvements being made from time to time to reduce costs, and it was this process that was intended to be used for the new product. However, it soon became

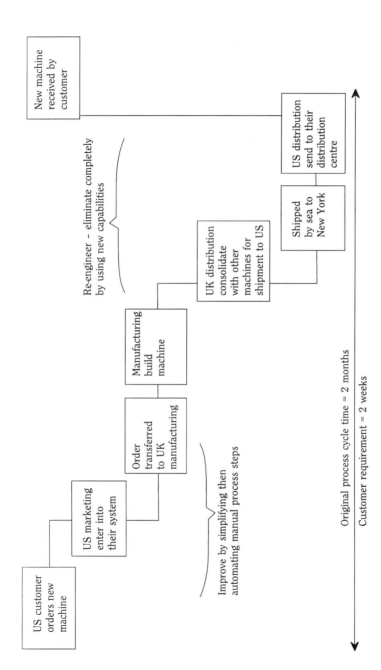

New machine received by customer

Re-engineer – eliminate completely by using new capabilities

Manufacturing build machine

UK distribution consolidate with other machines for shipment to US

Order transferred to UK manufacturing

Shipped by sea to New York

US distribution send to their distribution centre

US marketing enter into their system

US customer orders new machine

Improve by simplifying then automating manual process steps

Original process cycle time = 2 months

Customer requirement = 2 weeks

FIGURE 12.1 New product supply process

apparent that it would not be capable of meeting the customer demands in one of the new markets (the US market) now being served. The problem was that this process, if applied to the US market, far exceeded the customers' requirement in terms of turnaround time from submitting the order to receiving the product. The average process time for the US was calculated to be two months, whereas the US customers wanted a two week cycle time. The existing process was analysed and the major causes of delay were identified:

1 Order entry systems incompatibility. The system used to enter customer orders in the US could not talk directly to the production systems in the UK factory. Orders had to be transferred manually.

2 The company would only ship by sea to New York where it had customs clearing facilities.

3 It then had to ship the products to the National Distribution Centre where they were booked into stock and held until called for by marketing to fill a customer order. They were then shipped to a local distribution centre near the customer, and then finally to the customer.

The process clearly needed to be completely redesigned if it were to meet the new customer requirement. (That is, the change *driver* was the customer requirement.)

A process redesign team, principally from the UK factory, but also including UK and US distribution and US marketing (a genuine cross-functional improvement team), conducted a detailed analysis of the existing process and proposed alternative approaches that enabled the customer requirement to be met.

The key enablers were:

● The availability of affordable air freight that eliminated the need for sea freight, which reduced shipment time from 5 days to 8 hours.

● The availability of specialist world-wide door-to-door freight delivery companies, who could manage the whole distribution process from the factory right to the customer using their own distribution networks.

(That is, the enablers of change were the availability of new *capabilities*, not just new technologies.)

240

These new capabilities allowed significant parts of the process to be radically redesigned. The third problem area (that of incompatible computer systems) was solved by writing a new program that could provide a 'bridge' between the two systems. This change in itself was nearer to the continuous improvement end of the process change continuum than the other two, which were genuine radical changes. (Process redesign often requires a combination of *radical* and *incremental* changes.)

Problems encountered

Three major problems were encountered during this process redesign exercise:

1 *Vested interests*. Barriers to change were erected by people whose jobs were threatened by the proposed changes – the use of a contracted-out distribution service posed an obvious threat to the job security of the company's own in-house distribution function.
2 *The level of authority of the sponsoring manager*. Manufacturing management in the UK had the responsibility of designing an acceptable delivery process, but they did not have the organizational authority to make the required changes to the UK and US distribution systems. This resulted in a formal escalation to a senior executive who did have the authority to decide and implement.
3 *Acceptance of the status quo*. The delivery process had been in existence for many years and was operated by staff who were so familiar with it that they did not question the assumptions on which it was based. They accepted the constraints under which they operated rather than challenging them.

Process analysis tools

Two process analysis tools proved to be particularly effective during this exercise; the use of *raw cycle time* and *value-add analysis*.

Raw cycle time

This involves walking the process and establishing exactly how long it will take from start to finish if there are no delays, no problems and no need to correct errors. This approach is often very effective as a 'paradigm buster', convincing people that there is a need to change and that there is a significant opportunity for improvement. (In another process improvement exercise involving a paper-driven reporting process, the average cycle time being achieved was 5 days, whereas the raw cycle time was in the region of 15 minutes – a difference of such magnitude that it was difficult to argue that the existing process was acceptable!)

Value-add analysis

Each step of the process is examined to decide whether the activity performed actually adds any value when viewed from the perspective of the process customer, whether it is necessary to manage the business, or whether it adds no value at all. In many processes there are a surprising number of redundant activities that no longer serve any purpose. These 'no value-add' activities should be eliminated (Fig. 12.2).

USE OF VALUE-ADD ANALYSIS

Another good example of process improvement, one which stresses the importance of sorting all process activity into those that add value and those that do not, comes from a naval shipyard in the US.[3] The traditional approach to controlling indirect cost is the 'death by a thousand cuts' with the objective of reducing budget or headcount with no thought being given to reducing the amount of work being performed. When staff levels are reduced but work levels and methods stay the same, the results are delays, errors and poor morale. The result of this approach is to 'transform large, bloated, and inefficient bureaucracies into smaller, bloated, and (still) inefficient bureaucracies'.

The approach taken by the Charleston shipyard was to first construct an activity cost model of the entire shipyard, focused on business processes rather than individual departments. Analysis of this model showed some surprises; for instance it showed that at least half of all job-planning work was done outside the planning department, and that all departments spent excessive amounts of time processing travel orders, savings bonds, etc., activities that had no direct connection with the purpose of that department. This triggered a value-add analysis that identified opportunities for eliminating activities that were not necessary from the viewpoint of the ultimate judge, the customer. The way in which they evaluated whether an activity added value or not is shown in Fig. 12.2.

Three outcomes are possible from this analysis:

- *A*: The activity directly adds value in the view of the customer. Process improvement techniques should be applied to reduce cycle time and cost, and improve quality.
- *B*: Does not add value in the view of the customer, but necessary to the business. First revalidate the requirement (many will be found to be obsolete!), then apply improvement techniques to minimize resources consumed.
- *C*: Non value-adding, and unnecessary to the business (this can be as high as 80 per cent of the activity in some departments!). Eliminate completely.

BUSINESS PROCESS EXCELLENCE INDEX

Throughout this book emphasis has been placed on the regular review of all of an organization's business processes to compare their capabilities to current requirements, so that they can be categorized as candidates for either continuous improvement or business process re-engineering, and improvement priorities assigned. There now follows an example of how these reviews can be conducted, using a Business Process Excellence Index developed from the techniques explained in the earlier chapters. The Business Process Excellence Index combines some of the process assessment methods described earlier:

- performance measurements
- process maturity
- customer satisfaction
- relevance to business goals

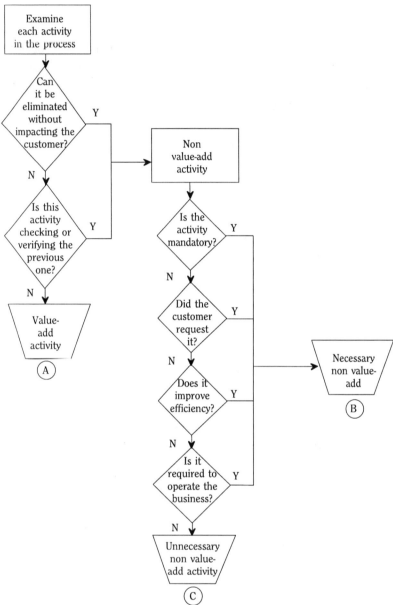

FIGURE 12.2   Value-add analysis

Source: Porter, T.J. and Keboe, J.G. (1993/4). 'Using activity-based costing and value analysis to take the pain out of downsizing at a naval shipyard'. *National Productivity Review*, Winter.

The method for using it is as follows.

Establish the current Business Process Excellence Index level for each process

For each process, each of these factors is assessed in turn and then the results are used to build up an overall index of excellence for that process (Table 12.2).

TABLE 12.2   Establishing the Business Process Excellence Index levels

(a) Process performance measurement

Assess each performance measure used for the process using the following, choosing the statement that it most closely matches:

0	20	40	60	80	100
No data available	Process measures are derived from organization's goals and CSFs	There is some performance trend data, which is compared to internal targets	Good trend data with no significant adverse trends, and meeting internal targets	Good trend data with no significant adverse trends, meeting internal targets, and compared to benchmarks	Excellent improvement trend with clear evidence of leadership in the industry and other benchmarks

Then add up the scores for each process performance measurement and average them to get an assessment of the overall process.

(b) Process maturity assessment

For each process, assess its maturity by matching its approach to one of the following statements.				
20	**40**	**60**	**80**	**100**
Ad hoc, chaotic	Dependent on individuals	Defined	Measured	Optimized
No system evident	Beginning of a systematic approach, reacts to problems	Sound systematic approach, a fact based improvement process, with emphasis on prevention rather than reaction	Sound systematic approach, emphasis on prevention rather than reaction, with refinement and improvement as a result of improvement cycles and analysis	Sound systematic approach, emphasis on prevention rather than reaction, with very strong refinement and integration

(c) Customer satisfaction

For each process, review the internal and external customer satisfaction data and assign a customer satisfaction rating based on the following.					
0	**20**	**40**	**60**	**80**	**100**
Not measured	V. dissatisfied	Dissatisfied	Neutral	Satisfied	Very satisfied

(d) Relevance to goals

Identify all the key business goals of the organization (which should be a mix of internal goals and external customer related goals), and then rate each business process in turn on how relevant it is to achieving each goal.

PROCESS	BUSINESS GOALS					
	Goal 1	Goal 2	Goal 3	Goal 4	Goal 5	Total score
Process 1						
Process 2						
Process 3						

Score 9 if the process is highly relevant to the goal,
Score 6 if the process is of medium relevance to the goal,
Score 3 if the process is of little relevance to the goal,
Score 0 if the process is of no relevance to the goal.

Add the score for each goal to get a total score for each process.

Plot the index for each process on the decision matrix

For each process, there are now four excellence indicators, three of which relate to its performance and one that relates to its relevance to the business. These are now plotted on the decision matrix (Fig. 12.3) with the sum of the performance indicators forming one axis and the relevance indicator the other – their relative positions in each quadrant then helps to guide management about what course of action is most appropriate for each process.

IMPLEMENTING PROCESS MANAGEMENT

Implementing process management in an organization requires something more than just superimposing horizontal lines on to the traditional organizational chart and then appointing process owners. In order to create a genuine process orientation it also requires changes to the organization's

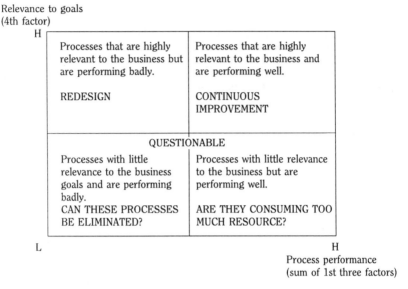

FIGURE 12.3   Business process improvement matrix

culture, values, and measurement and job evaluation systems, which in turn require a strong emphasis on education and training. In many respects the required changes mirror the factors identified by the CIRCA research as required for successful continuous improvement – a clear strategy, infrastructure, culture, tools and techniques, and process. In the case of a process-managed organization that maintains the vitality of all of its processes with either continuous improvement or redesign, these are as follows.

Strategy

The vision and goals of the organization must clearly be focused on delivering delighted customers and recognizing that the way to deliver that is via world class business processes. All re-engineering and improvement programmes must be clearly linked back to the strategy so that the changes are really beneficial to business performance.

Infrastructure

If we want to change the way people behave in their work environment we need to change more than just the organization charts. We need to change the way in which their personal performance objectives are set and measured and the way that their jobs are evaluated, change the reward and recognition systems from emphasizing individual performance to emphasizing the team, and change the role of the manager from one of control to one of coach (Fig. 12.4). Reporting lines have to consider an individual's process responsibilities as well as their functional ones. This in turn requires changes to the appraisal system so that more people than just the individual's direct manager influence their performance rating.

Culture

These changes require some fundamental changes to the culture of the organization. The culture is derived from the beliefs and values of the organization, and therefore these need to be changed to show a belief in customer delight, employee empowerment, and the development of world-class processes to deliver them. Not only do the words need to be changed, but the attitudes and behaviour of the senior executives in the organization must convince the other employees that the words are *real* values and beliefs.

Tools and techniques

Among the tools and techniques of process management are process mapping, process analysis, root cause analysis, value-add analysis, raw cycle time, and the seven basic tools of quality. These can be easily taught to all employees, but in order for them actually to use them as basic tools in their day-to-day work requires the right supporting strategy, infrastructure and culture.

In addition, radical changes to processes usually requires the availability of some form of new technology capability as an enabler for change.

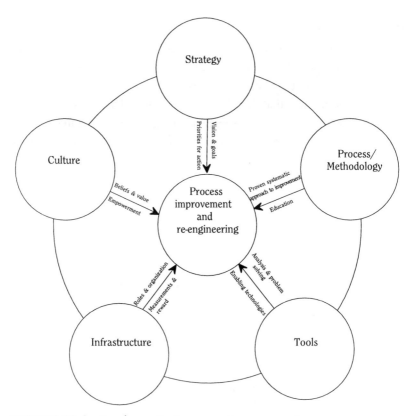

FIGURE 12.4 Implementing process improvement

Process

Various aspects of the process of process management have been explored throughout this book, with many different approaches explained. It is important that a process of process management is adopted by every organization and that all process owners, engineers and improvers are trained in its use. However, as has been mentioned on several occasions, neither the tools and techniques nor the process of process management are in themselves 'rocket science', and are seldom the root cause of failure. Failure is almost always caused by deficiencies in the strategy, culture or infrastructure of the organization.

Without *all* of these factors, any improvement programme will not be sustainable but will become just another short-lived flavour of the month. We all tend to focus on the tools and methodologies of improvement and re-engineering, but it is not these that cause failure – rather, failure is caused by an unbalanced approach that does not change or develop all five factors in parallel (strategy, process, tools, infrastructure, culture) in order to create sustained change.

REFERENCES

1   Randriamalaza, Y. (1994). 'Going with the flow'. *Corporate Business Re-engineering Journal*, Vol. 2, No. 1.

2   Hammer, M. (1990). 'Re-engineering work: Don't automate, obliterate'. *Harvard Business Review*, July/August.

3   Porter, T.J. and Keboe, J.G. (1993/4). 'Using activity-based costing and value analysis to take the pain out of downsizing at a naval shipyard'. *National Productivity Review*, Winter.

RECOMMENDED READING

Harrington, H.J. and J.S. (1995). *Total Improvement Management*. McGraw-Hill, New York.

CHAPTER 13

The way forward

The road to hell is paved with good intentions.
(Anonymous)

In the preceding chapters we have looked at the fundamental building blocks of continuous business improvement, which are:
- systems and processes
- benchmarking
- continuous improvement
- business process redesign
- self-assessment.

SYSTEMS AND PROCESSES

Both systems concepts and business process management have important parts to play in continuous business improvement.

Considering the system

Any organization is a system, a human activity system, and any improvement activity needs to start by taking a systemic view of the organization. Remember that a system is a complex set of processes that interact with each other and the external environment, and that these business processes are the means by which the system (the organization) achieves its objectives. A single process should not be addressed in isolation without considering the effect that it will have on other parts of the system.

This generally leads to 'sub-optimization' (see Fig. 2.1) which will make matters worse, not better.

Managing the organization via its business processes

Managing an organization by its business processes starts by identifying what the business processes actually are that the organization uses to deliver its products or services to its customers, with a process model of the organization being created so that the interactions between the processes can be understood (see Fig. 5.4 for an example). Each process should be assigned to an owner – a senior manager who will be responsible for its performance and improvement. Processes should be defined, mapped (using one of the methods described in Chapter 3), and performance measurements established, rated according to their importance to the organization's goals and their level of performance, and then finally prioritized for improvement.

BENCHMARKING

Once the improvement priorities have been established, the next step is to decide, on a process-by-process basis, what the 'stretch' targets should be for that process, and whether these can be achieved by continuous improvement or whether process redesign is needed. This is the reason for benchmarking: to set stretch objectives for the process based on the best that is being achieved externally and, by understanding the approaches used by the best, to decide whether those approaches can be introduced into your process via continuous improvement or whether more radical process redesign is required.

CONTINUOUS IMPROVEMENT

For processes in which continuous improvement is considered to be the appropriate approach, then a range of vehicles should be introduced to encourage and promote individual and team efforts aimed at identifying and implementing incremental improvements to the process.

BUSINESS PROCESS REDESIGN

For processes where a more radical approach is needed to bring them up to 'best practice', then process redesign should be adopted. Once the redesign is complete and the new process bedded in, it must not be left to stagnate but must be actively managed by continuous improvement; therefore at this point, continuous improvement becomes standard practice used across the whole of the organization.

Process capability should be regularly assessed to decide when the process is no longer able to meet its objectives by continuous improvement and is in need of further redesign.

SELF-ASSESSMENT

Self-assessment provides the framework for all continuous business improvement activity. Used regularly, the change in score gives confirmation that real improvement is being achieved, and the rate of change indicates whether the momentum is being maintained. The strengths and areas for improvement identified during each round of self-assessment give good indications of where previous improvement plans have started to become effective and which areas require further improvement focus.

CONCLUSIONS

These are the building blocks for successful continuous business improvement, and their use is shown in flowchart form in Fig. 13.1. The methodologies are described in some detail in the preceding chapters, and you have the option of adopting the methodologies as described, or following the examples provided and develop your own 'best of breed' methodology customized to your own organization's needs and culture. However, it must be emphasized again that there is no certain recipe for success. Organizations can be very good at using continuous improvement teams, benchmarking, process improvement, process redesign, etc., but they can also find them ineffective in making a positive contribution to business

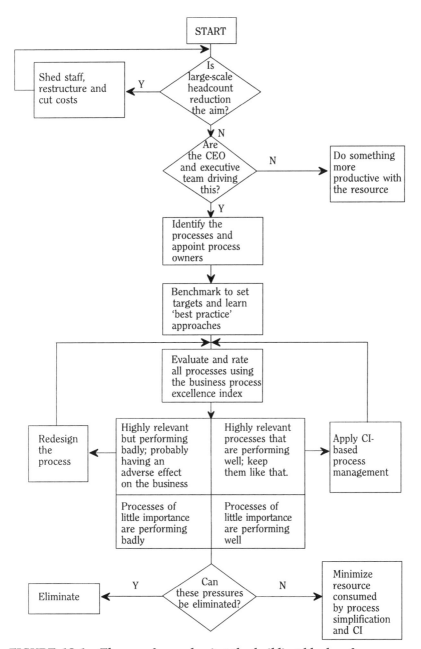

FIGURE 13.1 The way forward using the building blocks of success

performance unless the tools are used within the right strategic and cultural environment. The basic strategic and cultural ingredients for sustained business improvement are:

- clearly defined vision and goals
- clear strategic reason for adopting continuous business improvement
- committed and involved senior management
- enthusiastic middle management
- employees who are empowered, trained in problem solving and process improvement, and encouraged to use their training

If any of the first three are absent (see Fig. 13.1), then there is little point in starting on the continuous business improvement journey, as they are the enablers for middle management enthusiasm and employee empowerment (the people who in the main are the ones that actually utilize the tools of continuous business improvement and deliver the improvements to the organization). In their absence, resources would be better employed elsewhere where they might make some contribution to the business, rather than being wasted on ineffective improvement programmes. It is essential therefore to have defined strategic goals and reasons for adopting continuous business improvement, and the commitment of senior executives. These provide the foundations for an enthusiasm for continuous business improvement that ensures that tools and techniques are effective and that their use does make a positive contribution to the bottom line.

Index

Other titles of interest from the McGraw-Hill Quality in Action Series

Quality of Service – Making it Really Work
Bo Edvardsson, Bertil Thomasson and John Øvretveit
0-07-707949-3

Japanese-Led Companies – Understanding How to Make Them Your Customers
Nigel Holden and Matt Burgess
0-07-707817-9

Motivating Your Organization – Achieving Business Success through Reward and Recognition
Colin Pitts
0-07-707967-1

Quality Database Marketing – Valuing Your Customers
Angus Jenkinson
0-07-707950-7

Self-Assessment for Business Excellence
David Lascelles and Roy Peacock
0-07-709186-8

Strategic Business Transformation
Warren Winslow
0-07-707955-8

The Boy Who Jumped

By Terrence P. Nelson

ISBN 978-1-329-75439-3

To Brennan and Jess

Novels Also By Terrence P. Nelson

A Way Past Like
A Digger's Grave
The Snaker Boys
The Boy Who Spoke To A Stone
The Boy Who Forged A Masterpiece
The Bus To Destiny

This novel is written with a single sentence
on each line. This format is intended to appeal
to a wider range of readers.

"A journey of a thousand miles
begins with a single step."

Lao Tzu
Tao Te Ching, Chapter 64

This file contains the interviews, statements and observations compiled by
Detective Tony Wallace (Ret'd)
As told to
Terrence P. Nelson
concerning the disappearance
of Logan Fletcher

Gone

Detective Wallace:

11:36 PM July 23, a call is received on the Police Crisis Line.
The intake officer determines it is an Emergency: Level 1.
The call is immediately referred to the Summit Hill Station.

This is a transcript of the initial call:

(*A woman's voice*)
Hello*?* Hello? Oh my gosh! Oh my goodness! Oh no...no!
Please! Please send help. Send help right away. Help us.
How could this have happened? Oh no! Please help us.
This is Laura Fletcher. Something terrible has happened.

(*Sounds of sobbing from a man in the background.
The man speaks on the phone.*)
This is Gavin Fletcher. Please help us.
It's horrible. I can't believe this is even possible!
Everything was fine. It was an absolutely perfect day.
And then this. I just can't believe it. Oh my! Oh my!
It's completely unthinkable. Oh, what has happened?

Our boy Logan...Logan Fletcher is missing!
Do you hear me? Is anyone there listening to me?
(*The male caller begins screaming on the phone.*)
I checked in on him before going to bed like always.
And he was gone. My boy Logan was gone!!!
He wasn't in his room anywhere! Oh, he's just a boy...a boy!

We're on the 19th floor of a 23 story building...the 19th floor!
His window was wide open! Oh my goodness...wide open.

(*More sobbing*)
We are on the 19th floor...the 19th floor! Do you hear me?
Is anyone listening to me? Oh no...no...no!
And his window was open, as wide as it could go!
And our sweet boy is missing. Please send help right away.

We are at the Lakeside Condo Complex.
The security man will let you in. We are in Condo 19-6
Did I tell you his window was wide open? Oh no! Oh no!
(*More sobbing*)

Statement By Detective Tony Wallace :
Calvin Fletcher is a prominent lawyer.
Laura Fletcher is an investment counselor.
Logan is their only child.
The following interviews took place in their living room.
The time was 12:20 AM July 24.

An outdoor team was searching the grounds and roof.
Forensics was examining the boy's room and apartment.
Hallway security camera videos were being analyzed.
This would be assessed as a "Highly Secure Building."

Interviews With Missing Child's Parents In Their Living room
Laura Fletcher:
This had been a perfect day...tiring, but absolutely perfect.

Logan had just celebrated his 13th birthday with his buddies.
Multiple pizzas had been devoured by the eight boys.
They were eight hungry, frisky boys with bottomless stomachs.
The decision to have a pool party was a stroke of genius.

My husband and I watched the playful water competitions.
We saw variations of dodgeball, polo, and wrestle-tag.
An underwater hockey game was created on the spot.
Laughter...wild cries of joy filled the pool centre in our Condo.

We watched with a sense of satisfaction, Detective Wallace.
We were so proud of our son Logan, there with his friends.
How comfortable he was with such a diverse group of guys.

Some of the boys towered over him, but it didn't bother him.
Nope, not one bit. He seemed so confident with them.
Logan had a perpetual smile. We were so lucky.
We laughed as he pushed his black curls away from his face.
(Father begins sobbing.)

Laura Fletcher continues:
Most of these kids, I barely knew...
But Logan said they were his friends...he wanted them here.
I picked them up all over town, and then drove them home.
Some of their neighbourhoods were rough...to say the least.

I should have asked more questions...been more suspicious.
But they were all so happy...truly joyful in the water.
We watched these boys on the very edge of becoming men.
What is there about water that makes us turn into children?

We had reserved the recreation centre here as well.
And then the video games began.
Boys with turbans and ball caps shrieked with laughter.
In an instant, they became courageous, ancient warriors.
Each one seemed to step into the fantasy with enthusiasm.

They controlled their video characters with wild cheers.
Or if defeated, playful groans arose from the pile of boys.
Long legs criss-crossed on the floor as battles raged.
These kids challenged monsters, demons, and alien invaders.
They fought brutal mercenaries and marauding dinosaurs.

Around 9:00PM, I drove everyone home.
Detective Wallace, I was in neighbourhoods on the east side.
Honestly I was a little frightened. I had my car doors locked.
I had never ventured into this part of the city before.
I didn't tell my husband about where I had gone.
Logan gave directions and I wondered,"How does he know?"

When we returned home, Logan hugged us both.
He thanked us for such a perfect birthday party.
"It couldn't have been better. It was perfect in every way."
That's what he told us. "Thanks Mom. Thanks Dad...love you."

He went into his bedroom and fell immediately asleep.
How do we know? We could hear his loud breathing.
It was the heavy breathing of a weary boy in a deep sleep.

(Calvin Fletcher composes himself and begins to speak)

Calvin Fletcher:
I have been so proud of my son...so so proud.
He's an excellent student with near-perfect marks.
He's so popular among his friends, as we saw this evening.
And talented. He is the main soloist in his choral group.
Recent successes in basketball will likely lead to a scholarship.

My wife Laura was cleaning up the mess in the kitchen.
She likes things to be neat and tidy.
She was cleaning up the evidence of a happy party.
You know what I mean...paper plates, pop cans, old pizza.

I decided to check in on Logan before turning in.
I do that every time I'm home.
Sometimes, if he's still awake, we"ll have a talk...guy things.
He'll tell me about a play he made in basketball.
Or he might show me the latest book he's reading.
He likes those fantasy novels...mythical planets, warriors.

When I opened the door, I was stunned for a moment.
Then, I simply yelled, "Logan! Oh Logan!
My wife dropped the cake plate and it shattered on the floor.
She ran right over the glass in her bare feet.

Together, we stood at the door.
We were horrified at what we saw.
His curtains were pulled back and his window was wide open.
Yet, I was somehow in denial, refusing to believe the obvious.

We were frantic...absolutely frantic.

(Calvin Fletcher once again begins to sob uncontrollably. Laura Fletcher continues...)

Laura Fletcher:
Logan's covers were turned down and his bed was empty.
I flung open his closet, pulled back clothes and moved boxes.
Maybe he had a dream and began sleep-walking.
But he wasn't in the closet.

I looked under his bed, then slid in to see if he might be there.
I know it doesn't make sense, but we we desperate.
I found his set of weights. He was trying to bulk up a bit.
Some of the guys on his team were growing so fast.
He didn't want to get left behind.

In a plastic tub, he kept his fantasy novels.
He loved all those selfless, magical heroes who fought evil.
There was a half-eaten bag of junk food and a can of pop.
That was it...just a couple of pairs of sock and underwear.
They just got way-laid and didn't make it to the laundry.

I couldn't stop calling, "Logan! Logan! Where are you baby?
Are you here Logan? Please don't hide on us. Oh Logan!!!
But my boy was gone.
Logan was gone.
No matter how many times I called his name...only silence.

From under the bed, I could see my husband's rigid legs.
He was frozen in position on the far side of the room.
I slid from beneath the bed and rushed to my husband's side.
Calvin, my husband seemed stiff...saying over and over, "No."
He stood in front of the open window, unable to move.
As I gazed into the darkness, the horror of the situation hit me.

I screamed, "Our boy has gone through the window, Calvin.
My sweet, sweet boy has gone through the window.
We are on the nineteenth floor and Logan has...!"

It was too horrible to repeat.
We fell into each others arms, sobbing.
We saw that Logan's telescope had been pushed to the side.
The blinds has been raised to the ceiling.
Logan's little shelf containing his trophies had been moved.
It was always kept right below the window.

I had to do the unthinkable.
I had to force myself to look out the window.
I held my husband's hand and braced myself.
I stepped forward and stared down to the pavement below.
Nothing.
Logan wasn't there.
A little ripple of joy went through us...but not for long.
Calvin leaned over the sill and looked upward.
Maybe someone had descended from above and taken him.
But nothing was there...no dangling ropes...no tied sheets.

There did not appear to be evidence of a forced entry.

Once again, we simply held each other and sobbed.
"Where could he be?" we whispered in each others ears.
We called the police.

Detective Wallace:
Ten officers were assigned to the Logan Fletcher case.
Three investigated the grounds and another three...the roof.
An early consideration was that a kidnapping had occurred.
The Fletcher residence was assigned four officers:
Myself, **Detective Tony Wallace.**
Forensics Officer, **Aaron McKenzie**
Photographer, **Sam Tucken**
Computer Analyst, **Sheila Robson.**

Forensics Officer Aaron McKenzie:
It was quickly conclude that this was a secure building.
A doorman was always on duty as well as a security guard.
Doors and hallways have secure, touch-keypad access only.
There is video surveillance on every floor, and in the elevators.
All 23 levels of stairwells are under 24 hour video surveillance.

I was made aware that I would be in charge of the case.
This was due to Detective Wallace's retirement in one month.
He was to be assigned peripheral duties.
His focus would be on questioning and interviews.
The parents were terribly distraught, often weeping.
Calvin Fletcher brought us into Logan Fletcher's room.
The boy's bedroom was very typical of a youth his age.
The walls were covered with posters of sports heroes.
Trophies and medals filled shelves and hung from hooks.

Schedules for hockey, basketball and swimming were posted.
There were even a few stuffed toys, obviously well loved.

Walls were decorated with photos of Logan.
Every stage of growth and accomplishment was recorded.
Many photos show his arms around the necks of friends.
There is always a broad, genuine smile. He seems popular.

He is a slight, curly-haired lad with a scattering of freckles.
It is apparent that he has thrived in a supportive home.
Logan has received maximum academic opportunities.
Many awards and certificates adorned his walls.

These reflected his excellence in both sports and music.
Report cards were stuck in his mirror frame.
Logan Fletcher would be identified as a high achiever.

Three photos not typical of a 13 year old were above his desk:

Martin Luther King
Mahatma Ghandi
The Dali Lama
Malala Yousafzai

His parents were unaware of these photographs.
Attached to the photo of Malala was a short letter saying:

Dear Logan Fletcher,

Thank you for your note of congratulations.

Winning the Nobel Peace Prize was an honour for us all.

If there is a will...then there is a way.

Sincerely,

Malala

Forensics Officer Aaron McKenzie continues:

A desk is loaded with numerous fantasy books.

Other titles include: The Journey To Awareness

The Authentic Self

The Little Train That Could

Multiple Atlases were stacked beside his bed.

As I approached the open window, the parents wept.

Officer Sheila Robson accessed his laptop computer.

Photographer Sam Tucker took multiple photos.

I conducted a forensic analysis of the boy's room.

Detective Tony Wallace continued with interviews.

Detective Tony Wallace: Personal Observations

Having a teenager, I knew what temperamental meant.

So far, this case was not particularly unusual.

Boys this age, no matter how good, often become moody.

Maybe he slipped out unnoticed, due to rebelliousness.

Parties and get-to-gethers can be very enticing at this age.

Did Logan know how to turn off or avoid security videos?

Did he know exit routes usually used for deliveries?

Possibly, there was a family conflict they were not revealing.

My experience had tragically reinforced the sad statistics.

The most dangerous place for a child was in his own home.

We had to consider that the parents were lying.

The window could have been opened by them as a diversion.

Questioning the parents was not going to be easy.

(Confidential)

I knew I would have to proceed carefully.

Calvin Fletcher was an prominent provincial lawyer.

When children go missing, a family member is often at fault.

Disciplining may get out of hand, leading to the unthinkable.

Even easing a child's suffering may have sad consequences.

I realized that a child was missing...a bright, kind, boy.

This meant that no one was beyond suspicion. No one.

Detective Tony Wallace :Addressing the parents who are sitting together on the couch -Apt 19-6

We are moving ahead quickly, Mr. and Mrs. Fletcher.

Often, boys this age come home on their own, after a while.

So, we frequently wait to see if things work themselves out.

But in this case, with the open window, we'll proceed.

What was you son wearing when he went to bed?

Calvin Fletcher:

Logan was wearing a pair of old, black sleep pants.

They would be so easy to identify.

They had a basketball player jumping up the side.

The character was from the NBA, ready to dunk the ball.

The pants were definitely a little worn and tattered.

But Logan loved them. They were his favourite.
He had even cut them off below the knee a few days ago.

Laura Fletcher:
Logan wasn't wearing a shirt of any kind.
He liked to sleep a little on the cool side.
I remember this so well because I could see his muscles.
He was starting to fill out a bit...and had begun to lift weights.
He always kept his window a little bit open...just an inch or so.
Where ever my boy is, that's what he's wearing...definitely.

Detective Tony Wallace:
Mr. and Mrs. Fletcher, it seems that may not be the case.
The pants you are describing are lying on your son's bed.
It appears as if he got up and intentionally removed them.

Your son appears to be very organized and incredibly neat.
However, every dresser drawer was pulled open.
Drawers containing socks and underwear were left open.
The drawers with T shirts and jeans were also accessed.
Mr. and Mrs. Fletcher, your son got dressed for a reason.
Logan intended to go out.

(Mr. Fletcher covers his face and begins crying.
Mrs. Fletcher stares at me in apparent disbelief and shock.
The anguish they are feeling is truly tragic, but I proceed.
I allow a few minutes to pass, before I begin speaking again.)
Has your son...Logan...ever gone missing before?

Calvin Fletcher;

Of course not! I resent the fact that you asked that question.
You should be ashamed of yourself, Detective Wallace.
Logan is so thoughtful. He would never disappear. Never!

There is a short pause, then Mrs. Fletcher speaks up.
She gives no eye contact and is ripping up a serviette.

Laura Fletcher:

Actually, he has. Logan has disappeared twice...yes twice.
I didn't want to upset you Calvin. You were away on business.
And frankly, I was just so embarrassed that I had lost him.

Mr. Fletcher stares at his wife...looking stunned.

A Pattern

Laura Fletcher:

Logan was just six years old. Yes he was six.
I brought him to the big sandbox, in the Pinehill Park.
He was so happy playing with his little shovel and bucket.
My boy was all alone but he didn't seem to mind.
I could hear him speaking to himself and giggling.
I bowed my head and truly gave thanks for such a fine boy.

I looked up and he was gone.
I was absolutely frantic. I had only looked down for a second.
I called his name over and over but there was no answer.
I was sick with worry. "Logan! Logan! Where are you Logan?"
I screamed over and over. People came to help me.
We pulled back the bushes in case he was hiding.

I was shaking and began to cry. Only 15 minutes had past.
It seemed like an eternity. I had lost my sweet boy.
I asked everyone passing by, "Have you seen a little boy?
"He has a head full of black curls and a sprinkle of freckles."
I thought he may have been kidnapped.
Maybe it was someone that Calvin has tangled with in court.
I pulled out my phone to call the police.

At the last moment, a woman approached me, saying,
"Is your little boy wearing a sweater with a bear cub on it?"
I shouted, "Oh yes! That's my boy! That's my Logan."
I just couldn't believe what she said.

"I saw a small boy just like that at the Cedar Spruce Park.
He was playing happily in the sand with a little friend."

Detective Wallace, Cedar Spruce Park is 15 miles away!
Logan had only been missing 15 minutes at the most.
I didn't try to figure it out, I just dashed over there in my car.
And there he was, playing in the sand with a little boy.

I rushed up to him, saying "Oh Logan, mommy missed you.
Why did you come here? This is so far...so so far."
He just gave me a little smile and pushed his black curls away.
Then he said, "Mama, This is Ehsan and he was lonely."

That was it. He somehow traveled 15 miles across traffic. Why?
Because some little kid we had never met before, was lonely.
I never asked any more questions...he was only six years old.

Calvin Fletcher: *(very distraught and visibly angry)*
Surely Laura, this couldn't have happened a second time.

Inspector Wallace :
Actually, Mr. Fletcher, I think I can answer that.
I did a quick scan of the files from our Missing Persons Division.
You son, Logan Fletcher was reported missing a year ago.
He was gone approximately 8 hours, on the night of July 16.
Were you not aware of this, Mr. Fletcher?

Calvin Fletcher: *(glaring at his wife)*
No! No! I knew nothing about this...nothing at all.
Does this mean that our son is named in some police file?

Why didn't you tell me? This is appalling, Laura.
Our son was gone half the night and you never told me?
What's the matter with you? What happened?

Laura Fletcher: *(crying...trying to talk)*
It was around this time last year. You were away on business.
We had just finished up dinner and Logan helped to clean up.
Then as usual, he said that he was going to play basketball.
It was a nightly ritual, Detective Wallace.
We have a basketball court right here in the condo complex.
Actually there are several spread around the property.
After an hour or so, I decided to go down a watch him.

Laura Fletcher: *(struggling to talk)*
But he just wasn't there. I ran from court to court searching...
I called his name over and over, hoping and praying...
I found some of his buddies who played regularly with him.
Ian Brant, Dr. Brant's lad said he had seen Logan earlier.

They had taken shots at the basket together for awhile.
"I stopped to tie up my shoe, and Logan was gone."
That's all the boy could tell me...Logan was gone...
I was frantic. I decided to call the police.
I didn't want to upset you Calvin. You were in Ottawa.

Calvin Fletcher: *(shouting at his wife)*
Where was he? Where was Logan? My gosh Laura!

Laura Fletcher: *(increasingly upset by her husband's anger)*

I received a call at about one o'clock in the morning.
A police officer on patrol thought he had sighted Logan.
He wanted me to see what was "going on."
Somehow, he wanted me to see our son "in action."

I was terrified. I thought for sure it was something terrible.
If it wasn't for the GPS, I would never have found the place.
I drove for 23 miles into the far east side. It was horrible.
The buildings look as if they had been trashed or burned.
Windows were smashed or boarded up.
Bags of garbage were strewn everywhere.

The police officer had told me where he was parked.
I pulled in behind him and walked over to his car.
I climbed inside, totally bewildered by the situation I was in.
All I could say was, "Where's my boy? Where's my Logan?"
The Officer in the unmarked car pointed across the street.
I rolled down the window and stared in disbelief.

There was Logan. He was playing a game of basketball.
There was no court or even proper basketball net.
He was playing in a filthy, abandoned parking lot.
There weren't even proper basketball nets.
Calvin, they were using plastic hoops tied to the chain fence.

A barrage of laughter, grunts, cheers and groans poured out.
Logan had been absorbed into this neighbourhood team.
I would have been terrified simply to get out of the car.
Yet, there was our Logan having the time of his life.
He didn't look like the other boys but it didn't seem to matter.

Logan had his shirt off and was covered in sweat...dripping.
He just seemed to be wearing this wide grin.
Honestly, I've never seen him so happy...truly happy.

He played hard...and held his own against some big boys.
Some of them towered over him and were so aggressive.
But Logan thrived on it...he even encouraged it.
He certainly gave as well as he got...that's for sure.

It was after one in the morning on a sweltering night.
But people had begun to gather and cheer.
Folding chairs appeared from everywhere.
Grannies with babies on their knees yelled and clapped.
Brothers and sisters called out...shouting and teasing.

Logan relished the intensity of the moment...pushing himself.
Every pass, every dribble, every shot...was almost magical.
He jumped to heights I had never witnessed before.
He seemed to bring life to a ball that obeyed his wishes.

Logan shared his water bottle and high-fived everyone.
During a short break, he would put his arm around their necks.
He could tease so effortlessly...giving them nicknames.
Cell phones appeared and pictures were taken.
He was like a beloved soldier, surrounded by his comrades.

The police officer said, "Maybe it's time to get your boy.
I don't think you have anything to worry about, that's for sure.
You can be very proud of you lad, Mrs. Fletcher.
He's something special. That's a boy who's going places.

I'll watch you from here just to make sure you're safe."

(Laura Fletcher becomes more controlled.)

I walked over to the fence and gently called, "Logan."
He stopped, swung around, waved at me and grinned.
He said, "I've gotta go now guys...that's my mom."
And then he did the most amazing thing.

His pulled his hanging shirt, out from the waist of his shorts.
It was his favourite...the one signed by that Lebron fellow.
He was planning to have it framed and hung in his room.
And he gave it away to one of the boys...he gave it away!

And that's not all. You won't believe what happened next.
He sat on the asphalt and pulled off his shoes.
He gave them away too. He handed them to another boy!
Those shoes were his pride and joy. Logan truly loved them.
He had saved his money for so long.

He even had a special shelf in his room for them.
And what does he do? He just gave them away.
He gave them to a stranger whom he barely knows.
Then he playfully jumped over broken glass to get to the car.
For him, it was a game as he dodged the filth in his bare feet.

All the way home in the car, he talked about the fun he had.
The words seemed to flow out of him with such enthusiasm.
I couldn't even think of punishing him...he was so happy.
He shone...are you listening to me? My son's face shone!

Logan shone with the excitement of the experience.

As we drove home, I glanced over at Logan.
He was shirtless, and his skin was covered in glistening sweat.
His black curls were matted to his forehead and soaking neck.
His head slowly turned towards me and he smiled gently.
In a few seconds, he drifted off to sleep.

It was almost three in the morning when we got home.
My son had been away for about eight hours.
And where had Logan been?
Playing basketball...in the most dangerous part of the city!

He showered for about 20 minutes.
Every few minutes, he'd yell something out to me:
"Mom, that was the most fun I've ever had!"
"Mom, I invited Terrell and Martin over on the weekend."
"Mom, maybe we can play basketball on our court."
"Mom, they might like the pool and sauna too."
"Mom, can we pick them up? Is that okay with you?"

I sat in the kitchen in a daze, bewildered and confused.
When he left the shower, he walked up to me and kissed me.
He was all wrapped up in towels, like when he was a little boy.

"Logan," I asked, "how did you get there...way across town?
"It just sorta happens," he replied.
"It's a lot like breathing...you don't think about it too much."
And that was the end of it.
I didn't pursue it...I just hoped it wouldn't happen again.

We picked up Terrell and Martin the next weekend.

In fact, they've been here often over the past few months.

Both of the boys were at Logan's party, just a few hours ago.

Officer Aaron McKenzie : *(Laura Fletcher was interrupted by a knock at the door. The investigation unit which was under my direction checked in with me. A detailed search of the grounds and the roof revealed no evidence of the boy. A tracking dog was on its way from the Nipison Detachment. Mr. and Mrs. Fletcher were sitting on the couch at the time. I requested that they follow me into Logan's bedroom.*

I already had noted the genre of books on the shelves:

Techniques In Improving Basketball Skills.

Remembering Basketball Heroes of the Last Decade.

Great Moments In Basketball.

These of course were typical of a boy this age and interests.

Yet I had some questions for the parents regarding others.

Officer Aaron McKenzie:

Mr. Fletcher, What is your son's attraction to outdoor survival?

Look carefully here at all the books on this second shelf:

Living In The Wilderness

Edible Wild Plants

Constructing Outdoor Shelters

What To Do When Lost In The Wood

Orienteering Strategies

One might think that your son was planning to go somewhere.

It appears that your son has all the skills to avoid detection.

Calvin Fletcher: *(responding angrily and defensively)*

How dare you imply that. You're twisting the facts!

Logan has been part of an Adventurers Troop since he was 8.
He has mastered outdoor survival all over the province.
Logan is fearless but careful. Any weakness is practiced.
He's not afraid to tackle adversity head-on.
He sets high personal standards and overcomes obstacles.
That's just the kind of boy he is.

His endurance is spectacular. He can hike for miles.
He canoes, camps, and swims competitively at the pool.
Logan also has a Level 5 in First Aid.
Next week, he was to begin rock climbing with a local club.
He also thrives on white water rafting and rescue.
He loves these activities because they are challenges....
Not because he was preparing to run away. Am I clear?

Detective Tony Wallace: *(I could see that Mr. Fletcher was becoming very agitated with Officer McKenzie so I continued with the questioning with probably neither of them happy with me.)*

Where does Logan keep his equipment, Mr. Fletcher?
Where does he store his tent, sleeping bag...that sort of thing?

Calvin Fletcher: *(anxious to remove any suspicion or doubt about Logan)*
It's all right here...right here in his room.
Just open up that wooded chest pushed up against his bed.
You'll find a tent, sleeping bag, hiking boots, pack sack....
It's all pretty precious to him...look, I'll show you.
The chest was his grandfather's from the war, you know.

Detective Tony Wallace: *(Mr. Fletcher yells, "Oh no!"*

There is no equipment. Logan's chest is completely empty. His parents both begin sobbing...as they are forced to confront the possibility that Logan left intentionally.)

Officer Aaron McKenzie:

Maybe you should return to the couch next to your wife.

I know this is hard for you...there is so much to absorb.

I'll give you a few minutes to regain your composure.

(Five minutes pass...and the questioning continues.)

I realize that many of Logan's friends were in his room today.

There are several different fingerprints in his bedroom alone.

Getting an accurate footprint and fingerprint is challenging.

Could you tell us exactly where he was, before going to bed?

It might be best if we had a different source to access.

Laura Fletcher:

He had a shower in the small bathroom down the hall.

He uses it exclusively...even kept it clean himself.

Detective Tony Wallace:

(Forensic Officer Aaron McKenzie asked me to take over the interview as he directed the fingerprinting process in the two sites...the bedroom and bathroom. When a match was confirmed, Officer McKenzie explained the findings and suggested that I be the one to present the information to the parents, since they "seem to trust you."

Mr. and Mrs. Fletcher, please come with me.

(I guided them back into their son's bedroom...over to the window which was still wide open, letting in a cool breeze.)

Look carefully and you will notice something very revealing.

The powders and lamps used to detect prints are definitive.

Right there! You can see clearly, your son's footprints.

Do you see them? There they are...on the windowsill.

They match the footprints in the bathroom and down the hall.

Do you see the positioning of the toes?

They are clenched around the exterior lip of the windowsill.

They are positioned like a diver about to spring off.

I know this is hard for you to hear, Mr. and Mrs. Fletcher.

But your son definitely jumped out this window.

(increased sobbing by the parents)

However, there is something we don't know at the moment.

We don't know where he landed...or even how.

(Laura Fletcher extended her head out the window, peering 19 stories, down to the pavement below. She could see the investigation squad with two dogs, continuing to scour the concrete surface.

Powerful lights had been set up, illuminating the area below the Fletcher apartment. Part of the team had moved onto the landscaped grassy area which extended for several acres. The beams from their flashlights pierced the darkness as they searched for evidence of the missing boy...or his body. Calvin Fletcher gently pulled his wife back from the window.)

Laura Fletcher: *(bewildered)*

What is happening to us? We lead good lives.

We are good people. We haven't hurt anyone.

The day had been perfect, absolutely perfect.

Logan has exceeded all of our expectations.

His future is so bright and promising.

And now, everything is crashing down around us...everything.

Sheila Robson: *(The computer analyst has been examining Logan's computer and begins to address Mr. and Mrs. Fletcher as they sit on their son's bed.)*

I've examine your son's computer in detail over the last hour.

I've been hoping to find some information that proves helpful.

It is not often that a password is taped right on the keyboard.

Believe me, that is not typical of a boy who is 13 years old.

So far, there is no evidence of involvement in any social sites.

Or is there any history of using chat rooms of any sort.

Other than sites accessed for homework, there is little activity.

...Except in one specific area.

(The Fletchers appear to be jolted out of a trance and look towards the computer analyst.)

Secrets Emerge

Sheila Robson:

Mr. and Mrs. Fletcher, I see that your son has a bank account.

An account that he monitors on-line and can access.

Is that right?

Laura Fletcher:

Why yes. His granny passed away last year.

They were very close. She left him $20,000.

He's added to it by working on Saturdays as a landscaper.

Logan helps the maintenance staff with the landscaping.

He's so careful. He rarely makes an account withdrawal.

We never have any concerns about him handling money.

Believe me, Ms. Robson, Logan is not skimpy...just careful.

His plan is to put himself through university.

We could have handled it but it was his own idea.

He said to me, "Mom, I'm sure I can do it...I'll work hard."

I would suspect that there is about $23,000 in his account.

Sheila Robson: *(The computer analyst seemed to pause for a moment, contemplating carefully how she would present the information she had just discovered. She began speaking in a calm but straight-forward way.*

Mr. and Mrs. Fletcher, according to the most recent banking records, your son has exactly $152. 63 in his bank account.

Calvin Fletcher: *(totally shocked)*

Someone must have gotten into his account and robbed him.

That's the only possible explanation.

There must have been a breach in the bank's security.

Surely the bank's computers were compromised in someway.

Or maybe it was an inside job...an employee of some sort.

You people have to get onto this. What's the matter with you?

(Mr. Fletcher frustration results in accusations but is quickly silenced by further revelations.)

Detective Tony Wallace:

Well, I think I'm onto something, but it isn't at the bank.

I may have the answer right here in my hands.

I discovered this little tin box on the shelf beside Logan's bed.

It wasn't hidden in any way. It was sitting next to a golf trophy.

I opened it and discovered it was full of receipts...dozens.

They are all carefully attached with paper clips.

A fingerprint analysis shows that Logan put them there.

Actually, within this box, is a detailed record of his spending.

These appear to match up to the computer withdrawals.

(I scooped up several at random and began to read them. Mr. And Mrs. Fletcher seemed transfixed.)

1 pair of glasses from Uptown Vision Centre

10 receipts of groceries from the Price Right Mart

Dental work paid to Dr. Tom Beaconi

1 walker purchased from Home Assistance

25 games of checkers

10 bags of dog food from Pooky's Pet Emportium.

100 pairs of socks from Guy's Clothing Warehouse.

!00 pairs of underwear...same location

20 bags of concrete

6 twelve foot metal poles

6 basketball hoops

1 load of top soil

300sq feet of sod...delivered

Detective Tony Wallace:

Do any of these purchases sound familiar to you?

(As I looked at Logan's parents, it was obvious that they were baffled and confused. They were coming to the slow realization that their son, barely 13 years old was leading a parallel life, about which they knew nothing. One could see that Laura Fletcher was beginning to unravel emotionally. One could detect the exasperation in her voice.

Laura Fletcher:

Familiar? Do they sound familiar to me? Are you crazy?

Of course they don't sound familiar to me!

There's not a single thing mentioned that Logan needs.

A walker? Why for goodness sake would he need a walker?

Logan is in excellent physical condition...excellent!

And you're trying to tell me that he bought a walker?

His vision is perfect, absolutely perfect...what's going on here?

Why would he need glasses?...his eyesight is perfect!

And sod? Isn't that the grass that comes all rolled up?

Tell me, just what would he do with a truck load of sod?

Do you see a dog anywhere? Inspector...we have no dog.

There is no need for dog food around here, that's for sure.

(Laura Fletcher was becoming more frantic by the minute.)

It's absolutely ridiculous that Logan would buy underwear.

Officer Wallace, my son has dozens of underwear. Dozens!

If you pull open that drawer you'll see what I mean.

He has every possible kind and theme imaginable.

You'll discover stacks of athletes, and cartoon characters.

All the various action heroes are represented as well.

He would not buy underwear and definitely not at that store!

Officer Tony Wallace: *(I did as she suggested and opened the top drawer in Logan's dresser. Together we glanced inside. Neatly folder inside was a small pile of boy's boxers...may 7-8 in number...nothing at all like his mother described.)*

(Staring at me, Laura Fletcher began screaming...)

Laura Fletcher:

You people have done this...you're trying to trick us.

I know what you are all up to. This is some form of entrapment.

If his underwear are missing, what else might be gone?

Or maybe I should ask, what else have you hidden?

(Laura Fletcher opens her son's closet and becomes hysterical...)

Laura Fletcher:

Where are my son's clothes? What have you done with them?

This closet should be full, absolutely full.

Every shirt or sweater had some official emblem or logo on it.

I should know...I bought them for him...most are over $100!

All the basketball and hockey teams are represented.

He was so proud of his jerseys...of course he never said that.

But who wouldn't be proud to wear such stylish clothes?

And that's not all! His cap collection is missing!

(She continues to shriek accusingly.)

Where are Logan's baseball caps? He had a huge collection.

They all hung on hooks on the back of his closet door.

He's been collecting caps since he was seven years old.

Many were autographed by the most famous athletes.

The names of sports superstars were signed on the crests.

My husband knows many famous people you know.

Those caps must be worth a fortune and where are they now?

Laura Fletcher's eye fall on an empty Plexiglas cube that had been lifted from its place on a table.)

Who could have done this?

Why would anyone want my son's basketball?

He got the winning basketball in the Provincial Jr. Boy's Finals.

He was given the basketball as a souvenir.

It had been signed by every boy on his team...and it's gone.

This precious memento has just disappeared...disappeared!

You people have done this. I trusted you...all of you.

I thought you could help us but look what you've done.

You've stripped away almost ever memory of my sweet boy.

There's only several simple T shirts and an old cap.

They all look as if they came from a Dollar Store or Thrift Shop.

Laura Fletcher collapses in tears on her son's bed and clutched his sleep pants closely to herself. Her husband guides her back to the couch in their Great Room as the team quietly begins to pack up, with plans to return in the morning.

Officer Aaron McKenzie orders that Logan Fletcher's bedroom be taped off and that the window should remain open. The team left with Logan's laptop, books, assorted papers. Hundreds of photos have also been taken and have yet to be analyzed.

The team makes plans to return in the morning. Officer McKenzie asks me to question some of the boy's friends who attended the birthday party. That will be my first duty in the morning.

I had to admit as I headed towards the staircase, that the likelihood of a happy ending to this bizarre disappearance was diminishing my the minute.

A Myth From An Island

Detective Tony Wallace:

This portion of the report was not included in my original submission.

The rest of the team accessed the elevator together.

However, I decided to walk down the 19 flights of stairs.

The several hundred steps might help to build some stamina.

I also was hoping to reduce the ever expanding waistline.

After descending the first flight of steps, I knew I wasn't alone.

Sam Tucken:

Excuse me, Detective Wallace, I'm Sam the photographer.

May I speak with you as we walk down?

(I recognized Sam immediately. He's a young, lean man with a dark complexion and wide winning smile. I had noticed that he had moved around the boy's room and the entire Fletcher residence in silence, with efficiency, speed, and focus. I told him to go ahead and tell me what was on his mind)

Sam Tucken:

Detective Wallace, my name is really Samuctama

Actually, it's Samuctama Tuctawab That's a mouthful eh?

I go by Sam Tucken, just to make it easier for everyone.

I'm originally from Swashatuq Island in the North Pacific.

My home island was once part of the ancient land bridge.

It joined Siberia to the North American continent.

However, as the ocean levels rose, an island was formed.

We were surrounded by water on all sides.
It took several hundred years, and we adapted as a people.
All of our needs were met and we existed in happy isolation.
The ruggedness of the island certainly had its benefits.
"From-awayers" weren't attracted to a cold windblown rock.
My family still resides there.

Detective Tony Wallace:

This is all very interesting young man...fascinating.
I know you have a excellent reputation in the police force.
But, what has this to do with the missing Fletcher boy?
I'm in a bit of a hurry. I'm anxious to get home to my family.

Sam Tucken:

I understand Sir, I'll try to explain quickly.
My father is honoured to be the keeper of the old stories.
They might be called legends or myths by non-believers.
Yet they are called truths or inspired words by those who do.
I was trained to take his place some day.
However, here I am in the city, working as a photographer.
Taking pictures is strictly forbidden in our culture.

Some university archaeological students arrived one day.
They brought along video games, cell phones, and cameras.
Well I got hooked and here I am.
I guess youthful rebellion takes place in every culture.

Detective Tony Wallace:

Please Sam. Get to the point. Where are you going with this?
I just don't see how this pertains in any way to the missing boy.

Sam Tucken:

Sir, Logan Fletcher wasn't kidnapped or abducted by anyone.

Nor has the boy run away.

After seeing his parents, why would he even consider leaving?

They are loving people whose hearts are truly breaking.

They have exceeded by far, in meeting all of his needs.

No Sir, the Fletcher boy wasn't taken or has he run away.

Logan Fletcher was called.

Detective Tony Wallace:

(speaking somewhat impatiently...)

What do you mean? What are you talking about?

Sam Tucken:

On my island, through time, young boys have disappeared.

They were the brightest, bravest, and the most courageous.

These lads were those who pushed at the edge of everything.

This might happen every third or fourth generation.

A boy with the greatest potential would simply go missing.

It's as if there was some greater calling beyond our island.

Mr. Wallace, our island is not an easy place to forge a living.

We would eagerly look forward to a young man to guide us.

A young girl too, might show us through life's turbulence.

The Pacific Ocean is not a gentle friend, Detective Wallace.

Churning ocean currents can whisk away our fishing boats.

Our island is on a collision course with brutal unrelenting winds.

Glacier crevices and volcanic activity are constant threats.

Our needs may be great, but needs are more dire elsewhere.

So a boy disappears, Detective Wallace.

He disappears just like Logan Fletcher.

He is called by the challenge of some far-off place.

And his absence forces the weaker ones left behind...to act.

Sometimes they do...and sometimes they don't.

Detective Tony Wallace:

(I was rapidly running out of patience with all this silliness and mumbo-jumbo.)

This is absolute foolishness, young man...foolishness.

Maybe the boys fell into one of those glacial crevices.

They might have slipped into the bubbling volcanic mud.

This "disappearance myth" has emerged for one reason.

It is a supernatural way of explaining some kid's carelessness.

My son is a teenager right now. Oh my gosh!

I wish I could account for all of his late nights with a "myth!"

That would be a wonderful way to explain away his stupidity.

Plus, explain to me, how a kid disappears. Try that, will you?

We stop descending the stairs and sit in some chairs on a landing, about three flights up from the lobby. The young photographer puts his hand on my shoulder and looks into my eyes intently and begins speaking in a quiet, reverential tone.)

Sam Tucken:

The child...even a small child...hears a call...

A need is heard...and the child is there.

Just like Logan in the sandbox. It's like a practice run.

But the calls become louder and the needs become greater.
And the most startling of all: the distances become farther.
In an instant, Logan could be across town.
In the blink of an eye, he could have gone thousands of miles.

(I looked at this seemingly intelligent young man in disbelief as he continued with this story:)

Sam Tucken:

There are indicators that he has already traveled many times.
It's just that Logan's parents weren't aware of it.
Almost always, he begins to give away personal possessions.
These are looked upon as meaningless and having little value.
It's like stream-lining one's self before a great adventure.
He had eliminated the excess baggage weighing him down.

Logan is responding to some inner call...from out there.
It's as if over time, the volume of the calling is increasing.
As this happens, so too do the distances increase.
It is likely that Logan has traveled many times across the city.
It takes him barely a fraction of a second.

I would suspect that his present journey is much farther.
The need might be greater...at least in his eyes.
For others, such an effort might be hard to explain.
Sir, Logan Fletcher has been beckoned...and has responded.
The call has now become clear and distinct.

But most often, a boy does not...or chooses not to answer.
The tugging feeling is suppressed, ignored, and disappears.

A boy may choose to continue on with his life as it is.
Hundreds of boys may have been called this year alone.
However, it is possible that only Logan has answered.
It is likely that he has returned to his bedroom ever night.
That is, until now.

Logan might turn up in his bedroom as if nothing happened.
Or he may never be seen again.
His journeys have probably become more challenging.
They might involve just a single soul...or possibly thousands.

Detective Tony Wallace:

(I must admit that I spoke to Sam with sarcasm.)

Well just tell me this, Mr. Spooky Man from a distant island:
Who or what is exactly doing this calling?
Who is calling out to brave young boys to disappear?
Just answer me that.
Who is telling a perfectly healthy lad to jump out a window?
Are you listening to me, Mr. Spooky Man?
Who is beckoning a kid to jump out a 19 story window?

*I could see that my comments had hurt Sam...and his voice
dropped to a quiet whisper.*

Sam Tucken:

Sir, you must realize that once given a name, He is restricted.
Even saying "He" presents inaccuracies.
On my island, His name is never uttered.
We simply bow or heads to signify Him.

We nod slightly to acknowledge his presence and power.
The anthropologists have named him The Caller.
However, these "From-Awayers" are so inaccurate.
The word "Caller" signifies such a tiny part of all that he is.

Detective Tony Wallace:
(By now I was becoming quite exasperated and short tempered.)

So what am I to tell Mr. and Mrs. Fletcher?
That their wonderful son has deserted them?
They were abandoned because he listened to some Caller?
He followed instructions to fly out a 19th story window?
That'll sound just fine at a press conference...my gosh!
Hundred of kids will be flying out windows all over town!
Sam, there is one thing I don't need and that's fairy tales.
Look, I've gotta get home. I think we're done young man.

Sam Tucken:
Detective Wallace, Logan Fletcher did not fly out a window.
He jumped.
He jumped with a conviction of purpose.
And the moment those bare feet of his lifted into the air...
The boy...the young man...cracked open light.
Logan isn't a light-beam rider, although they exist.
He entered it. He became part of its essence.
A single beam has transported him somewhere in the world.
Logan Fletcher is on a mission, guided by only two words.

Detective Tony Wallace:

And just what might those be?

"Do Good"

replied Samuctama Tuctawab from Swashatuq Island.

Father And Son

Detective Tony Wallace:

(Information not included in my primary report.)

In the morning, I had breakfast with my 18 year old son, Rick.
In a few months, he would be moving on to university.
I was happy to have some personal time with my son.
Rick's a smart lad, though a little frisky at times.

He still wasn't certain what he wanted to do with his life.
Rick had narrowed it down to playing in a rock band...or law.
I thought without a doubt, my son would be a great lawyer.
He seemed to thrive on arguing...over every point, everything!
The idea of Rick playing in a band was unfathomable to me.
Maybe a quiet bonding breakfast was just what was needed.

Let's just say that Rick was not a shy boy...definitely not.
This table had been the site of some pretty lively discussions.
It wasn't easy for him having a single father as a police officer.
It must have been tough for him at school sometimes.
But having his own "garage band" had its perks.
If you go by phone calls, Rick was a popular guy.

We sat together at the kitchen table.
I was in my suit ready for work, and Rick was in his underwear.
He was blurry eyed and unshaven, after a late-night gig.
I had to admire him.
The profits from his band were funding his college courses.

We munched noisily on corn flakes for a few minutes.
Finally, I initiated a conversation about the Fletcher case.
Rick was fascinated by the case, and followed attentively.
He was particularly interested in my conversation with Sam.

Detective Tony Wallace:

Son, who could possibly believe such gibberish?
Sam is a well-educated and talented photographer.
He has a knack for noticing details often overlooked by us.
Sam is in demand all over the province because of his skills.
He could easily get work with any police force in the country.

Yet there he was on the staircase, talking foolishness.
He rambled on and on...it was truly bizarre.
It was a fairy tale, all about a Caller and disappearing boys.
Do you know what I think Rick? It's all a fantasy.
It's a way for those island people to explain their tragedies.
They made up some myth to give purpose to catastrophes.
They needed a reason to explain why a kid...or kids vanished.
Some kind of a sacred narrative was formed.

But really Rick, some know-it-all kid was just overconfident.
That's what I think.
He got swept away in his fishing boat...and that's about it.
Or maybe he fell into a pool of bubbling lava.
I'm sure that kind of stuff would attract lots of curious kids.
He wasn't on some magical, mythical journey.
He wasn't some holy saint on a mission.
These are all hapless boys yanked into the ocean by a wave.
That's closer to the truth than zipping around inside light.

I'd laugh if it wasn't so sad.

Rick Wallace:

(My son pushed his long hair away from his eyes, scratched his bare belly and looked at me directly, ready to take on a challenge.)

Dad, how could you possibly be so intolerant?
You always raised me to be broad-minded and accepting.
We don't have to agree with them, I understand that.
But we do have to give someone elses position respect.
Didn't you tell us that we once had a different family name?
Your grandfather felt that our name sounded too "foreign."
So he change it. Our name didn't bring about respect.

People just don't do that anymore.
And their ideas shouldn't be considered foreign either.
I took a World's Religion's Class this past year.
There are lots of faiths believing in instantaneous movement.
It happens to sacred people...maybe holy people.
In the far east, it's called "monojavah" but it has other names.
I think it means something like "as swift as thought."

Basically, they believe in instantaneous movement.
In some cultures it might occur often...or temporarily.
Some individual might reach a certain level of sanctity.
And then...away he goes.
Maybe Logan has traveled from Point A to Point B.
He just didn't move through the "in between space."
Dad, have you considered that Sam just might be right?

Detective Tony Wallace:

That's absolute foolishness, Rick. Consider the facts.

Logan Fletcher is a mere boy, barely 13 years old.

What level of holiness could he achieve in his short life?

The Fletcher kid is...or was...a good-natured, well-off boy.

He's parents have raised him to be sensitive to others.

But that doesn't mean he's some kind of a saint.

If he's so saintly, why has he put his parents through all of this?

Isn't he aware of the suffering they're enduring right now?

Wasn't he aware of their feelings before he jumped?

What kind of caring kid harnesses some "spiritual energy"?

And then apparently goes zipping around at will?

I don't see that as saintly...I see that as selfish.

Rick Wallace:

(My son responded, using the same combative nature that he likely inherited from me.)

Why do you think a kid's spiritual journey is of less value?

Who picked you to judge the truth about Logan's calling?

You seem to think that your own faith is inspired, but not his.

Why is yours apparently truthful and Sam's is gibberish?

Who died and made you king? Are you listening to me Dad?

Logan Fletcher is missing. That guy Sam gave you a reason.

Let all those other officers go searching for the facts.

You said some other guy is leading the investigation.

Let them go searching for all the concrete facts in the case.

While they do that, why don't you check out Sam's story.

If he's right, Logan has already been out and about.

He's probably left a trail of "doing good."

There could be "do good" evidence, strewn everywhere.

That's what you have to go after, Dad.

Follow the "do good" trail and that might lead you to Logan.

(My son looked at his watch, gulped down his orange juice, grabbed four pieces of toast and jumped up.)

Rick Wallace:

Oh gosh Dad. I've gotta go.

My band will be practicing in the garage in a few minutes.

Good luck with the case...keep me up to date.

Detective Tony Wallace:

(With four strides of his long, bare legs, Rick was out of the room, running pantless towards the garage. Oh Boy!)

I sat alone in the kitchen and stared out the window.

I began to feel ashamed of myself for being so close-minded.

Yet, at the same time, I was proud of my son.

As a father, I was grateful to have such an accepting boy.

His tolerance and sensitivity was a mind-opener for me.

He'll make a fine lawyer some day...or maybe a rock star!

I had to ask myself, "Just which one of us is the adult?"

(I decided to put a call through to Sam, hoping we could have another conversation. I also intended to apologize, something hard to do when you're a senior member of the force.)

(I called the office and asked Margaret, the desk attendant to put me through to Sam.)

Margaret Hamilton:

I'm so sorry, Detective Wallace, but that's impossible.

Sam resigned early this morning.

He transferred thousands of photos to your computer.

He left a note saying that they pertain to the Fletcher case.

Apparently he was here all night packing up.

However, the night crew noticed something very peculiar.

Sam left all of his own personal camera equipment.

He said, "I won't be needing this stuff, where I'm going."

His letter of resignation is right here in front of me.

You won't believe it, but he has signed the letter,

Mr. Samuctama Tuctawab

Keeper of the Old Stories...in Training.

Here is one extra thing, Detective Wallace.

Sam has printed four photos for you, along with an note.

Detective Tony Wallace:

Go ahead and read it to me, Margaret.

Margaret Hamilton:

It says: Dear Detective Wallace,

I have printed four photos taken from a surveillance camera.

The camera was located on a building across the street.

They are grainy due to the distance and enlarging process.

In the <u>first photo</u> you can see the boy standing at the window.
The <u>second photo</u> shows him in the air, beyond the window.
The <u>third one</u> is of a transport passing, and blocking our view.
The <u>final photo</u> shows a clear, well-lit view of the ground.

The boy isn't there, Detective Wallace.
Logan Fletcher...the missing boy...isn't there.
The kid never hit the ground...never.
All four photos were taken in less than a second.
Good bye Detective Wallace.
I think you are about to embark on a wondrous journey.
I hope we meet again someday. I am going home.
I am going home to Swashatuq Island.
Sincerely, Samuctama Tuctawab

Detective Tony Wallace:
(I sat alone at the kitchen saying to myself....)

What have you done Tony...what have you done?
I decided to take my son's advice.
I'd let the other officers do the technical grunt work.
And what would I do?
I'd follow the intriguing path unfolding before me.
It would be an adventure one could never have imagined.

My first step would be to find a certain neighbourhood.
I would visit the empty lot where Logan met Terrell and Martin.
This was the most recent place where Logan had appeared.
The location was retrieved from Logan's mother.
It was also the site where she always picked up the two boys.

The Lot

Detective Tony Wallace:

I drove cautiously through the blocks on the east side.
The area is only about 40 minutes from my home at the most.
Yet, it was like entering some far-off third world country.
I hadn't been there for about 30 years at least.
This was where "new police recruits" were often placed.
This was suppose to give them the experiences of real life.

But this was not real life...but rather an aberration of a dream.
Garbage and boarded buildings engulfed the landscape.
Gangs of kids darted in front of my unmarked car.
Some barely glanced as they moved about without concern.
Others paused in front of my vehicle, staring defiantly.

I could not even imagine my son Rick in such a place.
Would he still have dreams of becoming a lawyer or rock star?
Or would he be huddled with a gang on the nearby corner?
I watched as they blocked some secretive transactions...
Boys leaning in with furtive glances...always tense...on guard.
Boys always suspicious...uncertain...defensive...and angry.

Might he ever have known about all of life's possibilities?
Do glimmers of hope survive in such oppressive places?
Or do they ebb away...day by day...like a leaking barrel?

I parked the car and looked across the street.
I was astounded...maybe even stunned by what I saw.

There was no evidence of trash or abandoned cars.
No pieces of broken furniture were strewn on the pavement.
No threatening packs of kids were hanging about the lot.

It appeared as if the concrete lot had been transformed.
I gazed silently across the street at a magnificent sports park.
What I saw before me was beyond my wildest dreams.

Dozens of boys and some girls filled the entire park.
I viewed the most intense games of basketball ever played.
There were teams of sweaty boys, some shirtless, or in T shirts.
All were engaged in active, thrilling competition.

The air was full of laughter and grunts in the heat of the game.
Team members were calling out praises or giving directions.
There were no signs of cheap, plastic hoops anywhere.

Instead, there were six "top-of-the-line" basketball hoops.
Each one was attached to an adjustable pole.
All of the metal poles were anchored in concrete.
In addition, the pavement had been freshly patched.
And that's not all.
It had the recently painted lines of three basketball courts!

Benches and picnic tables were arranged along the fence.
These too were filled...some by grannies holding babies.
Fathers and mothers encouraged and cheered their boys on.
Families sat together and enjoyed sandwiches and drinks.
Everyone was caught up in the excitement of the moment.
It was truly a perfect summer morning.

And there was more.

Every boy wore a cap. Not just any cap I should add.

They were Logan's caps, perched firmly on their heads.

Some of the caps were positioned to the sides.

Others had the brims towards the front.

However most were turned around backward.

Logan Fletcher's ball cap collection wasn't missing at all.

It was there on full display, giving the boys something tangible.

They each wore a cap that reaffirmed their uniqueness.

It called out to everyone, "I am somebody."

The caps gave them an air of confidence as they dribbled.

Self-assurance poured out of them as they passed the ball.

And when a ball was dunked, the crowds erupted in cheers.

There was a joyous intensity of living a life.

I decided to get out of the car with my folder.

As I approached the boys, the games slowly came to a stop.

I guess they know a policeman when they see one.

The cheerfulness from moments ago faded away.

Everyone stood, firmly anchored to the ground.

Some of the parents left the picnic tables and approached.

The atmosphere was cold.

I was surrounded by about fifty guys, all staring in silence.

Finally, one of the boys, maybe 13 or 14 spoke up.

"We're not bothering anybody...what do ya want?"

I replied, "Maybe you can help me," and opened my folder.

"I have a photo of a boy who is missing.

Maybe he has been here before...do you know him?
His parents are desperate to find him."

I held up a photo of Logan Fletcher.
He had a broad smile, freckles, and black, messy curls.
And of course, he was holding a basketball.
In barely a second, voices from the crowd began yelling out:

That's Logan!
That's Logan, isn't it?
What's happened to Logan?
What do ya mean, he's missing?
Logan is missing?
Did somebody hurt him?
Do ya need help finding him?
Mister, what happened to him?
If he was around here, we'd know about it.
Mister, nobody here would hurt Logan.
That's for sure, Mister, that's for sure.

Stepping forward out of the crowd were two boys.
Each wore a cap with a signature of a professional player.
The autographed caps were likely worth hundreds of dollars.

Terrell:
Mister, that's Martin and I'm Terrell.
We were at his birthday party yesterday.
As you can see, he had gifts for everybody.

(The tall boy pointed to the caps on everyone's heads.)

Nobody here would have hurt Logan.

What's happened to him?

Detective Tony Wallace:

The ever increasing crowd moved closer, surrounding me in a tight cocoon of sweat, energy and muscle.)

I simply decided to tell them the truth.

"All we know is that Logan disappeared during the night.

He went out the window of his apartment, on the 19th floor."

There was an audible gasp from some of the boys.

Some fell silent while others mumbled to one another.

A few guys covered their faces, imagining the worst.

Some of their faces appeared stunned while a few cringed.

Most of them had never been in a building with 19 floors.

The thought of a friend going out the window was shocking.

The whole scenario was so difficult to even envisage.

These were tough boys, used to handling themselves.

They had developed skills to cope with life's harsh realities.

But it was obvious that they were deeply moved.

Logan's apparent fate was foreign to them.

They struggled with the thought of a friend going missing.

Worried faces reflected a disturbing depth of fear.

The gravity of such a dramatic disappearance was troubling.

Boys struggled to understand this bizarre situation.

In a few moments, questions came from the growing crowd.

An older woman holding a baby spoke up from the crowd.
She asked the question they all were afraid to ask:
"Was there any trace of Logan...well...down below?"

Detective Tony Wallace:
The police have searched throughout the night.
Yet there is no sign of Logan anywhere.
Some of the police officers are suspecting a kidnapping.
However, we are still in the early stages of the investigation.
What happened to Logan continues to be a mystery.
May I ask you folks how you got to know Logan Fletcher?

Once again, it was Terrell who responded.

Terrell:
Logan just showed up one night last year...out of nowhere.
He had that wide smile and those black curls flopping around.
Kids like him don't last long around here but he was different.
He seemed unafraid of anything.
He just wanted to play basketball...and man could he play!
His mom came and picked him up...but he returned.

Later in the week he was back...in the middle of the night!
People, some of them pretty tough, would find him here.
Logan always came to this cement lot.
We'd hear him dribbling and taking shots at the plastic hoops.
Gradually, night after night, guys would join him.
We'd turn off the TV, or end our video games.
Some of us would even climb out of bed.
Word would spread through the neighbourhood, "He's back".

Three or four times a week, Logan would just show up.
Over time, people would wait here hoping he'd come.
Teams were formed as guys arrived.

No one wanted to be left out or miss a chance to play.
Spectators began arriving, revving up the atmosphere.
A couple of the men turned on the headlights of their cars.
The lot was lit up each night and full of excitement.

And believe me Mister, Logan was no wimp.
He might be skinny and pale, but he had an edge about him.
He was fair but could be a little on the aggressive side.
That was respected around here...a sort of pushiness.
A bleeding nose from a high elbow was taken...or given.
But a hand was always extended to a fallen player.

After coming for three months, Logan showed up in a truck.
The sign on the truck said:
Mid-Town Sports Supplies—Open All Night—Free Delivery
Then the men began to unload those six basketball hoops.
Logan just grinned and waved as we all began to cheer.
Believe me, there isn't a lot to cheer about, around here.

We all gathered together to help...kids, parents, everybody.
Next off the truck came the backboards and the steel poles.
All the big guys helped to carry bags of concrete.

After the truck drove away, Logan looked at us all and said,
"Okay guys, let's get to work."
And we did.

Logan sorta stayed in the the background.
We knew what to do.
The bigger guys took over...leading and guiding.

We all helped to dig the holes and install the steel poles.
People scurried back and forth with buckets of water.
I had never mixed concrete before and it felt good.
I stirred until it was like thick soup and poured it into the hole.
Do you see that pole there, it's stuck in there nice and solid.
I did that...I did that Mister.

Food seemed to appear from nowhere...hotdogs and snacks.
Mamas and sisters and girlfriends...brought sandwiches to eat.
We guzzled down lots of cold water from buckets.
There was a bit of a party atmosphere, that's for sure.

(The crowd opened up as Terrell pointed across the lot.)

There was enough concrete to patch all the cracks.
We all worked hard with the neighbourhood united together.
No one really noticed that Logan was gone.
But, he showed up the next night with paint cans and tape.
He gave us a map or diagram full of lines and measurements.
It showed us how a basketball court should be painted.

Some of the guys took this over...everyone was so keen.
It's as if Logan lit a spark in the neighbourhood.
And it seemed to spread...
We have three basketball courts now...and we made them.
We simply got used to Logan coming and going at night.

Detective Tony Wallace:

The reality of the situation was beginning to sink in.

Logan Fletcher had built a park in the middle of a slum.

An oasis of joy was flourishing because of a 13 year old boy.

Terrell:

Mister, the surprises just kept coming.

One day a few months ago, Logan arrived out of the blue.

He huddled with the basketball teams and said:

"Guys, little kids need grass to play on and a sandbox.

Little kids need a place that's safe for bare feet."

Believe me Mister, you don't see many bare feet around here.

Just imagine what could jab us if we ever tried it.

While we were talking, another truck pulled up.

Written on the sides were the words, **Robert's Landscaping**

Logan grinned and said, "Time to use your muscles, guys."

The truck was loaded with grass and dirt.

Not just ordinary grass...and not just any old dirt.

Nope, it was grass all rolled up like strips of carpet.

I'd never seen anything like it in my whole life.

And the dirt was black and smelled real nice...kinda fresh.

And it had wiggly worms in it.

The little kids giggled as they pulled them out of the soil.

(Then Martin took over explaining what happened next.)

Martin:

All along the far side of the lot was a narrow bare patch.

It was only about100 feet long and 10 feet wide.

That was where Logan decided we'd put in a kid's play area.

Once again everyone chipped in to shovel the dirt.

Teams of people appeared to unrolled the pieces of grass.

New people...different people...watchers became doers.

A relay of water buckets moved along...really organized.

The grass was laid and soaked...all in a few minutes.

Boards were nailed together. Suddenly we had picnic tables.

And a few minutes later, there were a couple of sand boxes.

Bags of sand were lifted off the truck, dumped and spread.

Do you know what Mister?

I'm 13 years old, but I took off my shoes and socks.

For the first time in my life I felt cool grass and soft, warm sand.

Other big boys did the same thing.

We walked in our bare feet, touching the grass and sand.

It felt mighty good, Mister.

The little park was made for the kids but we used it too.

That's kinda funny, eh?

There we were, walking back and forth on cool, green grass.

Some of the guys are kinda tough, if ya know what I mean.

But there we were, all thrilled to feel grass between our toes.

Some of the boys took off their shirts.

They laid down on their backs or bellies, just to feel fresh grass.

It was our first time. It was our first time feeling grass.

I bet that's kinda hard to believe, isn't it Mister?

Mister, didn't the police find a body or anything?

I just can't imagine that Logan's missing.

He never asked for anything .

He never wanted anything from us...nothing.

Logan just gave us...well...he just gave us chances.

That's what he did...he gave us chances.

And not just us.

Have you visited the soup kitchen on the next block?

Logan was there lots of times, especially during the night shift.

This was news to me! I was completely unaware that Logan had visited other places in the neighbourhood. Before leaving to check it out, I spoke to the group that had gathered around me.)

Detective Tony Wallace:

Thank you all for being so helpful.

Logan is certainly lucky to have good friends like you.

I'm sure he would want you to keep enjoying this park.

I'll leave my card with Terrell and Martin.

Please call me if you have any more information.

I'm sure we will find Logan very soon.

As I walked away, I knew I had lied. Deep inside, I believed that no one would never see Logan Fletcher alive again. While exiting the hole in the fence, I saw a little brass plaque that simply said:

In Memory Of Grandma Fletcher
(I climbed into my car and headed to the soup kitchen on the next block...where some startling discoveries awaited me.

The Kitchen

Detective Tony Wallace:

I followed the directions that Martin and Terrell had given me.
It was just one block over, and definitely not hard to find.
Forming outside the premises, was a line of people.
Men and women stood waiting for the doors to swing open.
Some were animated, caught up in lively conversation.
Other were silent, and stony faced, staring at the ground.
An invisible wall had been erected around them.

Most surprising, were the number of children waiting for lunch.
Little ones ran in between the standing adults.
They wiggled and giggled their way around long legs.
But others, maybe 10 or 12 years old were less exuberant.
An awareness had begun to set in.
The beginnings of shame, bitterness, and anger revealed itself.
Right now, they were preparing to receive...
But soon, in the future, they would be preparing to take...

The actual kitchen looked like a former restaurant.
Likely, the owner was allowing a charity to use it.
It would be a tax right-off and then someday demolished.
On each side of the kitchen, buildings were boarded up.
Others had broken windows and unending, swirling graffiti.

However, the windows of the soup kitchen were spotless.
A crack had been neatly covered with tape.
It spread up through the centre of the left windowpane.

I parked the car up the street, hoping to be less conspicuous.
I removed my jacket and tie and left them in the car.
Just as I walked across the street, the door swung open.
A grim looking woman stepped aside as people entered.

She saw me and said, "You must be the new volunteer.
You're a little late you know...please be on time tomorrow.
Now you head over to the bread table.
There are about 200 buns that have to be sliced open.
Be careful, you're no good to me if you slice open your hand.
Some volunteers are more trouble than they're worth."
Then, away she scurried with her walker.

Believe me, I did as I was told.
I didn't have time to tell her I was a police office.
As I sliced the buns, I gazed around the room.
It was a good opportunity to examine how this place worked.
I tried to imagine Logan Fletcher being right here.
How might a young, sensitive boy react to the chaos?

And chaos it truly was.
Hungry people pulled out their metal chairs noisily.
Some giggled to themselves or murmured to no one.
Loud conversations, some friendly other hostile filled the room.
An old man with a coughing spell nearly fell on the floor.
A shoving match between two teenagers violently erupted.
Fists began to swing and noses were bloodied.
A burly security guard dragged them both to the door.
Believe me, you don't mess around in this soup kitchen.

I looked a the woman who had assigned me, "bun duty."
She was a short, stout, no-nonsense kind of woman.
Her gray hair was cut short, probably by herself.
She wore a simple house dress and a thick pair of glasses.
This woman had a tag with the name "Thelma."

She looked almost as rough as the people she was serving.
Her middle-aged face, was serious, lined, and tired.
There was no time for kindness or sweet-talk.
Her mission was to feed 200 people and that's what she did.
And she did it extremely well.

Thelma was tough because they were tough.
She had been hardened by the people she served.
An emotional callus protected her from quavering.
She had seen babies with black eyes, and men without hope.
Self-destructive boys and girls filled the chairs, day after day.

Volunteers floated around the tables as people ate.
Many were naturals, engaging in lively banter with the guests.
Others were driven by a spirit of good-will but were uneasy.
The loud clamor and many unpleasant smells, were unsettling.
These bizarre behaviours caused feelings of discomfort.
This sensitivity of the newer volunteers made them vulnerable.

My sliced bread buns were quickly swept up and devoured.
Some were eaten or used to soak in gravy, from the bowls.
Many were tucked into pockets for snacks later in the day.
Hoodies covered the heads of many angry, silent boys.
These hollow-eyed young men stashed food up their sleeves.

Some sat with friends, others brooded in moody solitude.
They gave off an aura that screamed out:
"Stay away...don't come near me..."
Thelma stirred the thick, nutritious stew and filled each bowl.
She looked no one in the eye, staring only at the waiting dish.

Eye contact meant "connection."
One could see that past connections had led to tragic hurts.
There was now only one thing that a tired Thelma could do.
She could feed them.

However, she couldn't give smiles,
They had long ago been used up over years of service.
She couldn't even touch them.
She now associated human contact with violence.
But, she could make and hand out stew.
So that's what she did. I guess we do what we can do.

If they wanted warmth and loving words of encouragement...
They wouldn't get it from her.
The deep well of kindness had long ago run dry.
Tears no longer flowed because of their suffering.
But something permeated this protective armour.
And it was equally important and of great value.
Thelma had a sense of duty...a purpose for doing good.

As the meal came to a close, some clients approached her.
They held out cups to be filled with any remaining broth.
Thelma scooped it up...and out the door they went.
But not everyone.

A group of 40, maybe 50 people of all ages stayed behind.
One fellow, maybe 20 years old, opened a cupboard door.
His ball cap was pulled low and a few teeth were missing.
Carefully, he removed a stack of several, thin boxes.
A subtle sense of excitement surrounded the group.
The boxes were distributed and pairs began to form.

I strolled over, trying to observe what the focus was.
They were about to play a board game.
A massive spread-sheet was sprawled across a table.
Some kind of a tournament had been diagrammed.

An extensive chart of lines and boxes was carefully consulted.
And then, the most intense games of checkers began.
Silence filled the room, in contrast to the loudness of the meal.
It was interrupted only by the odd cough and loud breathing.

Suddenly I felt a sharp poke on my shoulder.

Thelma:
You're not a volunteer, are you.
I can tell.
You weren't so bothered by what goes on here...not so much.
Some volunteers last only a few minutes...but not you.
You've seen this kind of thing before...the noise, the smells...
Who are you? What are you doing in my kitchen?

*(I pulled the photo of Logan from my pocket and handed it
to her. For the first time in a hour, a smile broke across her
face.)*

Detective Tony Wallace:

Thelma, my name is Tony Wallace and I am a police officer.
This young boy is missing. Do you know him?

(Immediately, the smile was gone and the few seconds of joy evaporated. The concrete-like burdens that she carried on her shoulders just became a little heavier.)

Thelma:

Logan...that's Logan...what would we all do without Logan?
Of course I know him. Everyone here knows Logan.
Several months ago, he just showed up in line, like the others.
I think it was at the midnight serving.
Some of my clients only come out at night, you know.

But he was alone...I was concerned but I didn't ask questions.
You learn not to ask questions around here.
He didn't really stand out in anyway.
He just wore jeans and a T shirt.
His curly black hair was pulled back with just an elastic.

He sat alone and ate his soup. That's just about it.
But when he was finished, he did something extraordinary.
At least it was extraordinary for around here.
He began to clean up! Not just his own table, but others too.
The boy moved quietly, collecting bowls and spoons.
He wiped down the tables and pushed in the chairs.

Officer Wallace, most of the people come here to just eat.
I wasn't used to having one of our "visitors" actually help.
At first, he said nothing to the other people.

If he was harassed or teased, he just ignored it.

If someone grabbed him, he'd yank his arm away.
That boy could give a stare that was cold and piercing.
No one messed with Logan. Bullies kept their distance.
I thought for sure that his family had hardened him.
Maybe they were even neglectful...but I didn't know.
I just wondered how he could handle himself so well.
Let's just say that this is not a cozy environment.

The next day, he skipped the meal and just began helping.
We barely talked. He just did what had to be done.
He expanded his self-appointed chores with every visit.
He peeled potatoes, chopped carrots, and scrubbed pots.
Somehow, he gravitated to the jobs that needed doing most.
He would look at me and I'd simply nod and try to smile.
He did the same. He'd just nod and a smile...and do the job.

One day, I could hear loud whistling, over all this clamour.
Yet I couldn't tell where it was coming from.
Slowly the arguments and loud chatter, began to die down.
Crying babies and noisy children settled down as well.
People began to quiet themselves and listen to the whistling.
Gradually, a wave of silence spread across the room.
Everyone was listening to the most joyful whistling imaginable.
It was some kind of classical music. It was beautiful.

Then the door to the washroom swung open.
Out stepped Logan, with a mop, a pail and rags in his hands.
He had been whistling while scrubbing the toilets.

Are you listening to me Detective Wallace?
That boy, just a wisp of a thing, had been scrubbing toilets!

Now believe me, those toilets are not like yours at home.
People here are far from careful, and are often sick in there.
Things are left in there that I can't even begin to describe.
What I'm trying to say is that they are filthy...absolutely filthy.
Just walking in there can turn the stomachs of our volunteers.
It is the least desirable job. Yet there he was...and whistling!

He looked up, surprised by the room of silent faces.
He grinned with embarrassment and said,
 "I guess I was a little loud. It echos in there.
I got a little carried away."

Then he put down his mop and walked out the door.
He was back the next night. I saw him outside up on a box.
That boy was cleaning the windows which was no easy feat.
I looked at him and he just nodded and smiled...that's all.
But really that wasn't all.

Over the next several days, things began to change in here.
Now there was no great transformation...let's be clear.
But some of the guys started helping out.
The young lad set an example and others followed.
See those guys scraping the plates and washing up?
Those are my clients...and so are the men doing the dishes.
I guess they thought, "I can at least do what that kid can do."

It's never easy here, but at least it's not as hard.

After a meal one night, Logan had a surprise.

He opened a bag and took out a flat box.

He placed it on a table and opened it.

Carefully, he began to set up a game of checkers.

And then, he waited.

Within a minute, an old man sat down, and the game began.

Reds jumped blacks and blacks jumped reds.

Checker pieces became marauding kings across the board.

A crowd began to gather, encircling the players.

A quietness settled over them, captivated by it all.

More spectators approached to view the competition.

When someone spoke, Logan simply raised his open hand.

A hush embraced the entire group surrounding the game.

A rule had been established. If you watch...you don't talk.

Who the winner was, I don't know.

But Logan stood and shook hands with his opponent.

That simple act set a pattern for behaviour.

People of all ages lined up to be the next ones to play.

They sat. They played. The crowds were hushed.

The players won or lost. They shook hands...and on it went.

Each day, Logan brought a few more games.

There are now 25 games of checkers being played.

That means 50 people are focused, calm and settled.

As you can see on the chart, he was planning a tournament.

He even brought in a trophy for the winner.

I have it put away in the cupboard.

(Thelma led me to a locked room at the back of the kitchen. The shelves were piled high with stocks of groceries. On a lower shelf was a trophy of a muscular boy, ready to dive into a pool.

It had been Logan's.

It seems he had won it in a swimming competition.

Nobody here will mind having a gold diver on their trophy.

As you can see, he pulled off his own name and the event.

It didn't seem to bother him at all.

Some of the guys have been making their own games.

They wanted to practice on their own board, away from here.

They've coloured in pieces of cardboard with squares.

Cardboard circles have been traces and cut.

Then they were coloured with crayons to make the pieces.

A few of the better artists have been selling their games.

I've heard that some of the folks are playing at home.

And it was Logan who started all of this.

That pale, slight boy who walked in here as if it was home.

So you say that Logan is missing...what happened to him?

(Thelma spoke just a little too loudly. Players who had been intently focused on their games, abandoned them and approached me calling out, "What's happened to Logan? Where's Logan?"

(As the 50 or so people stood around me, obviously agitated, I noticed that each one was wearing a sports shirt or jersey of a hockey team or basketball team. They were all wearing Logan's shirts!

Logos of sports teams splashed across the fronts of their jerseys. One little elderly man saw me looking at the shirts and spoke up:

Clifford:

My name is Clifford...Clifford Walkinnon.

Logan gave us these shirts, but we had to earn them.

First we had to play at least three games of checkers.

Then we became part of the official checkers club.

Do you know how it feels to be part of an official club?

We feel special...and I haven't felt special for a very long time.

Sometimes people will ask to buy my shirt right off my back.

But I say "No thanks, not in a million years.

I'm a member of Thelma's Kitchen Checker's Club."

What's happened to Logan?

(The other members of the club gathered close and hung onto every word.)

Detective Tony Wallace:

Well, we aren't exactly sure.

He went missing from his bedroom last night.

He lives on the 19th floor of an apartment building .

The only evidence we have is truly mysterious.

His bedroom window was wide open...on the 19th floor.

However, no clues were found on the ground below.

Even a search of the roof produced nothing.

Please let me know if you hear anything that might be helpful.

I'll leave my card with Thelma.

I see that some of you are walking towards the door.

Please don't do that.

I've never met Logan although I feel as if I have.

I think he would want you to continue playing checkers.

You can honour him by playing the very best that you can.

He's made a tournament schedule with all sorts of play-offs.

Please continue to play your checker games.

(For the first time, I seem to have gotten swept up in the spirit of Logan. What right did I have to speak on behalf of this boy? Yet I could see how this lad had given these men of all ages, a sense of purpose...a goal that was achievable. For the most part, they returned to their games.

For some, the stress of hearing about the missing boy caused them to rock back and forth...other mumbled or twitched. A few began to scratch at open sores. But there were those guys who directed the stress into the game. The sound of checkers jumping each other returned and a sense of relief settled over the room.

Detective Tony Wallace:

I guess that Logan Fletcher gave them something valuable:

Friendship, structure, and competition, all rolled into a game!

Thelma:

That's not all he gave us. Come with me.

(I followed Thelma once again into the cupboard at the back of the kitchen. It was about the size of a small bedroom.)

Thelma:

Do you see all those groceries? Logan brought them here.

I rely on donations to keep my kitchen open.

I don't get any help from government organizations. Nope!

I just "go it alone". That way, I can do what I want.
Sometimes, there isn't much to put in the stew.
It can be pretty watery, mostly broth, that's for sure.

The night after cleaning the toilets, he showed up in a truck.
And this is what he brought us. That lad brought us groceries.
That young boy with all those curls tied back...is feeding us.

From the floor to the ceiling, were shelves filled with cans of vegetables and fruits of every kind. Huge bags of potatoes were stacked high, along with numerous packages of pasta. Large jars of various jams and sauces loaded many of the shelves. Thelma opened the two old freezers and they too were well stocked with numerous cuts of meats and loaves of bread.

Thelma:
And there's more...lots more.
Logan saw me hobbling around with an old cane.
The next night, he shows up with a walker.
A walker of all things! It's like getting a pair of new legs.

I don't smile too often, Mr. Wallace. This is a harsh place.
But there was another reason. My teeth were in bad shape.
Before I got security here, I tried to stop the fights myself.
One night, I got in the middle of some swinging fists.
I had my four front teeth knocked out.
So what does Logan do? He pays for new teeth!

That little kid even provided dog food for the clients' pets.
If the people are hungry, just imagine their dogs!
There's enough dog food here for over a month.

I also have a shelf of underwear and sock...piles of them.

Some even have superheroes on them.

I know they are superheroes because I can see them.

Logan paid for my glasses.

Logan only asked for one thing.

He asked if I'd put this little sign on the door.

I looked at the small sign, handwritten in the strong, bold, script of a confident, young boy:

In Memory Of Grandma Fletcher

*(As I approached my car, I decided to check my messages from the office. **Fletcher boy sighted...call in....**was the message that lit up my screen.) I headed to the station immediately.*

The Beach

Detective Tony Wallace:
After arriving at the station, I went directly to see McKenzie.
Gathered with Officer McKenzie, was the rest of the team.
Sam Tucken was noticeably missing.
We updated each other on our particular findings.
The others continued to focus upon forensic evidence.

My report resulted in stunned silence.
I reported that a pattern had already been established.
Somehow, Logan was exiting his window regularly.
He was often "appearing" in troubled places across the city.
I was able to find objects from his room that were missing.
Some of the items that he had purchased were traceable.
Officer McKenzie interrupted my presentation.

Officer McKenzie:
Get ready for this.
It appears we have had a sighting of Logan Fletcher.

Detective Tony Wallace:
In my mind, I'm thinking...at Thelma's...at the lot?
However, I was wrong...very, very wrong.
We were stunned by his announcement.

Officer McKenzie:
Vancouver. Logan Fletcher has been seen in Vancouver.

Detective Tony Wallace:

The team looked at one another, totally bewildered.

Everyone was trying to calculate the time and distance.

In a second, they had all concluded that this was impossible.

Officer McKenzie:

I know what you're thinking.

How could the Fletcher boy travel 5000 kilometres overnight?

Even a direct plane flight couldn't get him there so quickly.

But we have to take a look at the evidence sent to us.

I sent out pictures of Logan to every police detachment.

I also faxed the list of missing articles from his room.

This video was received this morning from the west coast.

I'll play it for you.

Officer Dumarche:

Good morning.

One of our officers was making a nightly patrol of the beach.

We have a lot of people sleeping on the beach here.

Sometimes they are runaways, or the homeless.

Occasionally, there might be some noisy guys partying.

If everyone is not too disruptive, we leave them alone.

Life is already hard enough for them.

They don't need harassment from us.

I'll let Officer Laramer explain what happened.

Officer Laramer:

Hello.

I was on the night shift, patrolling the beach.

It was a fairly quiet night with several tents set up on the sand.
Most were filthy, having been retrieved from dumpsters.
They were crammed with snoring guys from across the city.
...All except one.

There was one tent that stood out.
It was in excellent shape and very high end.
This tent matched the description of the missing boy's tent.
I could see that it was set up with the skills of a true camper.
A tarp had been erected over it to deflect rain.
Gullies were dug around each side to carry any water away.
It was angled upwards to slightly raise the occupant's head.

I approached the tent that was so nicely nestled in the sand.
I opened the flap, hoping to see a 13 year old boy.
I desperately wanted it to be the missing curly-haired boy.

But it wasn't.

The sleeping bag matched the description exactly.
But not its occupant.
I shone my flashlight inside the tent and saw Xaviour.
He is a homeless man who is a regular on the beach.
Attempts to have him move into a shelter always fail.

It seems that Xaviour always drifts back to the beach.
I don't think I had ever seen him so contented...truly happy.
However, he was also confused and thought I was the kid.
This is what he said to me.

Xaviour:

Is that you boy? Is that the boy with the curly black hair?
Let me try to recall your name. Oh I remember now.
It's Logan. That's who you must be.
You are the boy who appeared on the beach.
You aren't one of the regulars but you acted like one.
You just seemed to know your way around...with no fear.

Let me tell you something, Logan.
I've never had such a cozy, little house all to myself.
At first I thought this might be heaven...all snugly and warm.
But apparently not. This isn't heaven after all.
It's a warm tent on the beach.
There is something I want to tell you, Logan, the boy with curls.
My heart is full. Are you listening to me?
My heart is full.

Why did you give me a little house, Logan?
Why did you tuck an old man into a warm sleeping bag?
I know I smell bad, Logan...I know.
But you tucked me in with gentleness and a smile.
You just smiled and pushed all of that hair out of your face.

Officer Laramer:

I finally told him I wasn't Logan.
The glow on his face evaporated.
He realized who I was and fell back on his pillow.
I handed him a sandwich from my mid-night lunch.
He took it but said nothing more.
Any questioning was only met with silence.

In the morning, our investigation team checked the area.
Photos and castings of footprints in the sand were taken.
Fingerprints from the tent poles were also gathered.
From the information you sent to us, there is a match.
Logan Fletcher was here.

Xaviour sat staring out at the ocean.
As we moved around him, he spoke up one last time.

Xaviour:
I noticed the boy...Logan...had no shoes.
So, I gave him a pair of mine.
I had two pair. Who needs two pairs of shoes, right?
One day, they just washed ashore, tied together.
They were clean, that's for sure, and probably fell off a boat.
But they were splattered with red paint.
He slipped them on and said with a smile:

> "Thank you Xaviour.
> Where I'm going, I'll sure be needing them."

Here's what I want to know:
How did he know my name?
How did that boy...a kid whom I've never met before....
How did he know my name?

Just tell me that.

Officer Laramar:
There have been no further sightings of the boy, Officers.
This is just as baffling for us, as it must be to all of you.

We have come to this conclusion.

Logan Fletcher is coming and going at will.

This does not appear to be a child abduction case.

I'll send along a copy of our investigation so far.

We'll continues to keep this case open.

However, you may wish to consider Logan as a run-away.

His case will be transferred to our Children Services Dept.

How this boy is getting around, only heaven knows.

Detective Tony Wallace:

The entire room of police officers sat in bewildered silence.

These professional investigators were used to logic and facts.

They were baffled by this bizarre situation.

After several seconds, the room erupted into wild outbursts:

How could this be?

This is absolutely ridiculous!

Do you expect us to believe that?

How did the kid get across an entire continent?

It's impossible...completely impossible.

Their procedures must be faulty or inaccurate.

And so it went.

A Narrow Tunnel

Detective Tony Wallace:

After dinner, my son Rick was lying on the couch.
He yawned, still weary after a late night gig with his band.
We both decided to wind down by watching TV.
His long legs extended down the couch and over my lap.
My little snooze was soon interrupted by Rick's outburst.
"Dad, you've gotta watch this!" he said as he poked me.

News Reporter:

The recent earthquake in Afghanistan continues to rumble.
The damage to buildings and the loss of life are devastating.
Ancient buildings from long-past civilizations have toppled.
Newer buildings are cracked and shaking in the aftershocks.

Centuries-old cobble roads have buckled high into the air.
Other have heaved and shifted, leaving massive holes.
Parts of this war-torn country have been literally swallowed up.
If you look behind me, you can see the depth of this tragedy.
Huge blocks of concrete are strewn everywhere.
Sections of the city are now completely impassable.
Re-occurring tremors spread fear among the survivors.

Bodies are strewn about as dog packs do the unthinkable.
And yet, the cries of the trapped are bringing forth the brave.
A small group of men have gathered to attempt a rescue.
The tiny whimper of a child has called these men to act.
Beneath the tons of rock, we can all hear a little baby crying.

These young men now seem galvanized to act.
The earthquake has thrust upon them a sense of purpose.
Their frustration is now redirected. One man is the father.
As you can see, they are removing the rocks and boulders.
Team-work and sweat have exposed a small hollow.
It is likely here, that the little child, maybe a baby, is trapped.

Unfortunately, these men are all too large to enter the tunnel.
Any attempt to widen the opening, is destabilizing it.
Further tremors are making this entire area dangerous.
I fear that it is unsafe to broadcast from this present position.
Tragically, we must leave the whimpering child to its fate.

Folks, something very dramatic is taking place in front of us all.
A young boy, maybe 12 or 13 years old has stepped forward.
It seems as if he just emerged out of the haze of dust.
He approaches one of the men who is sobbing.
It is likely that this is the baby's father...they exchange words.

The boy is slight in stature, wearing jeans and a simple T shirt.
He has long, black, curly hair tied back with a string I think.
He has a pair of running shoes with splotches of red on them.
I'm unsure if it is blood or possibly a paint stain.
The boy appears to be doing the unthinkable.
He is walking towards the high, trembling mound of rock.
He is lying down on his stomach as the ground rattles.

Folks, this young boy is entering the narrow tunnel.
He is making an effort to rescue the tiny, helpless baby.
It seems as if his body is the perfect size to enter this hole.

Oh no. The earth is trembling again. The rocks are shifting.
We can hear loud cracking noises coming from the debris.
It appears as if the entire mound of rocks has collapsed.
People are screaming with the horror of what has happened.
The air is thick with dust making it impossible to see.

Friends, I don't believe it. I can see through the lifting haze.
I see two running shoes with red markings emerging...
They are poking through a small opening in the rocks.
It's the boy moving backwards on his stomach.
I see his legs as he slides his body out through the opening.

He is carrying something in his arms. Oh my! Oh my!
It's a baby. He has actually rescued the tiny baby!
The baby must be healthy because we can hear it screaming.
Those are the screams of life, my friends.
As you can see, he is handing the baby to the sobbing father.
I'll send my translator over to listen in to the conversation.

The translator is saying that the father is asking the boy...
He is asking the boy who rescued his little girl, to name her.
It is a great honour to be asked to name a child.
The boy is saying, "Thelma. I think that's a good name.
Yep, I think that her name should be Thelma."

Well friends, I bet this is the only baby with that name...
In all of Afghanistan.
Oh my, the boy seems to have slipped away into the haze.
I would liked to have interviewed him but it's too late.
Folks, today you have witnessed a miracle, a true miracle.

Inspector Tony Wallace:

(*I could feel the perspiration pouring down my face. I turned to my son and said:*

Rick...that kid is Logan Fletcher.
That's the boy who went out the window.

Rick Wallace:
Are you sure Dad? If you are, then you've got to tell your boss.
Maybe it's time to share the conversation you had earlier.
You know the one I mean...with that photographer guy.
You've got to let them know that this kid is on the move.
And he has some special ability to travel great distances.

Inspector Tony Wallace:
Well, I'll give it a try but the team isn't very open-minded.
They are logical, fact-based investigators.
I think that they won't be too receptive to the concept.
The idea of a kid zipping around the world is beyond them.
And frankly, I'm still struggling with it.

Anyway Rick, I'll give it a try in the morning.
Wish me luck.
I'm going to need it.

A New Language

Inspector Tony Wallace:

I was fired.

Well that's not completely accurate.

I was taken off the case and relieved of my duties.

I was told to stay home and await my retirement.

For the next month, I would have no responsibilities.

All of my police investigations were terminated.

That's what happens when you go too far.

I simply said, "This boy can move across space instantly."

And I was gone.

For the next several weeks, I gardened with gusto.

I cooked great meals for Rick and washed the car...often.

But my mind continued to linger with the boy who jumped.

Where was Logan Fletcher?

Newspaper stories began to fade and interest declined.

He became one more of the missing who fade from memory.

One morning the phone rang, something that was rare now.

I was preparing to take our dog Chunker for a walk.

Since my retirement, Chunker and I had walked miles.

He seemed happy that we just might be delayed.

All of this walking for Chunker was less than embraced.

He wasn't called Chunker for nothing.

Maryam:

Hello, Mr. Wallace? My name is Maryam.

You don't know me but it's important that I speak to you.
It's about the Fletcher boy...Logan Fletcher.

Tony Wallace:
I'm sorry Ma'am..but I'm no longer with the case.
You should get in touch with Police Department.

Maryam:
I have Mr. Wallace but they won't listen to me.
They think that I'm crazy...hysterical...even superstitious.
The woman who answers the phone must have been listening.
It was she who gave me your number. Please don't hang up.

Tony Wallace:
All right...what do you want to tell me?

Maryam:
I know about the Fletcher boy...I know where he's been.
However the first sighting was seven years ago in a park.
It's not far from here.
My son Ehsan was playing in the sandbox, all alone.
We were new to this country...making friends was not easy.

Our clothes were different and our language skills were poor.
My family spoke a language called Farsi.
We were from Persia which is now call Iran.
Ehsan was only six years old but had no friends.
When we would arrive at the park, people moved away.
Parents would call their children out of the sandbox.

One day, I was preparing our lunch on a picnic table.
As usual, Ehson was playing alone with his bucket in the sand.
All at once, I could hear giggling, the most wonderful giggling.
A little boy had joined Ehson in the sandbox.
He said his name was Logan Fletcher and he was six years old.
He had curly black hair, a few freckles, and the widest grin.
For the next half an hour, they played like long-lost-friends.
The boy wore a sweater with a bear cub on it.

It was a joy to watch them as they made roads and bridges.
Towers were built and smashed with laughter and glee.
It was truly enchanting to watch them.
I was moved to tears by my son's happiness.

But soon my joy turned to shock and then disbelief.
Logan began to talk to my son...in Farsi!
It is not an easy language to master, Mr. Wallace.
Yet, here was a wee little boy speaking my son's language.
Not only that, but it was in the dialect of my own province!

Then a woman, Logan's mother, showed up.
She was overjoyed at finding her son.
She picked him up and swept him away from us.
And then he was gone.

Tony Wallace:
But you said that you've seen him many times.

Maryam:
Well, I didn't actually see him, but I know where he's been.

Two years ago, we were told that Ehsan was ill.
My son had inoperable brain cancer, Mr. Wallace.
The doctors told us that he had about 12-15 months to live.
I have seen great tragedies in my life...wars and famines.
But there is no suffering that compares to the loss of a child.
I spent day after day staying with him in the hospital.
I knew that we were now on "borrowed time."

His body, so thin and lifeless, was attached to tubes.
Machines recorded the various declining rhythms.
Gone was the body of a lean, muscular soccer player.
Gone was a boy filled with vigor on the brink of manhood.
Everyday, his energy seemed to ebb more and more away.

One morning, I arrived to find a little flicker of light in his eyes.
The nurse said, "Your son enjoyed his midnight visitor.
He arrived at about midnight and stayed until 4 a.m.
They certainly had a lively conversation.
We made allowances for his visit. It's good to be flexible."

Mr. Wallace, the only sounds Ehsan could make were moans.
Medication for the pain could only do so much.
With every visit, my heart would break.
But on that one morning, there was a sparkle in his eyes.
I checked the admission book and there it simply said:
Ehsan's Sandbox Friend.

I tried to stay late the next night to meet him.
It seemed that he would delay his appearances if I was there.
So, I let the visits unfold without interference.

Every night for many months, Logan visited my boy.

That is, until three days ago when my Ehsan passed away.

The last thing he said to me in a tiny, whispering voice was this:

Don't worry Mama. Don't you worry one little bit.

Logan has taught me the language of the angels.

When we journey through heaven there are still challenges.

We have to learn a special "angel language" along the way.

It will help us navigate the twists and turns up ahead.

But I know the language of the angels already, Mama.

I'll be just like a little puppy running to his Master.

My name will be called and away I'll go.

That's what Logan said.

"I'll be just like a little puppy running to his Master.

My name will be called and away I'll go."

Mr. Wallace, are you still there?

Mr. Wallace? Mr. Wallace?

(I have to admit that I was having difficulty maintaining my composure.)

It's important that you find Logan Fletcher, Mr. Wallace.

The nurse on duty over the past few weeks was concerned.

She said Logan still had a wide smile but he may be ill.

Logan's complexion seemed gray and his lips were cracked.

He had scrape marks on his elbows and limped slightly.

I think that Logan Fletcher is giving everything he's got.

The boy who knows the words of angels must go home.

It's time for him to stop and go home.

A Needle And Thread

Tony Wallace:

Months had passed since Logan Fletcher went missing.
Where was the boy who had jumped out the window?
He was nowhere...and everywhere.
I walked with Chunker to the park and rested on the bench.
He jumped onto my lap and snoozed as I read the paper.

When I was working, I would often see men doing just this.
They would sometimes gather at the park together....
Groups of old men engaging in animated conversation.
Somehow, they still pretended that their ideas counted.
In reality, they had become secondary characters in life.

Some benches now hold solitary figures, who simply stare.
Are they oblivious to the world around them?
Do they notice the teenagers walking hand in hand?
Do they hear their giggling conversations?
Are they aware of the odd hairstyles or the unique fashions?

Or...in their fixed gazes, are they mining past memories?
Are they thinking of the wife they should have forgiven?
Do they linger on thoughts of the child that died so tragically?
Do they wonder about a son or daughter who never calls?
Or maybe they called...but it's forgotten in the fog of time.
As I sat with Chunker, I realized I had joined this group.
But maybe not.

And now I was part of the crossword puzzle club.

I was one of those who read every detail in the obituaries.

I hadn't yet fed the pigeons although I had thought of it.

As I folded the paper, the word **Mystery** caught my eye.

That's all it took to get the attention of an old police officer.

I usually skipped this column. It was often hilarious and silly.

The topics were about Alien Abductions and Bigfoot Sightings.

But not this time.

The heading said: **Mystery Visitor Still Not Found.**

I read it carefully:

Last Thursday morning, a local farmer had a tragic accident.

Walter Stone, a spry 76 years old, will tell us all about it:

"Well I was out on my tractor turning the soil ya know.

I was in the north field about 2 miles from the farmhouse.

It was about 11:30 in the morning and I was getting hungry."

"My grandson, Nipper usually comes along at 12:00 noon.

I let him drive the pick-up truck.

He's just 12 years old but he's big for his age.

Plus it's nobody's business what I do on my own property.

I treat him like a man because he acts like one."

"He kinda shy though...doesn't mix with people too well.

I'm hoping he'll take over the farm someday.

He brings my lunch and we have a big spread together.

Well I did something foolish, there's no doubt about it.

A rock was stuck in the blade, causing it to jam up."

"And there I go, sticking my arm in, to loosen it.
I stuck it in right up to the elbow."

"Well low and behold, that blade starts a-spinin'.
It slices my arm open so deep you could see my bone.
There was blood squirting all over everywhere.
The gash was about eight inches long.
I was beginning to feel woozy and began to pass out.
I felt bad that Nipper would likely find his old Grandpa dead."

"I had so much to tell him.
I was hiding a thousand dollars from his Granny in the barn.
It was in an old coffee cup on a shelf above the door.
You know, important stuff like that.
The blood was oozing out all over the place.
It was just like those wells that shoot out oil down in Texas.
It was a regular fountain of blood and gore, that's for sure."

"Then, standing right beside me were two skinny legs.
Each leg was stuck into a shoe all splatter red.
I thought, 'My gosh, I've covered those shoes with blood!'

"It wasn't Nipper.
My grandson Nipper is 210 pounds. He's a big boy for 12.
And this kid was a skinny guy...but I'm guessing the same age.
Nope it definitely wasn't my Nipper.
it was a boy I'd never seen before.
He took his hand and touched my cheek."

"He felt my whiskers and said, 'Don't you worry Walter.
Don't you worry one bit. Nipper will be here soon."

"Then this mystery boy opens up his backpack and says,
'I've got my Boys Scout first aid kit with me.'
He takes out a little box and removes a needle and thread.
Then he just goes about sewing me up. He's a regular expert.
I did a bit of screaming but at least the bleeding stopped.
I could hear Nipper heading this way and said to the boy,
'How can I ever repay you lad? You saved my life.'"

"He started walking away, but paused a moment and said,
'Your son and his wife are going to have a baby boy soon.
Maybe you could call him Ehsan. Could you do that?'
And then he just kept walking across the field."

"Well I yelled after him, 'You're darn right I can do that.
You're darn right I can call him Ehsan.'
They were going to call him Blake but I put an end to that.
The little boy was born last night and his name is Ehsan Stone.
He might be the only kid called Ehsan Stone on the Prairie."

"Now Mr. Reporter, listen to me good. Are you listening?
That mystery boy is a real hero.
He saved my life by sewing me up and stopping the bleeding.
I don't know his name but his first aid kit had the initials: L.F.
You have to find him because he should get a reward.
That boy with the initials L.F. needs a trophy or medal."

"Now I was just a-wonderin...how did he know my name?
How did he know about Nipper coming with my lunch?
And how did he know about my boy Cal having a baby?
The mystery kid even knew it was going to be a boy!"

"And ya gotta find him for another reason.
I think he's sick. He's scraped up quite a bit.
There are cuts and sores on his arms and his lips are cracked.
His jeans are torn at the knees...ripped right open in fact.
I think his knees might even be bleeding..."

"He's got a bad limp too. I think the boy's in pain....bad pain.
So ya better find him soon Mr. Reporter.
He probably needs to sleep for a few days.
Then he should have a big meal of roast beef and gravy.
Then throw in a heapin' pile of mashed potatoes and carrots.
Soon he'd be lookin' healthy like my grandson Nipper."

"It seems as if he just had to keep going somewhere.
Mr. Reporter, I don't know were he's come from, that's for sure.
And I don't know where that heroic boy is going.
But here's something I do know...it's time for him to stop."

"Find that boy real soon.
There must be kids missing with the initials L.F.
That's a good place to start, Mr. Reporter.
Now you just come inside and my Ethel will fatten you up.
Don't reporters ever eat?"

Released

Tony Wallace:

I was stunned by the news but felt unable to act.

All the evidence showed that Logan Fletcher was in decline.

Every good deed was pulling something from him.

His soulful work was somehow causing his very soul to bleed.

His traveling and his many acts of kindness were taking it's toll.

According to those who saw him, Logan was very sick.

I sipped on my morning coffee and gazed out the window.

I could hear Rick in the shower upstairs.

He was getting ready for his admission test to study law.

He had decided to shave and dress a bit for the exam.

"Maybe freshening up might help with the right mindset."

That's what he had told me, anyway.

Becoming a rock star was now plan B.

Becoming a lawyer was now plan A.

I walked Rick to the car, gave him my keys, and hugged him.

He headed off (driving a little too fast) and into his future.

The phone was ringing when I returned to the kitchen.

"Hello" I said, expecting it to be a charity of some sort.

Officer McKenzie:

Hi Tony. This is McKenzie from the station.

I hope you're enjoying your retirement. We all miss you.

That's for sure. It isn't the same around here without you.

(Those of us who are retired have all heard that before!)

Tony Wallace:

Thanks. Why are you calling? Did I leave anything behind
when you sent me onto an early retirement?

Officer McKenzie:

Listen Tony. I'm sorry about that. I really am.

There was a lot of pressure to solve that Fletcher case.

Some of your input at the time seemed to move us "off-track".

However, I now wish we had listened to you more carefully.

We all could have been more tolerant of your comments.

The situation here is pretty desperate Tony.

Tony Wallace:

What do you mean?

Officer McKenzie:

There have been no breaks in the case in months.

Our investigation into a likely kidnapping has gone nowhere.

The people you interviewed have all been checked out.

Regretfully, we have isolated them by our suspicions.

We also ignored reports of distant sightings of Logan Fletcher.

We deemed it impossible for a boy to travel vast distances.

How could he be see in another country or even continent?

We entered this investigation "closed minded."

His parents are truly in a tragic state.

We thought that they would be constantly pressuring us.

We were expecting daily calls and demands for results.

This only happened during the first 10 days or so.
I visited them yesterday and they are in a sorry situation.
The Fletchers have not yet returned to work.
Since the lad went missing, they have barely left the building.
They have both slipped into some kind of depression.

They simply stared at me and made no effort to talk.
They seem to be just going through the motions of living.
They are both broken people...very broken people.
They appear unkempt and have a distant, unresponsive gaze.
Their have both abandoned all hope...almost.

The window in the boy's room is still wide open.
The idea that we might find him is no longer even considered.
They have absolutely no faith in the police.
However, there is a lingering hope that he might return...
Yet, it is obvious they think it will be through the window.
He'll re-enter the window that is 19 stories above the ground.
I still can't wrap my mind around this.

Tony Wallace:
What do you want from me?

Officer McKenzie:
I'd like you to come into the office Tony.
We have a grainy surveillance video I'd like you to see.
Your contribution would be much appreciated, Tony.

*(I knew that McKenzie was going out on a limb inviting me.
There would be team members opposing my visit.)*

(My ideas were still "mumbo-jumbo to them.
We would probably be meeting together in his office.)

Tony Wallace:

All right...but you'll have to send someone to pick me up.
My boy has my car.

(I was in his office within the hour.)

Officer McKenzie:

Tony, I was sent some surveillance video from Brockton Inlet.
As you may know, it's a town on the west coast by the ocean.
I was hoping that you would help me understand what I see.
What goes on is pretty bizarre.

If you look carefully at the screen, Tony.
You can see a figure walking beside a pool.
The quality of the video is poor...very grainy and blurred.
This is someone at night, walking inside the Dolphin Complex.
I think it's called "Come Swim With Dolphins."

He is not authorized to be there.
We don't know how he gained access to the premises.
It is heavily protected with high, electrical fencing and alarms.

There's a lot of controversy about this type of a setup.
Many animal rescue groups oppose the keeping of dolphins.
They view it as cruel and inhumane entertainment.
The demand for their release has been growing.
They object to keeping dolphins in concrete pools for years.

These are creatures capable of swimming vast distances.
They can navigate over a hundred miles in a day.

All sorts of attempts have been made to release them.
But this Complex brings millions of dollars into the community.
Governments are slow to act and it is obvious why.
The dolphin show provides local revenue and employment.
Hotels and restaurants are full for three seasons.
Tourists pour into the region for the dolphin shows.

Occasionally, an activist group will try to enter the complex.
Their intention is to free the dolphins by opening the gate.
This underwater gate separates the tank from the ocean.
It's constructed of steel bars with a free flow of water.
The ocean flows in and out of the tank through the gate.

The security systems have been very efficient over the years.
There's a combination pad with a secret code.
The pad is attached to the actual gate...underwater.
Someone attempting to open the gate must have two things:
First, they would require knowledge of the electronic code.
Secondly, they would require some kind of scuba gear.
One simply could not hold one's breath long enough.

Now...look carefully and tell me what you see, Tony.

Tony Wallace:
Well, the video is definitely grainy, that's for sure.
But I see a figure, a boy, walking along the edge of a pool.
He's extending his hand into the pool.

I assume he's touching the dolphins in the water.

And then there is a high pitched squeaking.

I guess the dolphins are making that noise. Am I right?

Officer McKenzie:

No Tony, you're wrong.

It's not the dolphins making the noise.

It's the boy. The boy, according to our experts, is doing it.

He is initiating communication with the dolphins!

Listen further and you will hear them reply.

Tony Wallace:

My gosh, I can hear them.

There seems to be a wild exchange between them.

Language is pouring out of the boy and the dolphins.

It's fascinating to watch...it's so exciting to hear everything.

Officer McKenzie:

Look carefully Tony, at what the boy is wearing.

Tony Wallace:

Let me see. He seems to be wearing just a T shirt and jeans.

And a pair of running shoes. I can't believe what I'm seeing!

There's red paint splattered on the running shoes!

Is this Logan? Do you think this is Logan Fletcher?

Officer McKenzie:

The video seems to say yes and logic seems to say no.

Explain what you see happening next.

Tony Wallace:

The boy is taking off his shoes.

Now he's slipping out of his clothes down to his shorts.

He's pausing for a moment...what's he planning to do?

Wow...he's diving into the water!

I know that Logan is a champion diver. I've seen his trophies.

He's amazing to watch...almost like a dolphin himself.

He thrusts himself into the air at an amazing height.

Then he enters the water, with confidence.

It's exhilarating to watch.

What does he do in there...swim with the dolphins?

Officer McKenzie:

Don't you realize what is happening Tony?

The kid explained to the dolphins his escape plan for them.

He dove into the water, and decoded the lock system.

He's released all of the dolphins through the gate!

All of the dolphin swam into the ocean. He freed them all.

(I continued to stare at the pool, looking for the boy to emerge from the water.)

Tony Wallace:

But where's the boy? Where's Logan Fletcher?

Officer McKenzie;

Logan never emerged from the water.

It is likely that he was swept out to sea.

All the searching up and down the coast has led to nothing.

I fear that the search for Logan Fletcher is over.

(Officer McKenzie reaches down below his desk and passes me a box, the kind often used to hold police evidence. I open it up and pull out a pair of running shoes, splattered with bright, red paint. I begin to tear up. There is something about this boy's worn, tattered shoes which caused me to become emotional. They were like abandoned companions who once shared an adventure with Logan Fletcher, full of risks and danger. I hold them, with tears streaming down my face, and say to Officer McKenzie...)

Tony Wallace:

Maybe not.

There's another possibility you haven't considered.

Logan is swimming with the dolphins.

Or maybe riding them.

There's one thing I've learned about this boy...

Nothing is impossible...absolutely nothing.

We now have to figure out, just where he's going.

Where would a boy on the back of a dolphin actually go?

Sighting One

Tony Wallace:
Life as at lighthouse keeper seemed to have a dim future.
Or so it was thought...but not for Bernard Spears.
The advent of oil tankers had breathed new life into the job.
The threat of a catastrophe made Bernard's job a necessity.
He was only 27 but knowledgeable, keen, and dedicated.
The young man had the latest "teckie skills" required.

Nothing had prepared him for what was unfolding before him.
He gazed through his binoculars at the ocean coastline.
Perched high on the tower, his vision was unhindered.
It was a clear, bright, almost windless morning.
This is a transcript of a later interview he had with me.
It was not included in the original report.

Bernard Spears:
At first I thought it was my imagination.
Being here alone can make your mind play tricks on you!
I had checked incoming reports but nothing was expected.
The shipping lanes were clear and a slow day was likely.
Smugglers always avoid this area knowing its well monitored.

In the distance I could see movement.
I recognized it immediately as a pod of dolphins.
I've often seen them as they migrate in schools over the years.
These were particularly active, leaping high above the water.
I decided to go down to the rocky shore to watch them pass.

I stood firmly on a flat rock close to the ocean.
As they approached, I was aware that they could see me.
They seemed to make an effort to come even closer.
It was exhilarating to see their collective joy as they swam.

As they came closer, I noticed something unusual.
One dolphin, the last one in the pod, appeared much larger.
It is difficult for me to tell you what I saw happen next.
But I'll just come out and say it. It wasn't a big dolphin.
Passing directly in front of me was a child.
It was boy...a boy was riding on the back of a dolphin!
Do you hear me? A boy was riding on the back of a dolphin!

He wore only a simple pair of shorts...and showed no fear.
His skin was dark from the warm ocean sun that poured down.
Long wet, black curly hair stuck to his neck and back.
His legs clung tightly to the sides of the leaping animal.

His face was one of total joy.
Happiness poured out of him.

He looked into my eyes, grinning with impish delight.
His great peals of laughter sailed across the vast ocean.
I extended my hand...and he did the same.
And I touched him. I touched the dolphin rider.

Instinctively, I asked him...I couldn't help myself...I asked him,
"Who are you?"
As he rode past me, he turned his head and yelled,
"I am the boy who jumped."

Sighting Two

Parker was ten years old.
Every summer he had come to his Grandpa's ocean house.
He had been told, "This is to give your parents a rest."
What they were resting from, he wasn't quite sure.

Parker had one month of total freedom.
When he was little, he and Grandpa did things together.
They'd walk along the beach, gathering shells and driftwood.
Sometimes they would dig up clams or go fishing.

But lately Grandpa had been sleeping a lot.
Actually, Grandpa was now snoozing most of the time.
Grandpa called it "getting forty winks."
But Parker thought, "It was more like 40 million winks."

Parker didn't mind it one little bit.
Never in his life would he ever have such absolute freedom.
He would never tell his parents that he was unsupervised.
At ten years old, he was onto an amazing realization.
Parker could do absolutely anything he wanted to.

He decided that clothes were bothersome and unnecessary.
He wore only shorts.
And really they might actually have been underwear.
But who cares!
Parker ate whenever he wanted.
And...he had taken a liking to eating cold hot dogs.

He would giggle to himself whenever he said those words.

"Cold hot dogs...cold hot dogs."

He liked to take them directly from the package.

Then he would eat them while standing in front of the fridge.

No dishes were needed and there was no mess to clean up.

Parker's mother would have had a fit if she knew about this.

That's what made it so much fun.

That's what he was thinking of while eating hot dogs...

standing up...

with the fridge door open...

with no mess to clean up.

Parker also went to bed whenever he wanted to.

Sometimes he stayed up all night...that was the coolest.

He had made a trap with a box and a stick to catch mice.

He put some bait in the trap and was successful.

On the first night, he caught two little critters.

He kept them as pets and fed them....hot dogs.

"One sure is getting chubby" he thought.

Soon, Parker would have many more mice...many more.

His only "sometimes friend" was Anna...also 10 years old.

She was visiting her grandparents at the cottage up the shore.

Parker was still having a difficult time figuring girls out.

She waved at him last week from her Grandpa's boat.

Parker returned her kindness in a very unusual way.

He decided to yell "Hey there Anna Banana from Havana!"

Anna was not amused by this greeting.

The next day, she squirted him with a water pistol.
And yelled, "Go and put some pants on, Parker.
I can see your bum !"

Parker was now planning his sweet revenge.
He decided to dig a hole in the sand and bury himself.
The only thing showing on the beach would be his head.
Parker was sure that this would frightened Anna Banana.
He relished the thought of her going past in the boat....
Then screaming when she saw his head lying on the sand.
It was so much fun being a ten year old boy.

That night, Parker slept peacefully in the hammock outside.
He jumped up in the morning, gleeful about his plan.
He didn't even bother to go inside to use the bathroom.
Parker was 10 years old after all.
And Grandpa just kept sleeping on the couch.

Parker's only goal of the day was to dig a hole in the sand.
Then he simply had to climb inside it and bury himself.
And of course leave only his head exposed.
As he slipped into the hole, he laughed at how smart he was.
He could barely wait for Anna Banana to come along.

Parker could hear lots of splashing.
Something was definitely coming around the bend.
Anticipation began to build as the seconds went by.
However, passing directly in from of him wasn't Anna Banana.

It was a pod of dolphins...playful, frolicking dolphins.

And on the back of one, wild and free...was a boy.
Parker could see that he was almost a version of himself.
The kid, dressed only in shorts, flew past like a rodeo rider.
He waved one arm frantically in the air for balance.
The other arm, he extended towards Parker.
Parker tried desperately to pull himself from the sand.

Parker was skinny and fast, but was a prisoner of the sand.
Finally, he burst from the deep hole he had made for himself.
He sprinted into the water screaming against the wind,
"I want to come with you...I want to come with you!"
Parker extended his arm towards the smiling dolphin rider.

Their fingers barely touched and Parker fell backwards.
He felt as if he was knocked off his feet by a bolt of energy.
He shouted as loudly as he could to the disappearing boy,
"Who are you?"

The answer came back, carried on the wind,
"I am the boy who jumped."

"T want to jump too!" hollered Parker with near bursting lungs.
"I want to jump too!"
"Maybe some day you will," replied the boy who jumped.
"Maybe someday you will."

Parker sat in the sand, dazed by the experience.
He felt an overwhelming sense of disappointment and loss.
Yet throughout his body, his skinny little body, was a strength.
He seemed to possess a new, emerging power.

It traveled through every fiber of his being.

Parker would need this strength within seconds.

He rushed to the cottage to tell his Grandpa everything.

The torrent of words poured out of him.

But Grandpa lay silently on the couch by the window.

He hadn't moved in three days.

The boy then realized that his Grandpa hadn't been snoozing.

Parker was only ten years old.

But he was strong...very very strong...

As an adult, Parker sat on the same beach.

The cottage of his youth was now his.

Next to him was his wife, Anna.

Anna Banana had long forgiven her goofy neighbour.

They watched with pride, their twin boys out in the ocean.

Two, strong lads, windsurfing with ease and confidence.

One day, after hearing Parker tell about the boy who jumped,

Anna asked, "What if he had actually grabbed your hand?

Would you have gone with him?"

Parker stared out into the ocean and replied,

"In a second."

She touched his hand, looking out at her sons and said,

"Maybe you did jump after all."

Sighting Three

Jacob Wabinook sat on his favourite rock by the ocean.
The thick, gray fog rolled in with the waves.
His entire body was surrounded by the cool, damp mist.
He picked up a pebble and held it firmly in his hand.
Jacob extended his finger across the top and flung it.
The pebble hopped and skipped its way across the surface.
Then, vanished from sight as it entered the water.

It was here years ago, barely into manhood, he had listened.
Today, the words from his father still lingered in his mind.
"Remember Jacob, a man always takes care of his family.
I'll say it again Jacob, a man always takes care of his family.
It will be your greatest honour and greatest responsibility."
But today, he felt like a failure.

Jacob was a sculptor....and a good one.
He had learned the techniques from his father.
As a little boy, Jacob watched his father work his magic.
Jacob was in awe of his father's power.

By chipping at a rock, he made animals slowly appear.
Fish and seals....whales and birds ...emerged fresh and lifelike.
His father had told him, "They are all hiding in there.
It will be your job to someday release them from their prison."

"When you pick up a rock, you must look and listen carefully.
Is a chubby walrus grunting, 'Let me out!' ?"

"You must use your mind's eye to see him locked inside.
Then slowly, carefully, patiently...you begin to chip away.
After many hours, there he'll be...poking through the rock.
If you are very quiet, he might even talk to you.
He might say, 'Thank you for rescuing me from my prison.
I have been waiting for you to come by...for a long time.'"

His father had been his hero.
Lately, Jacob had felt that he was close to equaling his father.
Rather that being overjoyed, Jacob was experiencing a crisis.
When he looked at a rock, it no longer spoke.
There was no shortage of rocks, only a shortage of vision.

Where were the voices that used to call out to him?
Where were the whisperings of the mighty coho salmon?
Why had the roars of the powerful grizzlies gone silent?
Even the howling of the wolves had fallen quiet.

His mind's eye had gone blind.
The shape of a rock meant nothing.
No clue was forthcoming .

His sculptures had sold well in the local craft shop.
He was not one to boast, but he outsold all of the others.
There were many fine artisans in his community, that's for sure.
However, Jacob Wabinook had the best reputation.
That was...until now.

For the first time in his life, Jacob had nothing to sell.
The shelf in the store with his name on it...was now empty.

There were no leaping fish, playful otters or mangy muskoxen.
The flame of his vision was extinguished.
And this was happening just when it was needed the most.
Jacob had expenses, and the bills were piling up daily.
His wife Nina asked for nothing...their love grew year by year.

But Jacob Wabinook had 5 sons...big strapping boys.
Each one was built like a war tank and he loved them all.
It was said around town, "Jacob's boys are all good boys."
And Jacob Wabinook ran a tight ship, with rules:

You kiss you mom before going to school.
Work hard...no acting up in class.
Stop in and check up on Grandma on your way home.
Chop and pile the wood when you get home.
Do your homework...minimum one hour.
If there's no homework, you read for one hour.
Eat supper.
Play hockey on our pond.

His youngest was 8 and the oldest was 17.
They were lively, happy, rambunctious boys.
And oh how they could eat.
He had promised his dad, "A man takes care of his family,"

The boys were in need of new hockey equipment.
They had never let him down, and he couldn't let them down.
He loved sitting around the table at night talking with his boys.
Conversation was lively and laughter was frequent.
And most of all, food was plentiful. Man could his boys eat.

There had been a little extra pasta lately...and more potatoes.
The older boys were aware that something wasn't right.
However, they said nothing. This was strange territory.
Their father had always been such a strong presence.
They talked among themselves but that's as far as it went.
His sense of pride and honour would be hurt...they felt.

Jacob sat on the same rock where he used to sit as a boy.
Where had his inspiration gone? How had it ebbed away?
He was about to toss another rock but held back .
Something was approaching from the south.

The dense fog was like a thick veil.
He squinted, trying to recognized the dark, hazy form.
Suddenly, a burst of sunlight shone through the clouds.
The intense light penetrated the mist.
Directly in front of Jacob Wabinook was a wonder to behold.

He saw a boy, filled with self-assurance and smiling with glee.
Before his very eyes, he saw a young lad riding a dolphin.
The man stood, unsure if this was a dream or more.
Maybe it was a a phantom emerging from the mist.

Barely clothed, the youth had long, black, curly hair.
His skin was a copper colour, tanned by the radiant sun.
And when the boy spoken, Jacob mind re-awakened.
The boy who rode the dolphin spoke in the old language.
He knew the language of the ancestors!
Dang gwa kaay.ying?
(Are you giving up?)

In an instant, Jacob's mind shot back in time.

These were the words last spoken by his old Grandmother.

He had not heard them in over 40 years.

Tears poured down his face as he reached back in time.

Jacob immediately responded in the ancient language.

Effortlessly, he retrieved the words from his distant memory.

Gam gina tlaa dii isda gaay.ya gang ga.
(I cannot do anything right.)

The boy stared directly into Jacob's eyes, saying,

Jacob...Dang sdaagasgida ga.
(Jacob...You are great at everything.)

At that moment, the dolphin bounded forward.

High into the air it leaped. The boy grinned and waved wildly.

Other dolphins surrounded him, leading him into the mist.

Jacob, filled with awe and wonderment, called out,

"I must know ...

Are you some ancient spirit, returning to guide me?"

Through the fog came the distant voice of the dolphin rider:

"I am the boy who jumped."

Jacob hollered into the now blasting ocean wind,

"Can I jump too...can I jump too!"

The last words he ever heard from the boy were:

"You already have Jacob...you already have."

Jacob's wife, Nina, was busy skinning rabbits in the kitchen.

Friends had been dropping off food items through the week.
"Oh we just have too many..." they would say.
"These meat pies were left over..." they would claim.
"My garden is just overflowing with vegetables." they told her.

But she knew that word had spread along the shore.
It was hard to keep secrets in this close-knit community.
Everyone knew that they had fallen on hard times.

And then she heard a sound that forced her to stop.
She dropped the bloodied half-skinned animal on the floor.
Leaving it there, she poured herself a cup of tea.
Nina walked slowly over to the long 4 plank kitchen table.
She sat down, sipped on her tea, and listened.

At that very moment, her boys came in from school.
They glanced at their mother.
They skipped their usual playful rowdiness.
No one made their typical mad-dash to the fridge.
Instead, they sat in silence beside their mother...listening.

The five boys and their mother listened and began to grin.
The youngest boy "Spooky" born on Halloween, began to cry.
They were listening to the most beautiful sound in all the world.
It wasn't the songs of birds or the nearby ocean waves.

The could hear...chipping.

From their father's studio behind the house...came chipping.
They listened intently to intense chipping, filing, and grinding.

Their father was working again. His purpose was restored.

Word moved across the community like a wave of smoke.
It twirled and danced through homes, yards and docks.
The distant sound of chipping caused people to pause.
Many gave thanks that "the old Jacob" had returned.

Jacob's youngest son, Spooky headed towards the door.
He wanted to race across the yard and see his father.
But the lad was stopped be his mother.
"Not now," she said. "Let him work for a couple of hours.
There is an energy pouring through your father right now.
This would not be a good time to interrupt him."

The boys did their chores while listening to the chipping.
The filing and scraping of rock were heard through dinner.
It permeated their thoughts as they did their homework.
They were desperate to see what their father was creating.

At ten o'clock, Nina gathered up her boys.
Together, the walked down the path towards Jacob's studio.
They could barely contain their excitement.
It was dark, but the path was well lit as they journeyed along.
They were guided by the light from the workroom's window.

However, even a better guide than light...was the chipping.
It was like a magnet that pulled and embraced them.
They slowly opened the door .
Jacob, covered in dust, looked up at his family and grinned.
On the table in front of him was a large stone.

They gathered around and were awed by what they saw.
Emerging out of the rock was a boy riding on a dolphin.
Actually, the boy seemed to be exploding into freedom.

The sculpture was far from finished but it's outline was visible.
A young boy...maybe a youth...had one arm raised up high.
He was like a rodeo rider, hanging on with steely grit.
The dolphin was leaping in a high arc with the boy on top.
They were both grinning joyfully as they dove into the wind.

Jacob had caught them at the height of their jump.
It was the very moment the pair of adventurers crested....
It was the apex of an exhilarating thrust above the waves.
His sons gazed in wonder at the creation...awestruck.
They viewed their father with a deeper sense of appreciation.
And Nina could see that her husband was transformed.
He had become the man he was meant to be.

She stepped forward and pushed his hair away from his face.
Dripping perspiration had made little rivers down his cheeks.
From his glow, she knew that he had in some way changed.
Jacob had been fulfilled.

Within hours of going on sale, Jacob sold his sculpture.
"The Dolphin Rider" became known throughout the art world.
Demands for similar sculptures poured in...
Jacob was constantly creating variations of the sculpture.
Sometimes the rider looked in different directions.
Maybe the tail of the dolphin flipped in a different way.
People began to notice changes in the dolphin's expression.

Over time, Jacob began using different stone as his source.
"The Dolphin Rider" had pink, blue, and black versions.
Some even acted like prisms, reflecting colours onto walls.
Jacob and his family prospered.

Often, Jacob was asked to speak at gatherings.
Sometimes he spoke to small groups in his community.
When he spoke at galleries in town, hundreds would attend.
Everyone wanted to meet the creator of "The Dolphin Rider."

He would tell the simple story of being in despair...
And being drawn to the rock of his childhood by the ocean.
He had lingered over the guiding words of his father:
 "A man must take care of his family, Jacob."

Then Jacob would tell his audience:

"Before my very eyes, a child appeared, riding a dolphin.
He showed no fear, no hesitation, no doubt about his journey.
This lad never wavered.
And yet he was a slight boy...weak in body.
His ribs protruded from his slight frame, and his arms were thin.
His long, wet, black hair flew wild and free from side to side.
But his face radiated such joyousness.
The rolling waves and blowing winds only enhanced this joy.
I could sense he had somewhere to go....but where?"

Many in the audience saw this story as a metaphor.
"It's a parable for life," they would say..."an allegory".
"It is an imaginative way to encourage others,"they said.

But Jacob knew better. He knew exactly what he had seen.
He had seen a special child on a dramatic, thrilling journey.
A child both weak and strong...a child who dared...
All his life, Jacob, would remember the boy's departing words:
Words accompanied by joyful laughter:

"I am the boy who jumped!"

Sighting Four

The old wolf was dying.
He dragged his weary body beneath a bush by the ocean.
Infected, dripping, open sores were already attracting flies.
Mangy, knotted fur hung from the wolf's flea-infested skin.
Overhead, a vulture circled...waiting for its afternoon meal.

The wolf knew he couldn't move another single step.
Every muscle ached. Pain wracked his joints and bones.
Chewing parasites gnawed away at his internal organs.
His teeth bled or dangled from his jaw, ready to drop.

He was no longer able to hold his once proud tail high.
The fur was filthy, ragged, tangled and burr-filled.
The tail bone had snapped.
He looked pathetic and subservient as he lay on the ground.
The symbol of his strength and power was lifeless and pitiful.

He was once the leader of an active, wild, thriving pack.
With firmness and strength, he guided, controlled and led.
Those who challenged him...would live to regret it.
He had led the pack on moose hunts lasting for days.
He had mastered strategy and taught his off-spring:

Chase....harass...tire...nip...bite....tear tendons...rip throats.
And then feast...gorge....feast...gorge...chew bones...
Then move on...

He had fathered entire generations of wolves.
He had brought to the bloodline, strength and endurance.
His cunning had enabled them to survive and prosper.

Somehow, he had steered clear of humans.
He had overcome the temptation for the easy kills.
Killing cows and sheep would be effortless, but fatal.
An easy meal might end with a bullet in the head.
He had seen it all before...and he had learned.

But others had not. The old wolf had been challenged.
It was his own young and frisky grandson.
The young wolf was both powerful and handsome.
The females were already fawning over him.
They were attracted by his flowing fur and muscular body.

The old wolf had to admit that his grandson had strengths.
His stealth and stamina in the hunt were unsurpassed.
But he had a fatal flaw of leadership.
The young wolf lacked vision.
He had wanted to attack the sheep within an enclosure.
It had led to a confrontation that the old wolf would lose.

The old wolf lay broken and bloodied from the battle.
As he waited to die under the bush, he could hear the bullets.
He knew that his entire pack had likely been slaughtered.
They had been led and gone willingly towards what was easy.
No one had said, "That's not right. Where will this lead us?"
Slowly, life was slipping away from the old warrior.

Splashing sounds along the shore aroused his curiosity.
He had to gather all of his dwindling energy to open his eyes.
The old wolf had seen dolphins before....and people.
Never had he seen a child...a human...riding a dolphin.
Maybe it was a dying hallucination brought on by weakness.

The wolf thought that he was well hidden beneath the bush.
He had to be.
He did not want his last moments to be violent ones.
As an aggressor, he knew how helpless the weak could be.

A hungry bear or wolverine could sniff the aroma of pain.
The floating smell of anguish and suffering was prevalent.
His body probably reeked of approaching death.
Was he visible to the boy who rode the dolphin?

Apparently so. The old wolf saw them pause.
The boy looked at him, stretched over, and touch his nose.
And then, from deep within the boy's throat, came a howl.
This strange human could speak his language.

A veil of darkness began to descend over the dying wolf.
But within the howling of the boy, he heard a message.

The Boy On The Dolphin:
Old Wolf, you are about to embark on a wondrous journey.
Set aside your fears and re-ignite the excitement of youth.
Your tired spirit is about to be reborn...do not be afraid.
You will soon enter the shadows and a surprise awaits you.
You will be called by your name...for you are precious.

Your leadership has been recognized in other realms.
A child awaits you. His name is Ehsan. Just follow his howls.
I have taught him your language and he will embrace you.
Now go Old Wolf. I can hear Ehsan calling you now.

With his last breath, The old wolf asked:
"Are you one of those spirits that we see in our dreams?"
The last thing the old wolf heard was the boy replying,

I am the boy who jumped.

Five Teens Missing At Sea: Presumed Dead

This was the tragic headline in the Rocky Cove Journal.
Rarely, did the newspaper use the word "dead."
It was always such a positive, optimistic newspaper.
Crime was carefully screened out of its pages.
In Rocky Cove, people wanted to hear about cheerful things.
They loved headlines that read:

Rocky Cove Oldtimers Win Baseball Tournament.

Or

4 Year Old Willy Weston Catches Monster Salmon

Or

Church Fundraiser Over The Top: Good Going Ladies!

Anything nasty or illegal, still made the rounds, that's for sure.
It just wasn't printed in the newspaper.
Those stories were whispered about in kitchens and garages.
They were shared over fences and in restaurants with coffee.
To actually use the word "dead" outside an obituary was rare.

If the newspaper said, **Moose Struck Dead On Highway**
Well, that was okay.
If the newspaper said, **Hundreds Of Dead Fish Wash Ashore**
Well, that was acceptable too.
But it just wasn't used in stories involving people.

And there it was, in large, bold, black letters.
They formed a headline that spanned the newspaper.
After three days of frantic searching, it was now time.
The truth for this tiny village had to be confronted.
Hope had been abandoned. Further searching was fruitless.
This grieving community had to accept reality.
The situation was now hopeless.

The boys were dead.

The village of 800 people were truly in the depths of despair.
This was the entire group of boys, graduating that year.
They were all 17 years old and the best of friends.
All five boys were first, second, or third cousins.
When walking through the village, one could hear sobbing.
Little brothers and sisters cried uncontrollably.
Wailing from distraught parents continued hour by hour.

Neighbours could not comfortable the mourners.
They too descended into a pit of unfathomable sadness.
A depth of grieving descended upon Rocky Cove.
The population seemed to be in a sorrowful trance.

An hour after graduation and still in their suits, they vanished.
Five boys, some barely shaving, but others not...disappeared.
Different sizes, different shapes...all were gone.

"Let's take out a boat," one had said.
"Let's look at the village from the ocean one last time."
"It will be our last act together, before we push along."

....before Tom heads off to university.

....before Jake works in his Uncle's garage.

....before Andy goes on the trap line.

....before Harold becomes a coach.

....before Sloan studies welding.

That's what they said.

These were good boys.

Oh there had been a few slip-ups along the way.

But, they watched each others backs.

They made certain no one went too far..or over the brink.

People said, "These guys will be friends forever.

"They'll all be the best man at each others weddings."

In sports, there were no heroes.

In studies, there were no geniuses.

In looks, there were no movie stars.

But in friendships, they were unsurpassed.

And then they were gone.

No one checked for approaching winds or storm warnings.

No one left word of their intended route.

No one said good-bye to grannies and mothers.

No one gave hugs to old, weary papas and fathers.

No one took the time to tease little brothers or sisters.

And only one person in the whole village saw them go.

Blesser had been fishing off the dock at night.

When he was born, the doctor had said,
"He's going to be a boy with special needs, Vera.
He's going to need a lot of care...and God's blessing."
So Vera, holding back tears, called him Blesser

Blesser didn't like crowds.
He was the only one in town not at the graduation.
As he watched in silence, five giggling boys walked past him.
They all said, "Hi Blesser...howya doin' buddy."
The boys headed together to the end of the dock.

According to Blesser, they borrowed a little aluminum boat.
The giggling boys pushed off, happy and carefree.
And rowed into the vastness of the rough, gray ocean.
Then Tom, Jake, Andy, Harold, and Sloan vanished.

However, the boys were not dead.

They had been blown far from the coast in the ensuing storm.
The rain had soaked their suits.
They overcame thirst by sucking the water from their clothes.
Initial embarrassment was overcome by the desire to live.
Shirts, socks and underwear were turned and twisted.
Every drop was precious and potentially life-saving.

By day three, the boys knew that they were in deep trouble.
Efforts to be optimistic were replaced by long silences.
Their bodies swung from shivering to roasting.
Pangs of hunger had set in early.
These were lads who ate meals made by loving mothers.

Hunger began to take its toll.
It began to ebb away at weaken bodies.
Strong, teenage muscles were being consumed from within.

All five began to drift away into a semi-consciousness.
Occasionally a moan could be heard, or maybe weeping.
Incoherent mumbling was interspersed with a boy's sobs.
And then there was silence.

At dawn, the boys were jolted back to reality.
Their boat struck something...or something struck the boat.
Their tiny vessel no longer flowed with the ocean's current.
Instead, it was being propelled by another force.
The guys shook each other awake and stare in disbelief.

Through eyes nearly swollen shut by the sun, they saw a boy.
He was younger than they were, darkly tanned, and fearless.
He rode high on the back of a dolphin, certain of his cause.
The boy and dolphin had bumped the boat intentionally.

High-pitched sounds shot out of his mouth, piercing the wind.
In seconds, an entire pod of dolphins encircled the boat.
With their noses, the dolphins pushed the boat towards shore.
The boys were transfixed by the power of this slight boy.
He guided the dolphins, looking at the guys with a wide smile.

Sometimes the boy's long black hair blew wildly in the wind.
He said nothing, only communicating with the dolphins.
Hours past and the dolphin rider never grew weary.
Often enshrouded by fog, the boy was often barely visible...

He seemed buoyed in spirit by the challenge before him.

The boys held on tightly to the sides of the boat.
The dolphins maneuvered it through the powerful winds.
They steered it through mighty, flowing currents.
It was Sloan who yelled, "I can see our village! I can see it!
I can even see Blesser still fishing on the dock!"

The dolphins guided the boat up the the dock at Rocky Cove.
It was the exact spot from where they had first departed.
The boys jumped up onto the dock and hugged Blesser.
"We're back Blesser! We're back!"

Blesser was a little caught off guard by this.
He wasn't know for his popularity and could barely speak.
Doing up the buttons on his shirt was a big enough challenge.
He still hadn't figured out his left boot from his right.
However, he kinda liked these newly found friendships.

The five guys stood on the dock, waving frantically at the boy.
Already, the dolphin rider was turning to leave the cove.
His dolphin leaped high into the air and the boy waved back.

The boys on the dock could see the rider in the noonday sun.
The fog had lifted and they saw his tragic physical condition.
While his strength of spirit soared, his body looked vulnerable.
The boys were shocked by his skinny arms and rows of ribs.
The legs that clasped the dolphin were just skin and bone.

Harold yelled to the dolphin rider, "Please come with us.

"Our mothers will feed you really good!
There'll be a lot of feasting today, that's for sure.
Please come."

The boy on the dolphin shook his head.
As the boy faded from sight, Tom whispered to his buddies,
"I wonder if he was a guardian angel or something like that."
The response meandered its way along the ocean currents.
The rider's words were caught up in the swirling ocean breeze.
Five boys, weary but alive, stood on the dock and heard:

"I am the boy who jumped."

The boys were bewildered that the dolphin rider heard them.
Jake hollered in response, "Is there anything we can do?"
"Yes" the boy replied, pushing his black hair from his face.

From some distant place,
Far beyond the cove,
Carried on the ocean winds,
Came two words that changed their lives forever:

"Do good."

And they did.

Tom discovered that he was bright after all.
He was accepted into a prestigious medical school.
One day a week, he volunteers at a soup kitchen.
He offers free medical advice and care to the visitors.

It's operated by a woman called **Thelma.**
A woman with a walker, thick glasses...and now a smile.

Jake went to work as a mechanic, in his uncle's garage.
Once a year, he'd fix up an old car and raffle it off.
Because of Jake, two boys from the city could go to college.
Jake called this award, "The Dolphin Boy Scholarship."
Only his buddies from Rocky Cove knew why.
The university chose two deserving boys:
The first two boys selected were called **Terrell** and **Martin..**

Andy became a trapper, and was often away from home.
One day, he approached the Town Counsel with an idea.
"Maybe I can teach trapping and bring back the old ways.
Maybe there is someone who has lost their way in the world."

"Find someone who wants to make a new beginning.
And I will show him the ways of our elders."
The first person who arrived...was three times Andy's age.
His name was **Xaviour**...who had no problem living in a tent.

Harold became a college football coach.
He was respected for being tough but fair.
One day, he saw a big but sad looking boy in the hallway.
"What are you studying?" Harold asked the gloomy student.
I"m studying Agriculture but it's kinda tough.
I was hoping to take over my grandfather's farm,
But I'm thinking of dropping out. People aren't too friendly."
And there, right in the hallway, the kid began to sob.

Harold said, "Young man, you listen to me.
First of all, you're not dropping out.
I need you on the football team. You'll be a star.
Now what's your name?"

"Nipper," replied the future star of the football team.
"My name is **Nipper**."

Sloan took an apprenticeship as a welder in the city.
He boarded with a woman and her daughter.
He had always been the teaser in his family.
His joking, laughter and happy ways brought joy to this family.
One day, the daughter and Sloan went for a walk.
She said to him, "You have changed our lives, Sloan.
Your cheerfulness has lifted a dark cloud from our home.
Since the death of my brother, my mother has struggled.

"What was your little brother's name?" Sloan asked

"My brother was called Ehsan," she replied.
My little brother was called **Ehsan**.."

A Phone Call From An Island

Tony Wallace:

At that time, I had no idea of the Dolphin-Boy sightings.
I had thought Logan Fletcher was dead. I truly did.
In all likelihood, he had been swept out to sea.
He probably had released the dolphins through the gate.
Then was sucked into the ocean by the surging currents.
It was now six months since Logan had disappeared.
The phone call I received was both a surprise and shock.

Sam Tucken

Hi Tony. It's Sam here. I hope you remember me.
The last time we spoke was on the staircase at the Fletcher's.
I have some news Tony. I think the boy is here.
I think that Logan Fletcher is here on Swashatuq Island.

Some of the boys came in from fishing and found a hut.
It resembled the style that boy scouts learn to make.
Our boys know the story of such travelers and tried to help.
Logan was nowhere to be seen, but they built him a fire.
They also cooked up some fish and left warm blankets.
Each boy also left him an article of their own clothing.

Tradition has it that a traveler must not be approached.
He has been drained of almost all of his energy.
His encounters have left others strong...but he himself is weak.
It seems as if this lad has been exceptionally giving.
His unending service may have left him very fragile.

It's as if too much sap has been drained from a tree.

The boys who found this tent know that they have a duty.
For them, it is like a great calling.
They must meet all of his physical needs.
They must keep the fire going and continue to bring food.
Logan's little lean-to must be kept in good repair.
They also must patrol the area and keep people away.

And they themselves must never look at him.
Just a simple glance could be fatal.
It could draw away, the wee bit of energy Logan has left.

Tony Wallace:
But where exactly is he?

Sam Tucken:
Well, that's a good question.
His footprints in the sand seem to be giving us a clue.
The kid's in bare feet so we know that he's coming and going.
The food that is left each day is always gone.
He devours everything. This is definitely one hungry boy.
It is likely that he's building himself up for another jump.

If you go by the trail of footprints, they lead to the cliff.
An earthquake hundreds of years ago shook the entire island.
A section of the island was severed and fell into the sea.
Left behind was a wall of sheer rock, hundreds of feet high.
Down below is the ocean, smashing against the coast.
Massive sharp boulders are piled along the shore.

It appears that he's making daily visits to the crest of the cliff.

Tony, I think that he's checking it out.

Logan Fletcher is planning his final jump.

We on Swashatuq Island will never know the outcome.

If his jump is successful, he will be swept up into his "final lap".

He will arrive at where ever he was destined to be.

Or, he may plunge onto the rocks below and be swept away.

The currents and tides will pull his broken body out to sea.

We will never know .

There is a pod of dolphins who are patrolling the area.

I'm unsure what that all means.

Tony Wallace:

If no one is able to look at him, how will you know....?

How will you know if he's even jumped?

Sam Tucken:

The boys who have been leaving him food will let us know.

If a few days go by with the food uneaten, that will be a clue.

They also will check for footprints as well.

They'll see if the lean-to has been kept up through the day.

I'll call you if I have an update on anything.

Tony Wallace:

Thanks Sam for all you've done.

I'm sorry about the way I acted, early in this case.

I could have learned so much from you.

I would have done things differently, that's for sure.

Sam Tucken:

That's okay Tony. Don't worry about it.

I'll call you when I've got some news.

I hear you're retired now...maybe you might like to visit us.

The folks here on Swashatuq Island would treat you well.

Bye for now.

Tony Wallace:

(That was the last I heard from Sam...for a while. My own son Rick was busy getting ready for college so that consumed most of my thoughts and time. Yet, my mind often drifted back to the fate of Logan Fletcher.

After Rick left, I filled my days walking my dog Chunker but the fate of the Fletcher boy continued to gnaw at me. Even sleeping became a problem. About three weeks after my conversation with Sam, the phone finally rang again.

Sam Tucken:

Hi Tony, I hope you can hear me. The weather is wicked here.

We've had a major hurricane.

Anyway, I'll bring you up-to-date on developments.

For three days, his food has gone untouched.

The lean-to is down completely, even before the storm came.

The fire, which burned constantly, was allowed to go out.

The boy has jumped....can you hear me Tony?

The boy has jumped.

The dolphins are gone too. I don't know what that means.

I thought you would want to know. He's gone. He's not here.

The boy has jumped...

The Last Lap

Gavin and Laura Fletcher awoke with a start.
They were unsure of the exact origin of the bang.
However, it was loud enough to startle them from their sleep.
Sleep was not something that came easily to them.
Since Logan's disappearance, order had gone from their lives.

The long, gray days had no purpose.
The Fletchers simply fell asleep when exhaustion set in.
They planned nothing. They looked forward to nothing.
And they did nothing.
Days were long expanses of nothingness.
Days seemed to have no beginning or ending.
Instead, they were just filled with long, meaningless hours.

The Fletchers never left their apartment.
They no longer allowed friends to visit.
They avoided those who said, "You have to get over this...
You have to snap out of it. Join a club or something."

They cautiously stepped out of bed, walking hand in hand.
They looked in the kitchen and then the living room.
There were no clues showing the source of the bang.
The sun was just rising over the city, casting a warm glow.
Millions of people were coming to life, beginning a new day.

They peeked into the spare bedrooms. They were untouched.
The only room left to check was Logan's room.

They both placed their hands together and turned the knob.

Gavin and Laura Fletcher slowly opened the door.

Laura gasped and held her husband as they entered.

The window was shut....after all of these months...

The window was shut.

Someone or something had shut the window on the 19th floor.

Someone had come through the window and then shut it.

They never had a chance to think beyond that realization.

Their attention was quickly focused elsewhere.

The shower was running in the bathroom.

They could hear someone moving about in there.

They stared transfixed as the door slowly opened.

Out stepped Logan.

His long ,curly, wet hair clung to his shoulders.

A towel was wrapped around his waist.

He was taller but thin...a bit too thin...

He said to his parents, through a broad smile,

"Hi Mom. Hi Dad. I'm starving! What's for breakfast?"

Epilogue

Logan Fletcher remembered nothing of what his parents call, "The Missing Months". Any questioning by the police was ended by the parents, who saw that their boy was both agitated and bewildered by the questions.

Gavin Fletcher immediately accepted a position with the United Nations and moved his family to Switzerland. As a teenager, Logan Fletcher never returned to the city of his youth...we think.

However, during a vacation cruise about a year later, a pod of dolphins swam up to the side of the boat, and began squeaking. To the amazement of the other passengers, Logan responded, and engaged in a lively conversation using squeaks of his own.

When he looked up, he could see that the other passengers were staring at him. They appeared mystified by what they had witnessed. Logan simply smiled and said, "I must have just picked that up somewhere. I am the boy who....."

However, he couldn't recall how to finish his sentence. The words just floated in that misty place....somewhere beyond memory. The same kind of haziness was evident a year later, on a biking trip he was taking with his new friend, Julia.

She found this boy fascinating and laughed when he would often raise one arm in the air like a rodeo rider as he coasted down the steep, Swiss mountains. He seemed not to know the meaning of fear, as the scars on his arms and legs revealed. He could only grin as the speeds increased and the blowing winds, gravity, and pumping muscles thrust his bike incredible fast along the treacherous, winding, mountain roads.

It was a dangerous thing to do but this young man with the wild, flying, curly black hair seemed to embrace the thrill of adventure. She liked him.

They stopped at a roadside park to rest and have lunch on a picnic table, deep in the Swiss Alps. Sixteen year old Logan, now tall and lanky, bit hungrily into a thick sandwich and grinned at Julia as strawberry jam dripped down his chin and onto his shoes.

He stared for a moment at the deep red blotches on his sneakers and for a brief moment, the curtain of memory was pulled open...and he said to Julia, "Do you know what? I am the boy...." and then the curtain shut tightly and his sentence just dangled there, unfinished...incomplete.

But we know...we know who he is.

He is the boy who jumped.

The End Of Part One

Printed in Great Britain
by Amazon